OUR SONG

OUR SONG

A Memoir of
Love and Race

Lynda Smith Hoggan

[swp]

SHE WRITES PRESS

Published 2022
Printed in the United States of America
Print ISBN: 978-1-64742-389-6
E-ISBN: 978-1-64742-390-2

Library of Congress Control Number: 2021925334

For information, address:
She Writes Press
1569 Solano Ave #546
Berkeley, CA 94707

She Writes Press is a division of SparkPoint Studio, LLC.

Book design by Stacey Aaronson

Dedicated to
all the star-crossed lovers

Author's Note

This book is a memoir based on my own life experiences. It's a cautionary tale about not letting go of your dreams. And it's my tribute to the exciting years during which my generation came of age—exploring without a map, believing that we were going to change the world.

Some individuals have been identified in the book by fictional names, nicknames and other details. See the Afterword for additional comments on the approach I have taken.

> *You own everything that happened to you.*
> *Tell your stories. If people wanted you to write warmly about them,*
> *they should have behaved better.*
> —Anne Lamott

> *And that includes myself.*
> —LSH

> *Ninety-nine percent of the world's lovers are not with their first*
> *choice. That's what makes the jukebox play.*
> —Willie Nelson

Prologue

June 2014

WHAT IF YOU FELL IN LOVE WHEN YOU WERE TWENTY, AND then you fucked it all up with the help of your lover and your best friend? And then what if, like a miracle, you had a chance for a do-over four decades later, at age sixty-two?

Yes, age sixty-two. Because I was still vibrant. Because I still loved him. Because maybe he still loved me, too.

We stood face to face in the parking lot of my hotel in Washington, DC. We had just spent two nights together, talking and playing our old songs and loving each other again. Nights during which he told me the answers to questions I had wondered about for over forty years.

"I never loved anyone the way I loved you," he'd said. And with it the unspoken words that he had not loved *her* that way.

"I know that we fell apart because of youthful folly . . . poor communication . . . and a bit of malfeasance on her part," he'd said. Malfeasance, such a smart word. I'd tried not to cry, but I was flooded with relief. To know that he finally understood what had happened. How I had loved him but made bad decisions. How she had manipulated us.

At age twenty I had been a long-legged, long-haired college student. I'd made it that far in spite of my disorganized childhood, nine different living situations by the time I was eleven. Although I was smart in some ways (definitely in English, definitely not in math) and not bad looking as I went from child to woman (deep brown eyes, olive skin, and a happy smile), I'd remained sensitive, insecure, and introverted. I read literature and wrote poetry. I covered my shyness with a growing bravado—progressive politics, sex, drugs, and rock 'n' roll. I'd chosen a school as far away as I could afford from my meddling mother and conservative town.

At twenty he was a tall African-American basketball player from the inner city. He'd been raised in poverty by his single mom and grandmother. Like a lot of city boys, he did OK in school but was more interested in playing pickup basketball at the local playground. He was still more potential than proof when he was recruited to play for a small white college in my hometown in Pennsylvania. There his coach groomed him to become a top scorer and local sensation. That accomplishment still didn't fill another, more private need: he curated the songs of Motown for their sweet soul sounds and poetic lyrics, as well as a deep longing for true love.

When we met in 1972, that love took off like a wildfire. One we didn't know then would burn us both. Badly. And there were complications that would fan the flames.

One such complication was geographic. While his school was in my hometown, mine was six hours away; neither of us had a car nor could afford the expensive long distance phone calls. So our fire took the form of long letters penned late into the night—poetry, prose, lyrics, witty repartee, and a tentative but growing trust and intimacy. And my occasional weekend home that was like a blast of oxygen.

Another complication was romantic. And it was a biggie: I already had a boyfriend. He was spending our junior year studying in England. I had thought I was in love with that man until I truly fell in love with this one. But that first man, also African-American, came from a terrible background and clung to his relationship with me. I told myself that I didn't want to break his heart while he was so far from home. The truth is that in some ways I was also a coward. It was a decision not to decide, and the worst I ever made, with repercussions for years to come.

Now, after two nights with my old love, out-of-the-blue magic nights after all these years, I was returning to my long ago adopted city, Los Angeles. But I had asked him to consider that, given where we both were in our lives—single, childless, short on family, long on regrets—maybe we could find what we'd lost when we were so young.

"I'm holding," he'd said. I recognized the poker reference. He was still in the game, neither folding nor walking away.

We faced each other in the hotel parking lot.

"Do you know how to Skype?" he asked.

"I never have. But I can learn."

"OK," he said. "We'll learn to Skype together." He put his arms around me and drew me close.

I tilted my head back and tried to memorize him. "How do you feel about PDA?" I asked.

"PDA? What's that?"

"Public Display of Affection," I said.

"I hate it," he said, as his lips slowly came down to meet mine. It was a kiss as long and deep as the years we'd missed out on, and as sweet as the promise of what we might still be able to recapture.

PART ONE

———

April 2014

Chapter 1

THE WILDFIRE WAS COMING.

It was blazing across the Southern California foothills with zero containment. I didn't know how long I'd have before the knock on my door, the order to leave: "Fifteen minutes to evacuate!"

I'd barely survived one ten years before. Drought, high temps, roaring winds, and miles and miles of dried brush—a perfect firestorm that raged through the Angeles National Forest just above my home east of LA. In the end all I lost was one tree in my front yard. But some neighbors lost their homes, and a few even lost their lives. That fire taught me a lot. I owned a fire safe where I kept jewelry, important papers, my few writing publications, and CDs of favorite old photos. And a pump to be able to wet things down with the swimming pool water. I had replaced my composition roof with fire-resistant metal.

Now another potentially serious fire was burning my way. There were things I still hadn't done, like protecting the plastic storage bins of memories still sitting in my garage. At one thirty in the morning, I lugged one bin inside and opened it on my bed.

There were surprises. The card from my little sister that, at six, she'd been too young to realize had a sexual connotation ("Baby, you turn me on"). Goofy notes passed between my best friend and me in high school. A nametag from a dance, tattered and faded, still bearing the faint scent of Jade East cologne from the boy who'd worn it.

I paused to think about those memories, but not for long. I

was looking for one thing in particular, and it would break my heart if it were not there. But no, there it was, a nondescript paper bag starting to come apart at the sides. Inside were twenty-two hand-written letters dated 1972. His love letters, the most beautiful letters anyone had ever written to me. In a fit of anguish, and coerced by my other boyfriend, I had torn them into scraps. Later I painstakingly taped each one back together and placed it inside its original envelope.

For a moment I just held the bag and let flashes of that year wash over me—the seasons, the songs, his smile, his smell. I sniffed the bag to see if, like the other boy's nametag, it still held any trace of him, but it did not. I knew I should keep sorting—the wildfire was coming! But I couldn't resist pulling out his first letter and thinking back to when we'd first met.

PART TWO

———

1972

Chapter 2

ON A COLD JANUARY MORNING, I WOKE IN HIS BED AND knew that I could, I would, I had to make him love me.

My high school friend Hannah had introduced us the previous September. She'd invited me to a dance at their small private school, Moravian College, in our hometown of Bethlehem, PA. I had noticed that more than one friend wanted to introduce me to a "cool" black guy they knew. Probably because I was involved with Will, a black guy from Philly who was spending the year studying abroad. I wondered if Hannah was attracted to JT herself but was afraid to date someone black; most of the boys in our local pool were descended from white immigrants, especially German, "Pennsylvania Dutch." Along with my friend Sharon, I was the one in our group who had started clubbing outside Philly, where we met guys from different backgrounds.

Yet I was curious about this Johnny Thomas, the Big Man on Campus. Outside the local area, few had heard of Moravian, but his skills on the basketball court were putting the school on a wider map. It wasn't so much JT's modest fame that intrigued me. It was the way Hannah spoke about him, like he was a religion that you'd want to convert to. Smart, funny, charming, handsome, and oh yeah, genuinely nice. He was the whole package, and maybe one that none of us, no matter whom we had dated, had yet to open.

My state college, Slippery Rock in western PA, was hours away, but I was home for the weekend. That Saturday night I got myself together to go to the Moravian dance. I washed and brushed my long dark hair, pulled on my one pair of bell-bottoms that weren't patched and faded, and slipped into some faux Frye boots (I couldn't afford the real ones). I was ready, but for what exactly?

At the dance Hannah produced him rather ceremoniously: "Lynda, *this* is JT." As if I had been waiting for him all my life. She was grinning and dimpling, clearly pleased, like she could take a giant bite out of him herself.

She was right about him. Tall and rangy, big Afro, high cheekbones, expressive eyes. Dressed like a jock in a windbreaker, shirt, and pants. We made small talk, and he leaned over so I wouldn't have to strain my neck looking up. I asked him if he wanted to dance, but he ruefully shook his head, "I might be the only black guy who doesn't dance." Even if JT didn't dance, his eyes did. They twinkled in a way that told me he knew exactly what was going on. I wasn't sure what Hannah had told him about me. I wanted to be up front, so I managed to slip my upcoming holiday visit to my boyfriend in England into the conversation. We chatted a bit more, the dance ended, and we all said goodnight.

The next day, on the bus back to my school, I wondered how Will, my boyfriend across the sea, was spending his Sunday at Durham University. Studying, probably, since he didn't have the money to do much else. The realities of his life seemed very far away, so my thoughts soon turned back to JT. For some reason, a song from one of my roommate's albums was stuck in my mind. Blood, Sweat & Tears, a song called "40,000 Headmen." The song's words didn't speak to me, but the instrumental bridge was both haunting and hopeful. It stirred me, and without words I began to lay down my own story, like wondering whether I would ever see JT again. I found myself picturing JT's dancing eyes, hearing that refrain repeat in my mind as the highway blew by.

♡

I got busy with classes. Partied as usual, celebrated my twentieth birthday. Made plans to visit Will in England at Christmas. A big deal because I'd never traveled farther than family car trips to visit relatives or drives with friends to the Jersey shore. I worked in the cafeteria to save money and borrowed the rest from Colleen, my best friend from high school. Then came the holiday break, and it was time to travel across the ocean to be with Will.

The size and bustle of the Philly airport was overwhelming. The speed and noise of the flight's takeoff was terrifying to me. Every time there was turbulence, my heart leapt and my palms started to sweat, as I knew there was nothing but the deep black sea beneath. After six hours of that, I was able to catch my breath once the plane landed. Then there was a new challenge, would Will be at the airport waiting for me? His university was a five-hour train trip away, and mail was sometimes slow. I wasn't even sure whether he had received my travel plans. But there he was, sporting a happy grin.

We spent two weeks together that included my first exposure to a whole new world, the culture of Great Britain. To me, it seemed like I'd stepped into the Shakespeare I'd read in school. In local pubs, the young Brits were drawn to Will's 'fro and army jacket. They were curious about America and liked to brag that their society didn't have the racial prejudice problems we had. But when we hitch-hiked to visit Will's friends in Birmingham 150 miles away, we spent much of the next eight hours standing in the rain with our thumbs out. Hitching was common to our youth culture, even worldwide, but it was still rare to see a black man and a white woman hitching a ride together.

When it was time for Will and me to say good-bye, he looked devastated. I stood there feeling only slightly melancholy even though it would be another six months before we'd see each other again. My lack of sadness confused me, and during the flight back, I wondered for the first time whether I really loved Will. When I arrived home, my parents asked no questions about my trip. They didn't approve of my black boyfriend.

I finished the semester and then went home again for winter break. During the day I hung out with my little sister Barbie, now seven and always ecstatic to have me there. I liked to buy things for her that matched the way I dressed, like a big, floppy suede hat—"hippie chick" clothes she called them.

At night I got together with my local hometown girlfriends, usually Sharon or Hannah. Then on the weekend, my best friend, Colleen, was home from the University of Pittsburgh. On our last Saturday night before Colleen and I would head back to school, she and Hannah and I were going to hang out.

Hannah called and told me that she'd heard JT was arriving back at Moravian that day. The winter athletes came back early to start practice for the upcoming games, so she'd hatched a plan: "How about if we three girls go visit his dorm with some wine and a trivia game?"

I'd met Hannah through Colleen during our senior year of high school. Both Colleen and I had left town to go to school, but Hannah had stayed in the area. She and I started hanging out more when I came home for holidays and summers. Still, Colleen was the one I considered my best friend. Back when I'd started tenth grade, lonely because my junior high best friend had moved away, Colleen had reached out to me. From that point on we talked on the phone every day and did everything together.

Hannah's plan sounded fun, but I did wonder about the dynamics. Hannah was pushing me toward JT, but her crush seemed obvious. Did he feel that way about her? Why wouldn't he—Hannah was petite with an hourglass figure, thick black hair, and an impish grin. And Colleen was cute with her red-gold hair, big blue eyes, and flirty demeanor. Why wasn't Hannah pushing JT toward *her*? Maybe because, although U Pitt had plenty of men (that's where I'd met Will), I'd never heard that any of Colleen's dates was black.

And what about me? Was I just curious about JT, or would I actually cheat on Will? And because of something so shallow as JT's minor stardom or extraordinary good looks? Or was there a deeper magnet pulling me to him? I found myself humming the melody of that BS&T instrumental, imagining those dancing eyes.

Lastly, what did Johnny Thomas want? Hannah said that he wasn't known to be dating anyone, but I was sure he had plenty of opportunities. I wondered what he'd thought of me at our first meeting. And was this just a cheerful last hurrah of a group of college kids before having to get serious about our studies again? Or was something more about to happen?

At around seven o'clock we knocked, and JT's eyes widened when he opened the door. I realized that if athletics were his priority, he might actually send us away. But no, he invited us in. Was he flattered that three young women had so obviously schemed to waylay him for the night? Or was he just used to this kind of attention? If he was, he didn't show it. He seemed humble, a happy smile playing about his mouth.

He put on a Crosby, Stills, Nash & Young album, Hannah and I poured the wine into plastic cups, and Colleen pulled out a joint. Amidst the talking, laughing, and self-conscious jockeying for our social positions, I saw JT's eyes keep dancing back to me. Soon it became clear: JT was mine, at least as far as that night was concerned. Nervous, I used my fallback strategy: project an air of quiet mystery, a good hiding place for my shyness. I could still flirt with my eyes and smile.

We played the trivia game. Whereas I was drawing questions with answers like "Mesopotamia" (answers I didn't usually know), JT kept getting the vocabulary questions that I would have done well on. But JT was also good with language. "What's a four-syllable word beginning with T?" "Tantalizing," said JT, smiling at me. I leaned forward just enough to tantalize with a bit of cleavage. A little while later he drew the card again: "What's a four-syllable word beginning with T?" It seemed even funnier stoned, and we girls all just fell out laughing. JT didn't miss a beat. "Titillating," he said, his eyes locked on mine. I titillated back with my mysterious smile.

Hannah sent me an approving look and private wink. Colleen watched him, her eyes bright with admiration. But seeing his attention like a beacon on me, she stood back.

I'd just about given up any hope of shining in this game, when suddenly a gift appeared in the form of sexual perversion. "Name a famous doctor starting with K." Confident because I'd learned it in a psych class, I gave my answer, "Krafft-Ebing." The others just stared. I explained that he was a psychiatrist who'd written the first reference book about sexual psychopaths, but they had never heard of him.

"You made that up," said Colleen, poking my shoulder. Hannah and JT agreed, and they all denied me the points. I grumbled but conceded, hoping that JT might at least suspect I had a vast array of intriguing sexual knowledge, which I most certainly did not.

At one point when we sat quietly after the game, JT put on a Blood, Sweat & Tears album. I was taken aback when "40,000 Headmen" began to play. As the instrumental bridge swelled to a beautiful crescendo, JT's eyes again met mine. I knew he couldn't know that the song had previously made me think of him, but I saw that he was just as moved as I was by the ways that music could touch us.

It was getting late. As we girls were leaving, JT gently pulled me back inside. "You don't go back to school till Monday, right?" he asked.

"Yeah, right."

He casually took my hand and looked down at his fingers playing with mine. "I have practice during the day tomorrow. Do you wanna come up later and hang out?"

My heart clashed like the school marching band, but outwardly I played it cool. "Yeah, sure, why not? I'll see you then."

I caught up with the girls, who managed to hold it in until we were out of earshot. "What did he say?" "What does he want?" They both spoke at once, and I laughed.

"Oh, just to see me tomorrow," I said innocently, pretending it wasn't the most important event of the night, the most thrilling thing that had happened to me in ages. But I couldn't pretend for long; he probably heard our screams echoing down the hall.

The next night I returned with rum and Coke. JT rolled a joint and put on a stack of records, and we began our communicative dance just sitting on his dorm bed. Politics, Tricky Dick, the Vietnam War. Then our shared passion for music. From what I could tell, he had a nice stereo and a large collection of albums. We listened to our beloved high school Motown classics like the Temps, the Four Tops, the Supremes. He also played some rock tunes like the ones from the night before and even more obscure artists I didn't expect, like the esoteric Laura Nyro.

We took turns choosing songs, and as the beats and melodies ebbed and flowed, the dance became more intimate. Our bodies leaned closer, knees touching, his arm brushing against mine. I found out about the neighborhood he grew up in, inner-city Washington, DC. His mother's illness and stays in the hospital, the fatherless hours on the local basketball court that finally paid off in his being recruited to play for Moravian, my hometown college (and oddly enough, my stepdad's alma mater). I told him about my own mother's mental problems, which were not certifiable yet but omnipresent, my two unloving fathers, and a lonely childhood shuffled back and forth between parents and grandparents. Though afraid to break the mood, I still reminded him of my distant connection to another man. He thanked me for my honesty but didn't ask more.

Rum in my arteries, THC in my veins. Oxytocin and dopamine bathing my brain. JT pulled me closer. Was it a dream, or was his essence now coursing through me too, his words, his smell, his smile all tinctures blending with mine? Those eyes flickering like firelight, his lips on me—lips coming back to kiss me, kiss me. Deep murmurs and soft tinkling bells of laughter. *Mmm* sounds and *huh* breathing. Sweating in January, my top coming off, jeans unbuttoned and unzipped—everything off! Skin to skin, his strong arms under me, my long legs wrapped around his narrow hips. Isaac Hayes's low rumble repeating, "Your love so doggone good." Hips grinding, wet on wet, and then the rumble was inside us. "I love you," someone whispered.

Afterward as we lay there recovering, and I was trying to take it all in, the room began to turn like a merry-go-round. It went faster and faster until I jumped off, lurching out his door and down the hall to the men's bathroom to throw up in the toilet.

JT followed. "Do you need help?" he asked from outside the stall. "No! Don't come in." A girlfriend could hold my hair, but I didn't want JT to see me that way. He stood watch at the door and then led me, shaking, back to his room.

"I'm sorry, I'm so embarrassed," I apologized. "I shouldn't mix pot and liquor, I get the spins."

"It's OK, I understand," he said and held me, stroking my face and hair until I was well enough to get up. Dawn was about to break, and it was time for me to go. My parents did not take kindly to my staying out all night.

"I'll write," JT said. "Me too," I answered. As my internal fog lifted, and as if I wasn't already ashamed enough, I realized that it had been my voice whispering that I loved him.

I paused at the door. "Back there, when I said I love you . . ."

"Mmm-hmmm . . . ?"

"What I meant was that I love what I see of you so far."

"Shh, I know," JT placed one finger on my mouth, then leaned over and kissed my sour lips as if they were still sweet. "Don't worry," he said, and his smile was more brilliant than the sun that lit his hair like a halo as it came streaming through the window.

That's how it started, the love affair that would turn my life upside down. It would take me many years to understand how the young me was a paradox—smart but dumb, passionate yet blasé. I was an explorer trying to find my way. And I didn't have a map.

♡

After I left JT, I thought of little else. I knew it could be days or weeks before he wrote—if he even wrote at all. But no, of course he'd write, wouldn't he? Because I immediately wrote to him.

A couple days later, there it was: a plain white envelope in my college dormitory mailbox. The handwriting, guy writing, kinda messy yet kinda neat. His initials in the return address. A small envelope but not unsubstantial—the letter had to be several pages at least. I wanted to tear it open right there, but I forced myself to carry it to my dorm room, hands shaking with excitement.

2 / 1 / 72
Hi there Lynda!

Yes, he'd written right away, just like I had. He even spelled my name right—and how sweet it sounded coming from him.

He'd intended to write soon, he said, but not quite this soon. Why, then? Because someone he'd been with when he was home for break told him she "might" have given him something. He hated the idea that he could have unwittingly passed it on to me:

I'm just mortified, he wrote, *but I wanted to make sure that you would go get tested, too.*

Well, I was the one who'd thrown up on our big night, so I guessed we were about even in the mortification department. I didn't like knowing there'd been another girl, but when he was with her, he didn't know that he'd soon be with me. And when he was with me, he didn't know that he might have gotten something from her. He even said that he regretted having been with her. What mattered most was that he did the right thing by telling me. Oh, Jonathan.

As I read on, it felt like coming down the stairs on Christmas morning. He wrote about how much he dug our night together. How he hoped it would happen again and again. How the way I communicated broke through his defenses and made him open up in a way he never had. That I'd turned his head around more than anyone he had ever met. Although he mentioned classes and basketball, it seemed he couldn't stop talking about us. Did I think that we would meet again soon? (Oh, could I stand it until we met again?) Did I feel as strongly about him? (What about me just wanting him like I had never wanted anyone before?) He was already thinking about what to say when he wrote again. (We were so alike. How fast could these envelopes fly anyway?)

He ended his letter:

Please take care of your sweet self,
JT

Suddenly the two most important letters in the universe.

Chapter 3

TWO DAYS LATER, THERE WAS ANOTHER ENVELOPE—ALSO MAILED before he would have received mine. Seven pages.

> *2 / 3 / 72*
> *"So far away . . ."*

He'd started with the words to a Carole King song. Then he wrote his own editorials in bright red ink, all wordplay on the lyrics to make them about him and me. I'd never seen anything quite so adorable. Like where Carole mentioned her dreams, he'd written, *are you my dream come true?* Of course, a lot of the song and his red comments were about how hard it was to be separated.

From there on it was a more typical letter. How was my life going these days? (What, like the four days since I left his bed? It did seem like ages ago.) How he missed me. (Of course he did, how many people knew who Krafft-Ebing was? He'd just said it himself: I was his dream come true.)

He'd made the winning basket in the last thirty seconds of his basketball game. Oh, I wished I'd seen that. Little did he know, I'd already gone to the library and read about that game. His basketball talk was kind of sexy, not tedious like when my basketball coach stepdad talked about the sport. But everything sounded sexy coming from JT. Why hadn't I asked my stepdad more questions about basketball so that I could talk intelligently?

School was busy already and he might not be able to write

for a while. I smiled to myself: yeah right, go check your mail-box, JT. Then see if you can resist picking up that pen.

He signed his letter simply:

Jonathan

Jonathan—I liked that. Instead of what others called him, Johnny or JT. I bet his mom and grandma called him Jonathan. I wanted to be the only other woman who called him Jonathan. But then he added a postscript, a worrisome reference to an Undisputed Truth song:

> *P.S. Please don't be just another smiling face that doesn't tell the truth.*

I'd been honest with him because I wanted him to trust me. But how could he trust me considering that I had another man? Whom I was now cheating on with him?

Fuck! What the hell was I gonna do?

♡

In the meantime, a letter from Will had arrived. He complained about bad weather, loneliness, and how difficult his classes were. No mention of our time together at Christmas; he just sounded sorry for himself. I felt sorry, too, yet I had to push myself to write back. It was February in northern Pennsylvania, and I was at school—in a similar dreary winter boat, just a 3000-mile ocean away. There was one difference: JT's letters were like spring melting the snow, giving me something to daydream about when my professors droned on. I couldn't tell Will about that.

A couple days later, another of those recognizable little white envelopes arrived. Six pages.

2 / 7 / 72
Hi Lover.

"Lover" he called me? I loved it! I knew he wouldn't be able to resist writing me again. He went on to say that he had planned not to, thought things were moving too fast, but my letter made him feel like everything would be OK. I guess I'd reassured him by telling him how smitten I was, but did I even have the right? He mentioned authenticity, and I was being authentic with him. But I was being untrustworthy with Will. Could I be authentic and untrustworthy at the same time? Why-oh-why did things have to happen like this? He said I had nothing to explain. But if I didn't explain, he might think the wrong thing, that I was faithless, selfish, cruel. He might not realize that I'd thought I loved Will and that falling in love with him, JT, was making me realize that I didn't.

He said his natural pessimism made him doubt we'd ever get together, but:

> *I guess it was important for both of us to let each other know we wanted it.*

Yes, we'd let each other know for sure. Titillating. Tantalizing. Those dancing eyes.

He asked if I'd gone to Student Health:

> *I couldn't stand it if anything bad happened to you, especially because of me.*

24

Sure, I'd gone. The doctor didn't even examine me, just left the room and then came up behind me and jabbed a needle in my butt. My punishment for being a "bad girl," I figured. It felt good to know that JT was concerned about me.

I'd been worried about what my parents might say if they knew I'd stayed out all night. Whereas JT said his mom would be mellow, and he was surprised that I didn't have a better handle on my folks.

He finished by saying he'd looked up Krafft-Ebing:

> *You were right! I hereby give you those points.*
> *Now I've gotta get to practice.*
> *Write soon,*
> *Jon*

He was lucky that his mom was so easy-going. But my parents—oh my. How could I make JT understand what had happened less than a year before?

♡

Spring semester of my sophomore year. I'd just gotten off the dorm payphone with my grandfather when my mother called back. What was up with this? Phone calls were so expensive, they usually waited until eleven p.m. when the rates went down.

"Your grandfather's had a heart attack," she said. "He's dead."

I couldn't believe it. Just a few minutes before, we'd been talking, or, to be more accurate, arguing. We argued over the letter I'd written asking for his help. I had recently started dating Will and had kept it from my parents, knowing how they would respond to his being black. When they found out, it was even worse than I'd expected: they kicked me out of my family home.

For now I had my dorm to go back to, but school would end soon, and then what? "Maybe your grandfather will help you," my mother said coldly, as I carried my suitcase to the door.

My paternal grandfather had been rejected by his Jewish immigrant family for marrying a *shiksa*—surely he would understand the pain of losing one's family over prejudice. Instead, after receiving my letter, my Grandpa called and we argued. I tried desperately to make him understand what a good man Will was, but he screamed into the phone, "My beautiful granddaughter— how could you go with a *schvartzah*? It's *dreck*!" Then he hung up on me. And died.

I laid on my bed and sobbed. I'd lost the one man who I'd thought loved me unconditionally—except that now I knew his love was, to an extent, conditional. I was even more distraught to realize that I had a hand in his death. "His own prejudice killed him," I told myself. I half believed that.

After my grandpa's funeral my mother told me that I could live at home on breaks until I finished school. And I could continue with Will as long as they didn't have to hear about him. My mother did ask to see a photograph. "He's not as handsome as Sidney Poitier, is he?" was her response. She meant handsome by white standards, i.e., light-skinned. I felt like saying, "And Dad's not exactly Paul Newman, either," but I kept that thought to myself. During the summer I worked at a job my stepdad got me at one of the local playgrounds. On Friday nights I took the bus to Philly to spend the weekends with Will.

The weekends I'd stayed with Will at Pitt during our sophomore year had already been quite an education. On the outside he looked tough, but starting from our first meeting after he'd stepped in to protect me, a stranger, from a dangerous situation, I learned that appearances can fool you. He was a sweetheart and a good teacher. He taught me that the Black Panthers he volunteered with were more about giving inner-city kids breakfast before school than about starting a revolution. I'd heard of the Malcolm X who terrified whites, but he taught me about the Malcolm who had ultimately embraced a loving Islam over the racist Black Muslims who may have finally killed him. Will was an anachronism who listened to both African-inspired jazz artist Pharoah Sanders *and* white soft rock group Bread! I'll never forget the first time I heard him singing along with "Baby I'm-a Want You." In many ways, Will was intriguing.

Back in the days right after my family had learned about Will and disowned me, after my grandfather's death, and after my parents accepted me back home, I spent most weekends with Will at his parents' house in Philly. During the week, I "worked" at the playground job I wasn't really suited for, always giving a mediocre effort at best in return for the paycheck. It paid for, among other things, my bus ride each Friday. On the first trip, I buzzed with excitement and nerves: Sharon and I had gone clubbing in the suburbs, but I had never seen the city.

Will met me at the bus station downtown and maneuvered me through my first subway ride. Everything moved so fast. I looked around like a wide-eyed kid—at the smartly dressed secretaries, old Italian *nonnas* with their stockings rolled down, a homeless schizophrenic raising voice and fist to the sky. The human landscape changed to mostly black faces by the time we reached our 42nd Street exit.

Will's parents lived in a brick row home next to a wall splashed with graffiti: "Black is Boss!" Inside, the furniture was a mix of second-hand pieces likely battered through the family's many moves up and down stairs. On the walls were prints of

John Kennedy, Martin Luther King, and *The Last Supper*. Everything looked used but clean.

I was nervous about how Will's family would react to his white girlfriend. Mom, Mary, was the matriarch, roly-poly with a big belly she rested her folded hands on. "Welcome, welcome," she said with a wide smile. Dad, Joe, was tall and fit from working construction. He gave a benevolent nod and mumbled something. I would learn that Joe was taciturn except when he was drinking. Will had told me that Joe was an alcoholic and described a nightmarish childhood, but for now, Joe was on good behavior. Various sisters smiled shyly or greeted me: "Hi, Lynda," or "Hey, girl." Not one person in the family gave me a hostile or suspicious look. They looked up to Will, and if he wanted me that was OK with them.

That first Saturday, Will and I were invited across the street to his older sister Hallie's for breakfast. As we entered the kitchen, whoosh! A scurry sound and a glimpse of movement, as if a genie had just waved a scarf over the room. I was stunned when Hallie said, "Don't mind them, tha's just the roaches." There had to be hundreds all taking flight at once to create that whooshing effect. I'd never seen a cockroach, and that day I eyed the cupboards uneasily. But I soon learned that the inner city was an occupied zone, and eventually I got used to them.

Hallie wanted to talk about the house party she was having that night, charging a small admission because she was short on the rent. She wanted Will to help her keep an eye on the crowd.

I was excited. My first party in Philly! I decided to wear my stylish new hot pants, short and snug, in a blue and white cotton cloud pattern. Will topped his bell-bottoms with only a brown suede fringed vest that showed off the lean muscles of his arms and chest.

A blast of steamy summer night hit us when we stepped outside. Down on the corner a group of male shadows were making music, harmonizing and playing African-sounding rhythms on hand drums. Their voices moaned, wailed, and called—as if for lost fathers, unfound lovers, and always the elusive justice. I wanted to listen, but Will tugged my hand, "Come on, Kitten." I got chills when Hallie opened the door on the first notes of Donny Hathaway's keyboard intro: "Whoa-oh-ohhh, mm-hmm. Yes, this is the ghetto. Sho'nuff now!"

I was the only white person at the party. A few guests raised a quizzical eyebrow, smiled, or said hello, but most just ignored me, too caught up in their own good time to care. The night was a blur of sight, sound, and screwdrivers. White eyes, teeth, and embroidered dashikis glowed neon under a blacklight. Every hue of brown skin shone with oil and sweat. Girls' hips shaking, guys' arms snaking, reaching for a drumstick or a woman's waist. Big Afros with combs sticking out like antennae—"where is she, is she here?" Petite shell ears with gold dangles that caught the light and reflected it back to his eyes when she danced. And always there was the laughter and the beat. The sense that something good might happen—even here in West Philly at a rent party in the ghetto, half a paycheck spent on admission and a new outfit. Yes, something good could always still happen, even here tonight.

Over that summer I lived two lives, between my mostly white town and the kaleidoscope that was the black community in Philly. Like Saturday afternoons when *Soul Train* came on, black dancers in wild clothes, the opposite of *American Bandstand* with its polite sweaters and loafers. Will and his sisters laughed, hollered, and tried to outdo each other's moves—and screamed loudest of all when one of them pulled me up off the couch, "Come on, girl!"

I became more comfortable with the family and they with me. And I almost got over my embarrassment at the loud squeaking noises Will's bedsprings made. Our privacy was respected, and I never saw more than a trace of a smile cross anyone's face when he met my eyes and gestured upstairs.

Occasionally something disconcerting happened out in the street. Like the time Will and I were out walking, and a black woman yelled from a passing car, "Nigger lover!" I was shocked. I thought only white men said things like that.

Eventually, I saw Joe come home drunk. He sat in his chair and mumbled, but now his mutterings had a new menacing tone. Gone was the good-humored teasing that the family usually engaged in. Everyone kept a quiet distance while their eyes never lost their sideways watch on Joe. Older sisters who stopped by didn't stay long before steering their kids back toward the door.

I was mystified as to how he could hold everyone captive without even doing anything; of course, I had not seen the years that preceded this. The growing anxiety waiting for a missing Joe to come home. Worse when he finally got there. Hours of threats, then slaps, screams, slamming doors, sobs. Desperate calls, white policemen tromping through the house. Courtrooms, restraining orders, tearful reunions. Promises, and broken promises.

For now, Will didn't interfere unless Joe got up and stumbled toward one of the girls or punctuated a rant by stabbing a finger toward his wife. Then Will would move closer to his sister or mother, never taking his gaze from Joe. From Will's mouth came a warning mumble of his own. It was enough to send Joe back to his chair to stare grumpily at the TV. I wondered if this were a language born of slavery—people lowing softly out the side of the mouth, a few words that could be understood only by the intended listener.

As mundane as it seemed, a drunken broken man, I knew I was privy to an inside view of something profound: the legacy of racism.

Yes, this too was the ghetto. *Sho'nuff now.*

And when fall came, I went back to school, while Will was off to his opportunity-of-a-lifetime as a foreign exchange student. We promised to remain faithful.

♡

So, no, I didn't have a very tight rein on my parents. I didn't have an easy-going mom like JT's. Would his mother be so mellow if she knew he was with a white girl? What if he had previously told her that he loved one white girl, and now he was telling her, no, I only thought I loved that white girl, but I was wrong, now I love this new white girl? Yeah, right.

The last page of JT's letter was the lyrics to a Temptations song, "Ungena Za Ulimwengu—Unite the World." No editorials from him on this one. But in my mind, I supplied my own.

We had grown up with the Cold War. We championed civil rights and other causes safely from our college campuses. But we knew, like the song said, that young and old on the front lines were being tapped, followed, harassed and worse.

Many of us couldn't even place Vietnam on a map. Yet it was as close to us as our nightly television news—footage of thick jungles, bomb blasts, tanks, bloodied soldiers, wrinkled old civilians cowering in their bamboo hats, children running, babies screaming. We were aware of the ever-present threat of the draft. Some guys we knew drew the unlucky numbers and shipped out. Luckily boys in college were deferred—for now.

Our elders judged people by the color of their skin, and as much as we younger people wanted change, we still sometimes feared each other. Was JT's song choice about racial equality, our differing skin colors, and to reassure me? Or did he suspect I'd been "misused" by blacks, as the song implied?

♡

It wasn't Will who had misused me. It was a guy named Curtis whom I had met the summer after high school. My friend Sharon and I went to a mixed-race club outside Philly where other kids from school had already been going to see better-known soul bands. George Clinton's Parliament Funkadelic was playing that night. They came out on stage dressed in white hooded robes like the KKK and blew our minds with their funky mix of deep south blues and acid rock.

After the show, a friendly-looking black guy talked to me. Curtis was from nearby Allentown and would be attending U Pitt in the fall, where my best friend from high school, Colleen, would be going, too. "You should come visit us," Curtis said. He seemed so confident compared to the guys I had gone through school with, and I was too naïve to get the concept of bravado. We agreed to meet again soon at a local summer dance series.

I figured he wouldn't show up, but there he was. We danced and then went outside to cool off. We lay down in the grass and started making out. Curtis moved fast. Soon he was opening my blouse, pushing my hand down. I resisted, and he backed off. I was too embarrassed to tell him that I had not yet had sex. I'd fooled around with my boyfriends in high school, but that was all.

The next time we met, he showed up in a sports car driven by a pretty, older black woman. She looked angry. I thought, is that his mother? He got out and proceeded to tell me that she was his lover, and she had told him to cut me loose. Since she was having sex with him and I wasn't, well, "You know how it is,

Lynda." Yeah, I guess I did. Suddenly my virginity didn't feel like a "special gift" but a weight that I didn't want to carry anymore. I was a grownup, after all.

A few days later I called Curtis. "I'd like to see you," I said. We both knew what that meant. I was nervous, but I met him in nearby Allentown at the address he gave me. Inside the older row home was African art, Sly Stone on the stereo, and several young men and women, all black, who were talking and sipping drinks while cooking up something good in the kitchen. I longed to know what it felt like to be an adult, have your own place, have your friends over. They were neither friendly nor unfriendly to me, watching as Curtis led me down to the basement. Maybe they smiled knowingly behind my back. Or whispered something unkind about what happens to a girl like me. But what was "a girl like me" anyway? I was a girl who didn't want to be a virgin anymore. A girl who wanted to be different from my parents, to understand people I'd been warned away from. A girl who thought broad shoulders and a confident swagger were the mark of a man.

There under a bare bulb was a soiled mattress. I should have been embarrassed or grossed out, but I was a girl on a mission. Curtis set about with very few preliminaries. He told me to get undressed and took off all of his clothes except his socks—yeah, he fucked me in his socks. He drew me down, skipped the foreplay from the summer concert, quickly entered me, and it hurt. He told me he'd pull out, but I didn't know whether to believe him. Afterward he got up, and I looked down to see blood on my thighs. I couldn't tell whether he had pulled out, either. "Don't worry, it'll get better," he reassured me as he put his clothes back on. I didn't see how. But those were his only kind words of the night.

Before I left for college, my mom took me to a gynecologist and told him to give me birth control pills. She didn't know that my period was already late. I spent my first six weeks of college worried that I was pregnant, and back then abortion was illegal. My roommate and I joked about her punching me in the stomach or throwing me down the stairs, but I actually considered it. I was terrified of a pregnancy and what it would mean to my life, to my family, to my reputation. Back in high school, girls who got pregnant were not allowed to graduate. Finally, after an afternoon of horseback riding, I started to bleed.

To my surprise, I received a couple letters from Curtis. "Believe it or not, I dig the hell out of you," he wrote. Why should I believe him? Maybe what I wanted to believe was that I hadn't been so used after all. And in a way, hadn't I used him, too? I made plans to go to Pitt, to see Colleen and Curtis as well. But when I did, he made very little time for me—just enough to have sex, which, contrary to his promise, wasn't better the second time. Then before I left, Colleen got a call from Will, a friend of Curtis's who asked me to meet him.

I was confused. What did this guy Will want? When I found out, I was in shock. He told me that Curtis had offered me to a group of his friends, Will included. A fucking gangbang! After Will refused, the others did too, but he thought I should know what kind of a guy Curtis really was. I was crushed. I felt so betrayed, and perhaps worst of all, foolish. Because Curtis's behavior the summer before should have been enough to show me who he was.

When I went back to school, I wrote to Will and thanked him, and we started corresponding. Within a year Will asked me to come visit again, and our relationship began. He was active and respected in black student politics (one reason the other men had followed his lead), and I was the first white woman he had ever dated. He called me "Kitten" because I liked cats. I think he saw me as a sweet girl in need of his care. With six sisters, a fragile mom, and an alcoholic father, he was used to giving care. And I did need it. I had a mother with psychological problems, a disappeared dad, and a disinterested stepfather.

Curtis's behavior had hurt and confused me. Did Curtis hate me? Or did he just hate white women? Did all black people really hate whites? Was that all that could exist between black and white, history and hate? Or was it a man/woman thing? I'd been pawed by white guys for sex, but the only one who had ever tried to gangbang me was black. On the other hand, Will was black, and he had saved me and then ended his brief association with gangbanger Curtis. I saw him as a protector. Will would take care of me and make sure that no one ever misused me again.

But now here I was, misusing Will because of my feelings for JT. What did that say about me?

☮

Chapter 4

IN THE SECOND WEEK AFTER I'D LEFT JT TO GO BACK TO school, his fourth letter arrived. Eleven pages. Tucked inside were three small photos. My heart skipped when I saw his smile. It started to trip as I read his words.

> *2 / 10 / 72*
> *Hi Baby!*

He started off happy, but then things took a downward turn. It sounded like he was having second thoughts about us.

> *Feeling pressure, too much writing back and forth.*

How was I pressuring him when he was the one writing all the time? OK, I was writing just as much. But still.

> *You have many captivating qualities, so tempting*
> *that I just cannot allow myself to enjoy them.*

Whaaat? Why not? There were so many mixed messages. Like the dilemma wasn't losing me, it was having me—huh? JT clearly was conflicted. I wished I could just take him in my arms and hold him. That was at least half the problem: he wasn't here. The other half? I wasn't there.

Next came the lyrics (by now I saw that this was his M.O.). A heartbreaking song called "The Harder I Try" by the Free Movement, about a man who could not get over the loss of his true love. JT's take was that such pain would not have to be suffered if only one stayed single and free. And it sounded like that was what he wanted. We'd barely begun. Were we already over? I was about to cry.

Until I saw the surprising turn of tide, in bold red ink:

Oh my love, I only hope you know how much you mean to me.

From there on, JT reiterated that he couldn't get over how much I had impressed him, more profoundly than anyone else ever had. And in just one magical night together. He said he didn't know whether to laugh or cry.

I know I've got to muster an army to resist your probable attack on my singletude, he wrote. ("Probable"? Excuse me?) But it sure didn't sound like he planned to resist very hard. Because there were eight more pages talking about school, me, basketball, and us, before:

> *It's 3:00 a.m. and I've gotta mail this and then try to get a little sleep. But just so you know, I miss you.*
> *Jonathan*
>
> *P.S. Here are some photos I got from some girl.*

I put down the letter to examine the pictures. Oh, how I loved seeing JT's face in the black and white photos, each one showing him with a different expression. In one he was laughing, like "some girl" had caught him unawares. In another he looked bemused, like "Hmm, why is this chick taking my picture again?" In the third he had a stern expression, like "OK, knock it off already."

Who was "some girl"? Did she mean anything to him? What did I mean?

His army, my attack—what was with the battle metaphors?

Yet I saw the gold nuggets in the shifting sand. My captivating qualities, so tempting—no one had ever talked to me that way. He said he read my letters over and over—what guy did that?

Who sent pictures if they planned to break up?

I imagined JT in his room, moving from bed to desk and back again, trying to study but unable to concentrate, head spinning, reading my letters one more time, reaching for a pen.

He mailed the letter at three a.m.? Probably to make the early pickup, wanting to get it into my hands. I could almost hear the hall door *shush*-ing in the quiet dorm, his sneakers pattering down the stairwell. The snow-covered campus silent but for the lonely cry of a night bird, giving voice to his longing:

"Oh my love, I only hope you know how much you mean to me."

Now I wanted to laugh and cry, too. I should have been studying, but instead I curled up on my bed and studied his pictures until my roommate burst into the room.

"Nixon's going to China," she announced, having just heard this in her Poli Sci class. But we had absolutely no idea what that meant.

♡

JT dominated my inner life, but my outer life was still that of a college student. Before I spent time on Will or JT, there was my roomie, Fran. We heard of legendary battles between other roommates, but in two plus years of rooming together, Fran and I had never been more than mildly irritated with each other.

When my parents had dropped me off at school, I scored a corner room and hoped I'd be as lucky with a roommate. Fran's mom barged in like an army sergeant, asking assertively, "Do you have a roommate yet?" Behind her, a tall girl with a heart-shaped face smiled shyly. I smiled back and got up to help them move Fran in.

I found out that she actually wasn't shy but an interesting mix of good girl/bad girl. She'd been president and valedictorian of her high school class back in Pittsburgh, balancing her accomplishments with plenty of drinking, smoking, and sex. I admired her mod Carnaby Street outfits and the way she coolly blew smoke rings when she lit a cigarette. Night after night Fran and I sat huddled on her lower bunk. Listening to our old soul records, we'd rehash high school and debate the meaning of life while she patiently transformed me from non-smoker to skilled blower of those sexy little clouds.

My first semester weekends were lonely, as Fran's boyfriend came most Friday nights to take her home. Still, she was torn: while he lavished her with gifts and was reportedly good in bed, his scary temper was why we privately dubbed him "Fuckface." I saw him smack her in the dorm parking lot one night because she and I had been drinking beer at a frat party. Eventually she'd had enough of Fuckface's volatile mood swings, and she dumped the asshole. I was relieved that she was no longer tempted by the pressure he exerted for her to "just quit school and come home." It also meant that there would be a lot more time for Fran and me to go out and play.

Our dorm room was in the center of campus, the only drawback being that it was on a sorority floor. Frat guys got houses where their drunken parties took place, while girls were relegated to dorm halls. Not only was visitation from guys extremely limited, there was even a rule that we had to leave a shoe in the doorway (an assumption that, if the door were slightly ajar, there could be no sex going on). We were embarrassed to reveal our school's provincial limitations to friends from other colleges, people who could practically have lovers living in their rooms.

The sorority sisters generally turned up their perky noses at us, but they were curious about what went on in our room. Our walls were covered in purple crepe paper and blacklight posters, and tie-dyed sheets hung around our beds. We were changing. We played less of our sweet old finger-snapping Temptations and more of the battle cries of Jefferson Airplane and Jimi Hendrix. Our dorm-mates also noticed the funny smells that wafted out from under our door. "Is that incense or marijuana?" the girls whispered in the hallway. "Both!" they decided.

On weekdays we went to classes, especially Fran, who was more studious than I. The only one of her siblings to go to college, she had a scholarship and a widowed mother who was counting on her to succeed.

Yet we also took part in campus activism, especially me, who was more political than she. Ever since I was a kid, I'd been outraged by a growing awareness of the many inequities in our world of white vs. black. Poverty, prejudice, beatings, and lynchings. In high school I had argued with my parents over civil rights, begged them to let me join other white youth travelling to the south to register black voters. Not only did they say no, but made it clear they were fine with the status quo, which included that the war, one that countless poor young men were fighting because rich old men forced them to, had escalated. Well, I no longer lived under their racist roof. Now in college, I was free to do what I wanted.

Protests, rallies, "love-ins," and "be-ins" were all surprisingly similar. Joints passed around by students who were varieties of us. Girls with long straight hair, big Afros, halter tops. Jesus-looking guys with low-slung jeans, bare chests, dashikis. Boots or bare feet, headbands, and earrings. The first chords of the anthem of the day, whether the Stones played electrically through loudspeakers or Dylan picked acoustically on someone's guitar. Happily dazed smiles or angry fists, depending on what some charismatic speaker was urging us to do: "End the war, protest the draft, let eighteen-year-olds vote damn it, burn baby burn, burn the fucking fascist flag motherfuckers!" Or "Tune in, turn on, drop out, love is all you need, love the one you're with, baby." And the ubiquitous "Power to the people. Power to the people! RIGHT ON!"

In the spring of 1971, our sophomore year, Fran and I traveled to Washington, DC, for the largest anti-war march ever before. We were in the front lines of half a million protesters who strode to the steps of the Capitol building. Amazingly, organizers succeeded in keeping it peaceful. I was particularly struck by an emotional speech from John Kerry, a veteran who made it home alive but changed. When he'd enlisted, he'd been a young man in blind support of his country's actions in Vietnam, but by the time he returned home, he was firmly anti-war. We all thought, who knows better than someone who's been there? We naïvely ranted to each other, "Where is that coward Nixon, who sends boys off to war but doesn't even have the guts to face us?"

All of this was a reminder that we were in the bosom of our tribe. A tribe that was going to change the world.

But our tribe was also going to have fun. By our second year,

Fran and I were getting high a couple times a week before going out to find an adventure on campus. Like the night we went to a concert in the gym to hear the band Chase, who were big for their hit song "Get It On." Before the music started, one of the roadies came and asked us if we'd like to party with the band afterward. Sure we would! We both danced our asses off at that off-campus party and then each made out with a member of the band.

Another night we had our first experience with hallucinogens, something called wood rosin, which Fran had gotten from a high school friend. We rode the mellow high from party to party until we started to come down. At the local pizza shop, two good-looking dark-haired guys slid into our booth. They were in a frat that had been kicked out of Greek life for drug use. "Come back to our place, we're actually good guys," they laughed, and they were charming, too. So instead of fizzling out, our colorful evening rekindled with slow sex at their off-campus apartment. We dated them for a while, which only added to our reputation— the coolest room, the coolest music, and those long-haired, slightly badass boys. Most of the time, we went to their place, but sometimes they came to us—and we even took the shoe out of the door.

There were also plenty of nights when it was just Fran and me in our room, debating some issue, watching TV, listening to music, or doing homework. I wrote a paper for her, she sewed a top for me. We were roomies to the end.

When I started seeing Will, more of my weekends involved finding a ride to Pitt. Fran didn't want to go home that often, so naturally she began looking for other girls to hang out with. She'd had her time with Fuckface, and now it was my turn with Will. It was working out just fine.

♡

Apparently, JT was not breaking up with me. His fifth letter in two weeks was ten pages long.

> *2 / 14 / 72*
> *Well, so much for trying not to write you. It's impossible!*

He explained that he thought he had what his psychology textbooks called an approach-avoidance complex. I'd looked it up in the library, and it meant both wanting and yet not wanting, or fearing the consequences of, something. He did not say how he intended to resolve it. I'd written of my various worries regarding my parents, and most recently, how sneaking around might feel to JT. He said he didn't care as long as he could be with me.

Then he wrote out the lyrics to Bobby Taylor's beautiful song, "Does Your Mama Know About Me?" For some reason he spelled it Momma. I didn't know if that was a black thing, or maybe just a southern thing because my mom said momma too. The song asked if I understood what I was getting into, the reactions of parents, other family, friends. And how would my people treat him, would they accept him as a man? I hated that it was even an issue, and of course I knew that my parents would be horrified. But the weight of loving him was heavier than what people were going to think of me; it was the knowledge that eventually I'd be breaking someone's heart.

JT fantasized about our next meeting:

> *I think it won't be like the first time. We know*
> *each other so much better now.*

43

Maybe, but I sure would have no problem if it were just like the first time, the happiest night of my life.

He wrote out another whole song, this one by Smokey Robinson, "Here I Go Again." Such a sweet falling-for-you song. I could feel Smokey's yearning, and JT's too, as I read the lines about "your laughter" and "your lovely hair." And oh, did I have yearnings of my own. Like the Valentine's Day that came and went, and I had no Valentine to kiss me. Couples sped around campus through the winter sleet and wind, holding hands and laughing into their woolen scarves. I wanted to be one of them. But I had chosen differently: two guys, neither of whom was a student at my school.

JT ended his epic communiqué like this:

> *In spite of my conflict, I just can't afford to lose*
> *you and miss you for the rest of my life.*
> *Jonathan*
> *P.S. So you write poetry you say! How come I*
> *haven't received any?*

Hmm, approach-avoidance, huh. I wondered to which side JT was giving the greater weight. And why hadn't he told me? (Or was ten pages his way of telling me?)

My favorite part of the letter was about the next time we'd see each other. No matter what else, we were both thinking the same way about that.

Till then, JT wanted a poem? I would write him a poem. After all, I was the winner of my high school poetry award.

I'd been writing poetry since the age of six. And throughout school my nerdy bookishness had been every English teacher's dream.

Writers usually read, and books were my escape from a lonely childhood. From mystery heroine Nancy Drew to the leatherbound classics in my grandmother's antique bookcases. When I stumbled upon Sammy Davis Jr.'s autobiography, *Yes I Can*, it changed my life. My prejudiced parents had taught me that black people were "different" from us. But there was Sammy—insecure, yearning, aching, loving. He was a man and black and a celebrity, but his heart sounded just like mine. I wondered what else my parents were wrong about.

No one advised me about college. I just thought all colleges had the same majors. Had I been aware that some schools were known for their English and maybe even creative writing programs, I would have chosen one. But I wasn't aware. I picked Slippery Rock, a state-funded (i.e., cheaper) school as far away as possible from the long arm of my mother.

A new world of reading opened to me at the college library. Elia Kazan, Sylvia Plath, Nikki Giovanni, Norman Mailer, Anaïs Nin. I read James Baldwin's *Another Country* over and over, wondering what it would be like to live in a brownstone overlooking Central Park, go to cocktail parties in Greenwich Village, and have friends who were black and white, straight and gay, writers, artists, musicians.

Sophomore year, I took a creative writing class. Our first assignment was to write a short story, which I had never done before. My story "Introspection" fictionalized my grandfather's recent death. At the next class after turning it in, I was nervous but excited to see my grade. Besides an A, there were two underlined words: See me.

My instructor, a kindly, bearded guy, told me that he was impressed with my story and hoped that I would keep writing. That could have been my opportunity to ask him to mentor me, but I didn't know about such things. I earned an A in that class, which felt so good. Maybe I could write after all.

Now here was JT, wanting a poem. I got to work.

POEM FOR JONATHAN
(who thinks it may be utopian to be alone)

you said you had to be a runner, so run, go on, run along
if you can make it that way, then who am I to say
I was right, or you were wrong

but some silent moonlit midnight, madly
feeling alone, and not really so free
don't you know you might think, a little sadly
you didn't try to find out what I'm all about
and share something of yourself with me . . . just a little

oh go on and run, my fleet yet fearful one
jump high, pass it by, don't even try
but just hide from your heart what you knew from the start:
while you're running alone, so all on your own
you're passing up a chance to fly . . . just a little.

☮

Chapter 5

I WAITED WITH ALTERNATE FEELINGS OF CONFIDENCE AND self-doubt for JT's reaction to my poem. It took a few days longer than I thought. And only five pages? Already I was spoiled.

> *2 / 23 / 72 (and it's way late!)*
> *Hey Love,*
> *I love it! I love it sooo much. Your poem is a*
> *masterpiece. I can't stop reading these great lines.*

Then he quoted just about every phrase from the poem! The best part:

> *I'm on cloud 9 after reading this. And instead of*
> *running from love, I think I should run toward it.*
> *Don't you agree?*

> *Yours always,*
> *No longer a scaredy-cat*

> *P.S. Sorry this is so short, but to make up for it,*
> *here's a dull newspaper article.*

He loved it. He loved it so much. And it may have changed his mind about whether to approach instead of avoid me, I guessed.

I looked at the newspaper clipping. It was a large feature article: "Small White College Welcomes First Black Star." There was his gorgeous smile. It was all about how his small-college coach had gone to a big-city high school to recruit. Jonathan Thomas's accomplishments had included All-Conference (whatever that was), six scoring records, an average of twenty-seven points a game, and leading his team to two Division titles—despite that he was still only a junior.

Wow. I knew I'd caught a big fish in a small pond. But I hadn't realized how big a fish JT actually was. Besides excelling at his sport, the article said that he was a dorm counselor and was involved in clubs and student government.

I smiled to myself: some dorm counselor. He'd snuck a naked girl into the men's bathroom so she could puke. Still, I was impressed. For all my supposed activism, going around saying "Fuck the establishment" meant I didn't have to do much. How did he make everything look so easy? And find time to write pages and pages of letters to me.

I read on. It said he'd had difficulty adjusting to small-town life. Of course, it didn't mention the prejudice of small-town life. In fact, just the opposite, "The fans just want to see Johnny T. They don't care whether he's black." I doubted that, I knew my town. On the other hand, who wouldn't want to go see that handsome, talented man? I sure did.

There was more. And in his words to the reporter, I could hear his humble confidence:

"People made fun of the way I shot the ball. They said, 'No way you'll play college.' But I think they're real proud of me now."

Why did my heart fill with pride, too? As if I'd had anything to do with the making of Johnny Thomas. No, I was just the woman that he hoped to see again soon.

Yet I was so far away. For the first time, I regretted that distance away from my parents had been my main criterion for choosing a college.

♡

To get home, first I needed bus money. My parents would send it, but they might question why I suddenly wanted to come around. "I miss my little sister," I told them (which was true), and "I'm homesick" (which was not.). I was fed up with my mom's meddling, my dad's needling humor, their prejudice, their fights.

I'd have to lug my suitcase through snow and cold to be at the bus stop early. Then six tiring hours of bumping along pothole-studded roads. The smell of exhaust, a dirty bathroom, stopping at every small burg. At the tail end of winter, there would be only a dull brown landscape rolling by.

But oh man, the excitement when my travel day finally arrived. I brought homework and a novel, but I couldn't concentrate. All I wanted to do was fantasize, and it began and ended with JT. What would it be like when we first saw each other now that it had been over a month? Would we make love immediately or take a little time to get comfortable again? My parents would probably let me use the Chevy they'd inherited when my grandfather died, and I'd tell them I was going out with Hannah. Would I do it all again the next night? Hell, yes.

In the midst of my fantasies, troubling feelings about Will surfaced. His letters sounded so unhappy. He was disgusted with the covert racism of the Brits and how he hadn't received the full stipend he'd been promised. Did he realize how much his letters had decompensated into complaints? At times it sounded like he even blamed me for encouraging him to go. How would he feel if he knew I was on my way to be with another man—again? That this man and I already had songs that we called "ours," and that sex with him was "making love." Guilt squeezed like a vise around my heart, so I turned my thoughts back to memories of JT—that night with Hannah and Colleen, his dancing eyes, our love so doggone good.

When the bus finally dropped me at the dreary little one-room station, I called home and my stepdad picked me up. Dinner was ready, so I sat down with the family.

"How's school, honey?" Mom ladled gravy onto her mashed potatoes and chicken. She'd never gotten away from her childhood on a farm, with its huge homestyle meals.

"It's OK. I'm really enjoying Social Psych." The instructor made it interesting, but what was really fun was the fact that JT was taking it too. I enjoyed picturing him in his class learning the same things I was.

"Social Psychology. That sounds like some typical hippie hoo-ha," said Dad, chewing with his mouth open, as usual.

"Dad, could you eat with your mouth closed, please? And it's not hippie hoo-ha. It's science. Like we're studying about the Kitty Genovese stabbing in New York. It's fascinating that so many people heard her screams but didn't do anything."

"I'll tell you why. (Chew, chew.) They arrested a colored guy and turned out he had done other violent crimes. (Smack, smack.) No one wanted to get killed by a nigger, that's why. (Swallow.)"

"Dad, please. Don't say colored guy. Don't say nigger. Call people what they want to be called. Call them black or Afro-American."

"I'll call them whatever the hell I feel like it, when they're going around killing people," Dad said with a scowl.

"They aren't all going around killing people. That's one case, and now I'm sorry I brought it up. Mom, how can you stand him?" Mom gave her nervous giggle, the one that showed up when my dad and I discussed a topic she didn't know much about. But I knew her views were similar to his.

My little sister's head swiveled from one to the other as she tried to make sense of what we were saying.

"I know a black person," she said. "A boy in my second grade class at school. Darryl."

"Well, I hope you're nice to Darryl and would never call him bad names, baby." I tried to look stern but loving.

"I wouldn't, Sissie." She smiled a self-satisfied smile and ate a green bean.

"Sooo . . ." I nonchalantly took a bite of salad, acting cool like everything did not hinge on my next question. "Can I use the car tonight?"

"But you just got home. Where you going, hon?" That was my mom, always up in my business.

"Over to Hannah's." Even though she went to the local college, Hannah had her own apartment. "We're just hangin' out. I'll be around tomorrow."

Mom glanced at Dad, and he nodded his assent. We finished dinner in silence. Of course, they never asked how Will was doing. I certainly didn't tell them about JT. My dad had to know who JT was. JT was the local college basketball hero at the same school where my dad had once played and captained the team. My dad was now the local high school basketball coach. I was sure the name Johnny Thomas would come up that very evening, when my dad went out to the Republican Club to drink beer and talk sports with an assortment of assistant coaches, former players, and lonely geezers. That was how he spent nearly every night, while my mom sat home watching TV. A pretty boring existence for her, but I was too caught up in my own life to think much about their marital experience.

I helped with the dishes before excusing myself to go shower off bus fumes, cigarette smoke, and nervous sweat. Then I holed up with my sister in "our" old room, and we chattered and giggled while I got ready. She picked out a pair of paisley bikini panties: "*Ooh la la*, Sissie, wear these." I didn't even own a bra, but since I was slender, my favorite light blue bodysuit would give enough support to my small breasts and show them off a little. My softest pair of hip-hugger jeans did exactly what their name suggested, and I finished off the look with my worn brown boots and olive fatigue jacket. I kissed my sister, already sad-faced to see me go, and said goodnight to my parents. I slid behind the cold steering wheel and headed for JT's campus.

First, I stopped to visit with Hannah. We had to get our stories straight in case my mom got nosy, and I couldn't wait to fill her in on what was happening between JT and me. "Six letters?" "Yes." "But it's hardly been a month." "I know!" "And he's already saying 'love'?" "Yeah, can you fucking believe it?" We hugged each other, bouncing like we were still thirteen.

"What about Will?" she finally asked, and the mood turned.

"Well, of course he doesn't know anything. I don't know what I'm gonna do, Hannah," I said miserably.

She slipped an arm around my shoulder again. "Don't worry, you'll figure it out." I wondered how she felt about the fact that she had brought me and JT together. Maybe she thought we'd dig each other, have a one-night stand, and that would be that.

I drove the few blocks to his dorm and parked. It was already later than I'd planned to arrive, but on my car radio the Cornelius Brothers and Sister Rose were singing "Too Late to

Turn Back Now." For a moment, I just wanted to sit and listen to their sweet harmonies as they sang about falling in love. The cold night air kissed my cheeks, and the warm adrenaline buzzed through my body like a drug.

When the song ended, I ran inside and took the stairs two at a time, heartbeat accelerating with every stride. I knocked. There was no answer.

For a minute I stood wondering what to do, puzzled over why he wouldn't be there. Maybe he didn't get my letter. Maybe he feared that I might not show. Maybe he just didn't want to appear too eager.

It couldn't possibly be that he didn't want to see me. Could it?

I set out on a treasure hunt: where would I find my prize? The library was closest, so I went there first, but the stacks and tables held no sign of him. When I got to the gym, the sound of a ball dribbling on the court raised my heart rate again, but it worried me, too. I imagined our precious minutes dribbling while he finished a game and showered before finally back to his room. Instead, there he was in street cloth goofing around with a couple guys. He saw me, grinned, threw the ball to one of them, waved, and walked toward his love. It was already too late to turn back now.

♡

He was as handsome as I remembered.

The sad truth was, I had never really been that physically attracted to Will. I admired him, and part of that admiration included appreciating the way he looked—part Black Power radical, part hippie flower child, part math nerd. His Afro picked out or occasionally in cornrows. Round wire-rimmed glasses.

Dashiki, army jacket, peace sign, Che Guevara T-shirt. At 5'9"
he was shorter than most guys I had gone out with, but he had
muscle, the kind of muscle a teenage boy builds when he wants
to stay out of a gang or be ready to fight his own father. Dark
skin, full lips, broad nose—his features spoke of Africa to me. Of
course, what did I know of the shapes and shades of Africa? Will
could look intimidating. But he had the heart of a teddy bear.
Yes, I admired him. I just didn't particularly desire him.

I had assumed that admiration meant love and love meant
desire, and that had drawn me to him. I didn't know that those
were three separate things, till now.

At 6'2", 6'4" if you counted his hair, JT was tall. Tall like my
stepdad (also a former basketball player). And JT was lean—the
kind of lean like my dad said made his players fast on the court.
JT's hair was a little less wiry, his skin a little less dark, his nose a
bit narrower than Will's. In other words, he probably had more
white ancestors.

Was that why I found him so much more compelling? Was I
unable to let go of European standards of beauty, or did his look
just seem a little closer to my own tribe? Or was it simply that I
was falling in love? I didn't really care. I just wanted him.

In the gym, his long legs made short work of the space between us. And then we were holding hands, crossing the quad
past the old stone chapel, following paths shoveled between
snowbanks, fueled by our own little puffs of steam. Faraway winter stars winked at us. Yellow lanterns lit everything gold.

In his room, we turned suddenly shy. I felt larger than life,
filling the small space too full with my body and bulky clothes
and out-of-breathiness. He moved slowly, which I would learn
was his trademark everywhere but on the court. His keys made
no sound as he set them down, nor did his arms slipping easily

out of his nylon jacket. He looked around as if to see the room as I saw it, nodded his approval at its casual neatness (no jockstraps on the floor). I took my coat off, too, and perched on the edge of his bed.

He took the few steps to the stereo. "I've got something I think you'll like," he said, still not looking at me. He slid an album out of its sleeve and put it on, handing the cover to me. Plaintive guitar notes and rhythmic conga beats danced into the room.

"*Santana III.* I haven't heard it yet." I was excited, and music was our safe zone.

I started to feel a little more at home. Scooting back against the wall, I pulled off my boots and socks, crossed my legs and lit a cigarette. He handed me the makeshift ashtray, still there from our last/first night together, then pushed off his sneakers and unbuttoned his shirt. For the first time since I saw him in the gym, our eyes met. We both smiled. Shy smiles that turned into wide-mouth grins. Grins like suckers that last all day, like holidays, like snow days, like Today Is The Day. He sat down and slid one long arm around my shoulders, tipped his head so close that his hair tickled the side of my face.

"Now tell me," he said, in his honey voice with just a hint of southern clover, "how did this happen? How did you get here? And how did I get so lucky as to finally have you all to myself?"

"It's a long story," I said, taking a drag, "but since we have the time, I'll share my harrowing tale."

We didn't really have much time. Only two nights, magic nights that would fly by like witches on brooms. Countdown nights like the hours before execution, when first light would pull me out of his room. But the start of those hours felt rich with unused time. And already we were fixing the pattern for spending our riches: talk before love, love around midnight, an hour or so of sleep sometime before the dawn, joy all night long.

I woke in the early morning hours to feel a weight on my chest and realized that we had fallen asleep with him still on top of me. One arm was up under my neck, the other gently holding my hip. Legs tangled, faces nearly touching on the pillow. In the dim light I noticed a little whorl behind his ear, soft as a baby's hair, a vulnerable reminder of the boy he'd recently been. I reached up to stroke the silken circle, gently so as not to wake him, but already he was stirring and opening his eyes. They widened when he saw me. We both lay still, holding our gaze, coming conscious of all the ways we were commingled. The night came back in flashes:

"It's been so long."

"But doesn't it feel like yesterday?"

Santana moaned, *How slowly time passes without you.*

"And how did your parents react?"

"You have three psych books? I only have one."

"I'm so glad you're here."

Santana cried, *Let's go girl, let's go dance!*

"Did you see those POWs?"

"Terrible. Fran and I went to the protest."

"I can't believe you looked up those basketball scores." Yeah, I'd gone to my school library to check the hometown newspaper. What did people do before libraries anyway?

"Come here."

"Wait, listen to this part."

Santana urged, *Open your eyes to a new way of living.*

"Here, have some of this."

"Maybe you should have a little of this."

Laughter. Silence. Lips speaking without words.

Much later, just before sleep, my solo whisper, "I love you." No spoken love back yet. Just his arms pulling me tighter, his beard softly rubbing against my face like a cat.

And the next night, we did do it all over again.

Chapter 6

JT'S NEXT LETTER WAS SIX PAGES.

> *3 / 6 / 72 (middle of the night)*
> *Bonjour Mademoiselle,*
> *Maybe I shouldn't write because I'm in a fucked*
> *up mood. But I know that feeling closer to you has*
> *got to make things better.*

He didn't say what had him feeling down. Instead he reminisced about what happened on our last night together, or to be more accurate, morning. We had overslept. He knew I could be in big trouble, but he just hadn't been able to bring himself to wake me right away. Oh my god, was anything ever as sweet as him telling me he watched me while I slept?

When he woke me, I'd wondered for a brief moment, did I drool, was I snoring? I had a feeling that it wouldn't have made any difference. One song he had played for me by Jesse Colin Young talked about my sunlit hair, my sweet mouth. I realized that it was the way he saw me—a long-legged colt of a girl with a mane of brown hair, a loving free-spirit who would roll in a field and pull him down with lips that wanted to taste him.

Was that girl really me? Yes, but.

For us, the only sun was the dreaded dawn calling through his dorm window. The only summer's air would be when the weather got warm and we had to open that window to keep from having heatstroke. Our time together was circumscribed by the walls of his small room and single bed. And all because I feared my parents finding out.

What was I afraid of? It wasn't their judgment. They had already judged me plenty for being with Will. If they knew about JT, would that force me to decide between JT and Will? I knew I would have to face that in the long term, but I was scared to face it now.

In the short term, secrecy was a matter of practicality; I feared the barriers that my parents could erect to my seeing Jon. They could refuse to give me bus money or to let me stay at the house and use the car, and the best prevention was for my parents not to find out. Being black, handsome, and a local celebrity, JT stood out. I did not, but with him I would, and a lot of local sports fans knew me because my stepdad was the high school coach.

So yeah, I was anxious when I overslept that last morning. I imagined what I'd say if my parents had stayed up. Car problem—no, I would've called. Too drunk to drive—nope, they never asked me about drugs and alcohol, and I preferred it that way. The only thing I could come up with was that Hannah and I stayed up late talking and then I fell asleep on her couch.

When I pulled up to the house, every sound seemed magnified. Could my parents hear the growl of the engine, the clunk of the car door? By the time I reached the porch I regretted not having used JT's dorm bathroom before I left. I hopped in place as I tried to get my key in the lock, and I didn't even flush the toilet for fear of waking them up.

I hated the sneaking and hiding, but it was a means to an end. Did JT feel that way? Or did he feel like some kind of lesser backdoor man? If he did, he kept it to himself.

His letter continued by chastising me for flattering him so much, thinking he was all suave and sophisticated when he sometimes felt so dumb and tongue-tied around me. (Did he really not know that I sometimes felt the same way?) He finished with a joke that would become part of our regular teasing back and forth, that he was my therapist, I was his patient, and he could help me if only I would come into his "office" and tell him all about my childhood and my dreams:

> *Cuz I'll be dreaming of you,*
> *JT*

I was smiling through tears as I finished and then read it all over again. JT's adorable humor, my psych major playing psychoanalyst to me—yes, I would love to lie down on your couch, Dr. Thomas. But what would I tell him about my childhood?

♡

Growing up, I always heard that I looked "exotic." People asked if I were Italian, Greek, Spanish, Puerto Rican (if they were from the East Coast), Mexican (if they were from the West); and occasionally—when I was tan and had curled my straight hair—I was asked if I were mixed with black. No one ever guessed Latvian-Jewish, Scotch-Irish Canadian, Welsh/German/French/Native-American.

My mother, Dorthy, was the daughter of a Dust Bowl farmer who transplanted his family to Los Angeles, worked for General Motors, and eventually bought real estate. My father, Bill, was the son of two immigrants, a doctor and nurse who worked the night shift at a Pennsylvania hospital. My parents met at a college in Kansas. Bill was a tall, dark, and handsome charmer studying to be a journalist. Dorthy, a busty, long-legged blonde was probably going for her "Mrs." Degree—she wasn't stupid, but in her day, pin-up girl looks were more compelling than smarts. They'd moved us to LA, but their union didn't last. My mother said my father liked bowling more than working, and she divorced him when I was only three.

My father's parents offered to help her financially and with child care, so my mother and I moved back east to live with her ex-in-laws in Pennsylvania. I didn't want to leave my daddy. To me he was a hero who took me for special overnights. What did I know about a father who didn't pay child support and took his little girl to his bachelor apartment only when it was convenient for him? Fortunately, his parents were the opposite of him. They lived in a huge house full of fascinating antiques and had a summer cabin in the Poconos where I could swim every day. They were loving to me, and my grandmother especially entertained me with bedtime stories of growing up in a huge family in Canada. Night after night, I'd demand, "Tell me about that roo-ga-roo creature again, Grandma!" *Rougarou*, a French-inspired werewolf.

When I occasionally received a letter or a gift from my father, my mother took me aside.

"Your grandmother sent that. She just put your father's name on it so you'll think it came from him."

A little later my grandmother took me aside, too. "Don't pay any attention to your mother. She just wants you to think bad things about your father."

Secrets and lies. Who was telling the truth? I kept a secret of my own: my mother regularly beat me with a belt. Between beatings and secrets and moving and adults embroiled in their own dramas, I was already a misplaced child.

To his parents' dismay, my father's younger brother, Jim, began taking my mother out. Soon my mom went off to live with Uncle Jim in a small New Jersey town where he was a teacher and coach, while I stayed behind. I spent third grade with them but it wasn't a success; I was unhappy and broke the rules a lot, and Mom asked if I wanted to go back to my grandparents. With a new relationship to manage, it was probably easier on her, too.

In sixth grade it was decided that I would live with Jim and my mother again. It would be a fresh start back in his hometown where he'd just been hired to coach the high school team. They were trying to have a child together. They (and I) would suffer heartbreaking losses—several miscarriages and a son who died the day after birth—before my little miracle sister was born.

Jim never adopted me. He let my mother wield her belt. It took years before I got over a feeling that at any time I might be sent away. Then when they found out that I was dating Will, I was actually sent away.

Later my mother would ask me, "Do you think not having a real father is what drove you to be with a black man?" That sounded ridiculous to me. Wouldn't that have driven me to be with an older man?

When my father, Bill, was thirty-six and I was twelve, he moved back to his parents' home because he was dying of cancer. The adults were too lost in their own preoccupations to think much about me. Except for the moment when someone handed me the veteran's flag that had been on his casket, it was as if I weren't even there.

I was sure that he would be all alone in heaven. I thought about killing myself so I could be with him there.

⟡

But I didn't. Somehow, I got through the two awful years that started with my baby brother's death, then my father's, and lastly a disfiguring car accident that required cosmetic surgery and years of reparative dentistry. Then my long-awaited baby sister brought happiness to our disjointed little family. Complications came as she got older and needed structure. Jim (now "Dad") would not back up my mother's attempts at discipline. This led to many shouting matches, slammed doors, him storming off, and my mother crying alone at night. The older I got, the more it led to my not wanting to be at home.

By high school I had girlfriends, and then boyfriends, with cars. The more I left, the more obsessed my mom was with where I went. She rifled my purse, followed me, and sometimes even called my friends' mothers to discuss her fear that I would get pregnant. Why did I have to be subjected to this kind of oppressive parenting? None of my friends' parents acted that way.

Was that the start of my mother's later diagnosis of bipolar disorder? Maybe she came from beautiful but flawed genes. Maybe her two husbands' neglect just finally wore down her psychological resources.

One thing I knew for sure was that the adults in my family lied. The closest thing to truth was what I took in through my own eyes and ears. I couldn't wait for the freedom of college.

Yet now that I was there, I didn't feel all that free. And I had become a liar, too.

☮

Chapter 7

MY LOVE AFFAIR WITH JT BY US MAIL WAS NOT HAPPENING in a vacuum. Will was still writing, and the tone of his letters had gone downhill. "I feel I've changed," he wrote. "I hate." I didn't know how to respond as Will flip-flopped between angry rants and desperate pleas to love him, marry him, never leave him.

Will knew that I still owed my best friend, Colleen, money for the loan that helped me get to England to see him. He had said he'd help me repay her, but as the weeks went by, he no longer mentioned it. I was becoming embarrassed about how long it was taking to return her money. I was going to have to do something, but what?

Will did say that he had made a friend named Brenda. "I would die before I would ever cheat on you," he wrote. Why was he even saying that? Apparently, Brenda had helped him out with money when he was at his most destitute—and had invited him to spend spring break at her parents' house in London. It confused me to feel a twinge of jealousy toward Brenda. Did she want my Will? Did he want her? And how could I even call him "my" when I no longer felt like "his"? I worried that there might be something wrong with me psychologically.

Will's troubling letters were in stark juxtaposition to the shy teasing and gentle longing I felt from JT. Yet I tried to understand what Will was going through. He was in a strange place, cut off from everything familiar and without money. Whereas

Jonathan was in his element—the darling of the campus, the press, and me.

I was reminded of that when I received an envelope from my high school friend Sharon back home. Inside were just a brief note and a newspaper advertisement: "Johnny Thomas To Sign Autographs at the Friedrich's Grand Opening." There below the department store headline were those eyes, that smile. I thought, how strange that people would actually line up to get his name on a piece of paper. I already had several "autographs" and had moved on to a new desire—for him to just put his arms around me and never let go.

Sharon's note was a proposal: "How about if I go to the opening and bring him a message from you? Do you think he would like that? And what should I say?" I loved the idea. A little piece of me in the middle of his hectic, meaningless, me-less day.

"Just say, 'I have a message from Lynda. She asked me to tell you that she loves you,' " I wrote back. I smiled to myself as I dropped my response to her in the mail. Unlike some other things I was doing, this felt innocent—like being back with my girlfriends in high school, plotting about the boys.

The complicated, confusing "grown-up" things I was doing included cheating on Will. I certainly hadn't planned it. But I couldn't say "it just happened" either. Things didn't usually "just happen." I chose to go to that dance to meet JT and to visit his dorm with Colleen and Hannah. I deliberately titillated and tantalized. And when he invited me back, there was no question that I would go.

Another "grown-up" complication was how much I was blowing off classes. Not that this was grown-up, it wasn't. What felt grown-up was having a choice, every day. If it was snowing, if the class bored me, if I'd stayed up too late the night before—I could simply choose to skip class, to stay in bed. And because my new, complicated, "grown-up" life included an increasing amount of drug use, I was staying up late far too often. My grades, never great, were genuinely suffering.

In freshman year, Fran and I had attended only a few beer-soaked frat parties and then tried marijuana. Still, I ended up on academic probation because of missing class.

By sophomore year, Fran and I had a twice-weekly date with Boone's Farm and a nickel bag. After meeting our flirty rebel frat guys the night of our wood rosin trip, I failed an eight a.m. judo class due to sleeping late in my guy's bed. At times, I tried to bring my grades up: Fran and I took easy Sociology, Jazz, and Art classes together and did well. I aced Psych 101, Shakespeare, and Creative Writing. When I started seeing Will, he didn't drink or smoke anything, so the weekends with him were a respite from getting high. But one weekend when I was home, my mom took me to the family doctor. I had gained ten pounds thanks to unlimited food in the cafeteria plus the way-too-convenient vending machines in the dorm, and she thought I needed my first prescription for amphetamine "diet pills."

Then for junior year, Will was in England, and Fran's and my drug use accelerated, especially mine. We'd heard the stories of people losing their minds from getting loaded, but we believed that those were just scare tactics to keep us away from drugs.

"Lynnie, you're never gonna guess what's on TV tonight." Fran teased me by calling me Lynnie the way my grandparents did. We had just gotten back from the dining hall, and she was looking at the TV Guide.

"What, Frannie?" I was distracted, busy separating the

stems and seeds out of our stash. Then I'd turn it over to her because she was better at rolling.

"Our favorite *Dragnet*! The one where the parents get so high on mari-jew-wanna that they let the baby drown in the bathtub."

"Oh my god! Did I tell you they actually showed that episode to my senior class at an assembly? They thought it would scare us, but it just cracked us up."

We were smoking regularly, and no one had died yet. No one died the night we did wood rosin, either. Soon we added mescaline and various kinds of acid to our repertoire. I used the diet pills to keep my weight down, often staying up all night to read and write and only occasionally study. After I met JT, nights were for responding to his letters while playing the songs we loved. I shared the diet pills with Fran when she asked, although she wisely chose to abstain and sleep most nights. Occasionally I gave one to someone who needed to pull an all-nighter.

That wasn't the only thing that I sometimes shared on our good-girl sorority floor. I'd discovered that taking just a few birth control pills could bring on a late period. The snooty Greek sisters didn't like having non-Greeks on their floor. They fostered a reputation for being virgins, but their occasional knock on my door suggested otherwise. And I helped them because I still shuddered when I remembered my first-year pregnancy scare. In our "free love" era, guys acted like that love was equally free for both sexes. But an unplanned pregnancy could still turn a girl's life upside down, while the boys, who could just walk away, didn't seem to worry about it.

Much later I would learn that my pill dispensing was the precursor to "emergency contraception," which ultimately led to a safer Plan B.

But that was then. Abortion was illegal. Like most kids, we didn't have a plan b.

Then there were the other pills, mostly hallucinogens. Some claimed they did them for a spiritual experience. I'd spent the better part of two years discussing serious existential questions with various people, questions that I came to realize had no answers. After that, drugs became mostly about the party. I'd never had a bad trip, but a few times were touch-and-go. Like the night Fran, Pam (one of the two other non-sorority-sisters on our hall), and I dropped purple haze and decided to go for a drive—bad idea. When I told Fran she was driving down the wrong side of the country highway, we made it to Pam's parents' house nearby to come down—good idea.

The worst was the Sunday that Cathy (Pam's roommate and the other non-sorority girl) and I went home with two townies, Davy and Buddy, to do some THC. Soon Davy maneuvered Cathy into a bedroom, leaving me with Buddy. He had sex with me only because I couldn't move away or even speak the word "no." Afterward, he caressed me as if we'd just made love. When Cathy stumbled in wearing just her T-shirt and panties, we dressed and asked them to drop us off at the pizza place. We sat with our heads in our hands, too sick to even order food.

"Was that the THC?" Cathy asked me.

"I dunno. I've never done THC. But that's what gets you high on pot or hash, so it shouldn't be that different, right? Did you sleep with Davy?"

"Yeah. Did you sleep with Buddy?"

"Yeah, but I didn't want to. It was like I couldn't move or say anything. Ugh!" I was remembering Buddy slobber-kissing me and removing my clothes with his sweaty hands. Years later I would wonder if we'd been given PCP instead of THC. Did the guys know? Did they secretly not take any themselves? Or did the drug just not hit guys as hard? I knew I couldn't tell JT, my handsome stand-up JT who would never slip me a drug and then take advantage of me. Just the thought of JT knowing made my face burn with shame.

Drugs were unpredictable. Their very unpredictability made us feel like rebels, pioneers, renegades. Our tribe did drugs, protested the war, marched for civil rights, fought for Vietnam draftees to have the right to vote. And we partied. We laughed every day. We felt bold and brave every day. But I also felt scared nearly every day, and it didn't occur to me that maybe the others all did, too. Sometimes I just thought, oh JT, why am I here doing these crazy things, and you are there, so very fucking far away?

Meanwhile, back home, Hannah had an idea about how I could pay Colleen back. Hannah was seeing a guy who was a small-time dealer. Tucker ("Tuck") had good acid and offered to front some for me to sell at my school. He seemed to be a cool head who liked to help people out. He rented a big house and sometimes let people stay there when they were between pads or fronted them drugs if they needed cash. A hundred tabs at three dollars apiece would get me more than enough to pay Colleen and give Tuck his profit.

We agreed that I would take the LSD back to school with me the next time I went home. When I wrote to Will about it, he begged me not to do it. But he didn't offer an alternative.

I didn't tell Jonathan about the acid, either.

☮

Chapter 8

TWO WEEKS WITHOUT A LETTER FROM JT. NOW HERE HE WAS, in six pages. The first thing he did was apologize for his absence.

> *3 / 17 / 72*
> *Pardonne-moi ma belle dame!*

He had previously explained that he had gotten behind in school assignments and made sure to add that his silence didn't represent any diminished interest in me. In fact, he suggested that my last letter to him had sounded bitter. Maybe I hadn't taken him seriously when he warned that I might not hear from him for a while. Nothing could take away the disappointment of walking down to the front desk to find out that there was no letter from JT. Still, I didn't want to sound bitter to him. Everything about him was just too damn sweet. It was the situation that was one bitter fucking pill to swallow.

The good part was that he was floored by the surprise that Sharon had laid on him at the store opening. The only thing he would have liked better was if I had been able to deliver the message in person. Oh, if only it could have been me instead of Sharon going to that autograph signing. If I'd gone up to him and we'd walked away holding hands. Everyone would have known that he had chosen me, and I him. I wanted to tell the world, but I could not. But it was still fun to have sent him a surprise message.

He mentioned that he preferred to live a drama-free life. A drama-free life? Really, JT? Between school and sports and the media and now me—another man's woman? I wouldn't exactly call that drama-free. But then he got back to playing therapist, teasing me about how he'd like to send his secretary home and focus on my "treatment."

And the best part of all:

> *I'll get back from spring break on Monday April 3.*
> *Then I'll finally get to lay tired eyes on a tranquil*
> *sight.*
>
> *Avec amour,*
> *J.*

There in the last paragraph were the words I'd been waiting for: it was only two weeks until I'd see him again. Our breaks overlapped and we'd both get to "lay tired eyes on a tranquil sight." What a poet! Just those words on the page made my speed-fueled, bumpety-bump heartbeat slow to a calm, regular pace. Forgetting the work that I should have been doing but wasn't, the drugs that I shouldn't have been doing but was, I sat in my dorm in the bright afternoon, reading his letter on my narrow college bed. It was miles away from his and yet so much like his. My longing to be there instead of here felt like torture.

Until I could be there, I had things to do. Write to my parents for travel money. Make sure that Hannah would be available to be my alibi. Find out if Colleen would be home from Pitt on her break. Thank Sharon for playing our little prank on Jon at the department store autograph signing. Write to my little sister, Barbie, and let her know, Sissie's coming! Go down to the head shop off-campus to buy a hippie trinket for her.

I had to deal with my classes. One weighed on my mind the most heavily: Advanced Rhetoric, what the fuck was that? I'd been told that it was the next level writing class after my first one, but didn't rhetoric mean talking? And that instructor sure liked to hear himself talk. "The juxtaposition of unparalleled glory and angst created by this author blah blah blah." Then there was the balmy spring day when he decided he wanted to teach the class outside. It took six guys half the period to carry his gargantuan wooden desk down from the second floor, while we students sat uncomfortably in the still-soggy grass. What an ego.

Our first writing samples were due halfway through the course, but instead of encouraging me, he'd humiliated me. Thank God it was in a private meeting in his office. He told me my poetry, which often rhymed, was old-fashioned and out of style. I held back stinging tears as I practically ran out of there and decided to never go back to his class. With the exception of the poem for Jonathan, I completely stopped writing poetry. I knew I should deal with the situation (this was an important grade), but I didn't know what to do. So, I chose just to not think about it. Not much different from how I was dealing with Will.

Instead, I did enough in my other classes to keep those grades up. I did excel at writing papers. I could write papers about books I hadn't even read. I could write papers for other students about books neither of us had read. It was academic dishonesty, but I rationalized it. I told myself that academia was just part of the corrupt "establishment" that I spoke out against (even while hypocritically wanting that degree). I viewed my little writing business as a writing exercise, a mental challenge, and sometimes the source of a little spending money. My roomie even made it fun by promising to be my "servant for a week"—to do any chore or errand I asked for.

"Lynda, you really need to wash that purple top." Fran no longer smoked and didn't like it when I re-wore my clothes, with the cloying smell of stale cigarettes wafting about the room.

"Go fuck yourself," I answered with good humor, but the next thing I knew, she had flung me onto the bed. Taller and stronger than me, she actually held me down and wrestled the shirt off of me. We were both laughing. Then I had the last laugh.

"I dunno, Frannie my servant, I really think *you* need to wash this purple top."

(Pause. Sigh.) She climbed off, grabbed a pile of her own clothes too, and headed to the laundry room.

I lit a cigarette. "Frannie."

"Yeah, Lyn?"

"This is my last cig."

"Yeah, well, you should quit anyway."

"I don't want to quit."

(Pause. Big sigh.) "OK, got any change?" There were vending machines, including one for cigarettes, in the basement.

Maybe I overdid the servant thing a bit, but our teasing went both ways, and it was all in fun. Until, after more than two years of peaceful cohabitation, we began to have problems.

There was nothing I could point to that started it. Just a bunch of little irritations that began to add up. She'd watch *Star Trek* reruns over and over, so I'd take JT's last letter, my writing pad, and cigarettes and head down to the rec room.

I'd play and replay JT's and my albums, and she'd go hang out with Pam and Cathy across the hall.

I knew she was unhappy about our biology class. We'd agreed to take it together and buy one book. But the only section available was at eight a.m., in an auditorium all the way across campus. On cold, rainy, snowy days (and there were a lot of those in Pennsylvania), it was so hard to drag ourselves out of our snug beds that she often made that freezing trek alone.

She had a sarcastic sense of humor; there were times when she used it at my expense.

She didn't like for me to smoke in the room; some days I did it anyway.

One of these little incidents sent me to the dining hall alone the day before spring break. On my way out, I saw Ricardo, a guy I knew, talking to a girl I didn't recognize. Ricardo was from Colombia and had an outgoing personality, and it was just like him to wave me over with a big grin as if we were old friends. He was also tall and good-looking; not many people kept walking when Ricardo called out to them.

"Leen-da," he said in his sexy Spanish accent. "How are you? I want you to meet my other friend, Leen-da. She has your same name. I think maybe where she comes from is not too far from your home as well."

Linda was Afro-American. It was a little hard to call her "black" when everything about her was some shade of honey, from her reddish-brown hair to her gold skin to the tan fairy dust of freckles across her cheeks. But her fluffy 'fro made her ethnic identity clear. Her outfit—army jacket, faded bell-bottoms and peacenik T-shirt—was almost identical to mine.

I smiled and raised my hand in greeting. She nodded an acknowledgment but didn't smile back. Was she the kind of angry black woman I'd read about who didn't like white girls? Or was she just shy? Well, I was shy. I hoped Ricardo would fill the awkward silence, but he didn't.

"Where you from?" I asked Linda. It turned out that our home towns, on the eastern side of the state, were about an hour apart. Both of us were going back there for spring break the next day—which for me meant JT, ecstasy!

"You live in the dorm?" she asked, and I pointed to the building next to us. Finally a tentative smile: "Me too." From her room number, I knew that hers was directly above Fran and me.

"I wonder why I haven't seen you before," I said.

"I dunno, but let's hang out when we get back."

"OK, cool. Have a good break. You too, Ricardo." I waved again and headed for my room, smiling a little inside. Maybe this Linda and I had things in common. Maybe it would fill the void that Fran's new friendships and our petty rifts had caused.

♡

The number of times that I changed schools when I was growing up had taught me the pain and pleasure of being "the new girl": boys found me intriguing, but girls were suspicious. This happened in third grade when I joined my mom and stepdad in their small New Jersey town.

My mom already knew of two other girls my age who lived on our block, and it didn't take me long to realize that we weren't in the same league. Whereas my parents rented the upstairs of a small old farmhouse with abandoned chicken shacks in back, one girl was well off (with her father a doctor, their large home and its well-manicured yard) and the other one downright rich (her father a businessman and their home a literal mansion with an indoor swimming pool). Their facial expressions and tone of voice suggested that they were none too happy to have me show up.

I was trying to fit in with my new family. My mom was working, trying to get pregnant, and stressing out over my periodic misbehavior (not eating my dinner, not telling her when I went for a walk, bringing home a feral cat that crapped all over the apartment). Her belt was a frequent visitor to my behind.

One day I was jumping rope on the playground when a little black girl jump-roped her way over to me. She told me her name was Cassandra, "but just call me Cassie." We had one of those instant connections that are hard to explain. We couldn't stop smiling as we showed each other our jump-rope moves. She asked me if I wanted to come over to her house after school, and I said yes, but I'd have to stop and tell my mom first. That was a rule that had been beaten into me.

Because my mom wasn't home, I figured it would be OK to go with Cassie. The town was small, and I was allowed to roam.

Cassie's parents greeted me with hellos and friendly smiles. Then I was surprised at how Cassie's room upstairs was actually the attic, which she shared with a brother and sister. It had cool sloping ceilings like my grandma's attic did, and the beds were all under the eaves. In the middle was a play area, and there were bathroom facilities in the corner but with no door. It would be embarrassing in front of company, but I thought it sure must be easy to use the toilet in the night.

We hadn't been up there very long when Cassie's brother loped up the stairs two at a time.

"Hey, Cassie. Lynda's mom is outside. She don't look none too happy neither." I wasn't surprised that my mom had found me. It was a small town, and other kids had probably seen me with Cassie and pointed the way. What surprised me was that she hadn't come into the house and been mannerly the way she had always told me to do.

"I better go. Thanks, Cassie. See you at school tomorrow." Cassie ducked her head and smiled.

Downstairs, I said good-bye to Cassie's parents and thanked them the way Momma had taught me. Then I went out to the car.

As soon as I saw my mom's face, I knew I was in trouble. She sat rigid behind the wheel, her eyes narrowed, and her full lips in an angry pout. She didn't even look at me when I got in, just put the car in gear and pulled out.

"What's wrong, Momma?" I asked, my heart already thudding in my skinny chest.

"Boy, are you gonna get it when we get home."

"What do you mean?" My voice squeaked with fear. I could almost feel that belt searing my butt. "I stopped by the house to tell you where I was going, but you weren't there. What did I do wrong?"

"You know exactly what you did," was her cold response.

"No, Momma, I don't know!" I was crying outright by now.

She was silent for the rest of the ride. When she pulled into the driveway, she turned the engine off and just sat there. Then she turned to me with an icy stare.

"You're supposed to be polite to colored people. You treat them like they're the same as us. But they're not the same as us. Whatever you do, you never, ever go to their houses."

Mom did not beat me that night. The next day on the playground, I saw Cassie watching me, but she didn't approach me. Maybe her parents had their own talk with her, and later I would realize that it was a talk black parents always had to have with their children, to prepare them for the rejection, or worse, that they would face in the white world.

I didn't go to Cassie, either. Instead, we told each other of our sadness with our eyes.

☮

Chapter 9

IT WAS DRIZZLING AS I HANDED MY BAG TO THE BUS DRIVER and watched him throw it into the cargo area. I climbed the steps and picked a seat alone in the back—the bus was almost empty at this early hour anyway. Maybe it was the gray day, but I was in a pensive mood.

I thought about Will, wondered if he was on his way to London with his "friend" Brenda. Were they on the same train that we'd taken when he delivered me back to Heathrow Airport? Was it possible that train ride was only a little over three months ago? Three months during which my heart, my mind, and my life had changed so dramatically.

Now, in spite of the rain outside, there were signs of the shifting Pennsylvania seasons—yellow and violet crocuses in front yards, sprouts of green on stark tree branches. The tires of the bus droned *shhh-shhh-shhh* against the wet road. Eventually, little peeps of sun lit the raindrops like crystals, and soon even a faint rainbow appeared. Like a treasure that I'd saved to open later, I started fantasizing about where I was going and why: JT—I was on my way to him. I thought about how he would look when I first saw him. How long before he would kiss me. What exciting new music he'd play for me. The fascinating things we might talk about. How we'd laugh and flirt and begin to touch. And then the kisses would become more serious, the words turn into soft moans, and our clothes start coming off...

But none of it would happen right away. For the first half of my spring break, he'd still be home in DC, while I'd be a dutiful daughter and a good big sister in Bethlehem. I'd see my girl-friends when I could. Hell, maybe I'd even write something for that Advanced Fucking Rhetoric class.

Then JT would arrive. And we would have four (count 'em, four) whole nights together before I had to leave. What was that saying from childhood Bible school? "Like manna from heaven." JT was my manna.

But first, my parents had news.

"Guess what, honey—we're moving to Texas!" crowed Mom with the biggest smile I'd seen from her in some time.

"Now Dorthy, it's only for a year and not until August," cautioned Dad. They said he'd received a sabbatical leave—whatever that was—to attend graduate school. My mom missed her father and brother who had migrated there from LA, and she'd talked Dad into attending West Texas U.

"Wow, Mom—what does that mean for you?" I was being polite, but my mind was swirling.

"Oh honey, you know I can't wait to see my daddy and brother. I'm sure they could use help with the motels and restaurants." She was referring to her family's businesses on Route 66. Her voice took on that slight southern cone-pone flavor when she said "MO-tels," an accent that returned when she interacted with her family. I realized that, to pull this move off with my stepdad, she must really miss them. I knew I would miss my sister. Would I ever feel that way about my parents?

So, they would be gone for my senior year. They would turn over control of the government benefits from my father's death that paid most of my college expenses. I would be on my own a year earlier than expected. If they liked it there, they might even stay. It was almost impossible for me to take in. I knew I'd have a lot to think about.

For now, I just had to get through now. That meant five days with my family followed by four nights with JT that I had to cover with convincing alibis.

Time slowed down, as it has a way of doing when something special is in the offing. I slept in to help move the days along. I took Barbie out to the mall or the Dairy Queen drive-in. DQ had good burgers, and she liked watching the teenagers cruise in and out. She'd loved the suede peace choker I'd brought her, even putting it back on after every bath.

But she was worried. "Sissie, I don't want to go to Taxes." She looked ready to cry into her root beer float.

"Why not, baby?" It killed me to see my little sister hurting. It had been hard enough on her when I went away to school.

"It's far away. (Sip.) I won't get to see you. (Sip.) And besides, Mom and Dad fight about Taxes." She shook her head, her big eyes serious. "It can't be good. (Slurp slurp.)"

"That's taxes they fight about, baby. It's not the same as Texas. Taxes mean you have to pay money, that's why they don't like them. But Texas is a place, like here. It's where mom's family is. You'll go to school and play with friends, just like you do now. There will be horses and cowboys. And maybe," I tickled under her chin, "I can even come to visit." That put a little smile on her face. Crisis averted for now. In truth, I wasn't happy about my little sister going to Texas. Mom's family was prejudiced. I was sure a lot of people there were prejudiced. I didn't want those ugly attitudes to rub off on my sweet little girl.

At night, I either hung out at Hannah's apartment or picked up Sharon and went for a bite to eat. After I'd left for college, Sharon had continued going to the cross-cultural dance clubs.

Now she was dating a black guy she'd met there. Her proud Greek parents didn't know about him yet, but they could know soon. "We're thinking we might get married in the fall," she told me. Wow, married. It was hard to imagine.

Then Colleen came home from Pitt for a couple days. We met up over at Hannah's. Hannah was still seeing Tuck, and we were going ahead with the plan to have him front me some LSD. Colleen frowned and asked why I couldn't get work-study, or why Will didn't find a job.

"Because the work-study is all taken. And Will says there are no jobs for Americans." I shrugged. "It'll be fine. I'm only going to sell to people I know."

Colleen changed the subject. "How's that basketball player? He sure is cute."

Hannah was grinning, as usual. "Yes, he is. And he is crazy about his Lynda."

I laughed happily, reminded of what was to come. "He'll be here in two days. I can't wait."

"I bet you can't. And you'll be getting laid. I wish I was getting laid," Colleen sighed. "Sooo . . . is what's on the inside as big, black, and beautiful as what's on the outside?"

"Do you mean does he have a big dick?" I asked. She smirked.

Starting in tenth grade, before we had ever even seen a penis, we speculated all kinds of things about men and sex. When it came to JT, the gossip made me uncomfortable. I didn't like him being talked about like a piece of meat.

"Maybe," I smiled. Then I changed the subject.

♡

While I waited for JT to come back, I spent time daydreaming. What was he doing in DC? I tried to picture him at home with his mother and grandmother, but I had so little to envision. Were they as poor as Will's family? Did his religious grandmother make JT go to church? And what about the woman he was with right before we started seeing each other? At least since then, it didn't sound like he had any interest in seeing other girls.

Meanwhile, was Will in London? What was Brenda's family home like? Will said she had money, but like horses-and-servants type money? I wondered about the sleeping arrangements; were Brenda's parents liberal, or did they have to sneak in to each other at night? These were idle musings. Whatever possessiveness I'd started to feel when I first heard about her had mostly dissipated. I felt detached.

The hours dragged by.

Finally came the day that JT was to return. I didn't even know how he was getting back. Did he get a ride or come into the same bus station I did? Did people recognize him, or was he just a suspicious-looking black man when he wasn't on the basketball court? I could hardly keep my heart rate from skittering out of control every time I remembered that I would see him soon.

That night, dinner with my family seemed interminable. My mom with her chatter about Texas. My dad with his silence and his crumbs.

By now they were used to my taking the extra car. Dad would go out to drink with his buddies like he always did, while Mom stayed home with my sister and the TV.

At the head shop where I bought Barbie's peace necklace, I'd found a new top. It was paisley, my favorite pattern. Swirls of pink and maroon, light blue and navy crisscrossed over my breasts and hugged my waist. I couldn't wait to wear it for JT. It had been over a month since my last visit. How would we look to each other? I was almost sorry there weren't any more basketball games. I hadn't gotten to see him play, and now the season was over.

But playing ball would just mean that he'd get back to his room later and I'd have to wait longer to see him. This was my payoff, more hours in his arms.

I parked in the same lot behind his dorm and raced up the stairs. Just like the last time, he wasn't there. So, he wanted to play this game again. Was it a game or just his nervous energy needing to ricochet out of the room? Now that I knew his habits better, I was in good humor as I set out to search for him.

I didn't even bother with the library, considering his reaction last time after I told him I'd started there:

"You went to the library? Like, first?" His smile had been incredulous.

"Sure. You could've been there. You know, studying or something. On a Friday night." I had to smile, too, at my naïveté.

He'd thrown back his head and laughed. "I guess that just goes to show that you don't know me very well—yet." I noticed that he identified as a jock, lazy about his studies, not the intellectual type. But the way he wrote and talked belied his intelligence. If his grades weren't what they should be, our late-night soundtrack-driven letters had a lot to do with that.

This time I tried the gym first. The door was open, but the lights were off.

I cut over to the student union. I'd never been inside before. Suddenly I felt self-conscious and wished that Hannah was with me. The place was set up in one huge room divided by railings— snack bar area, pool table area, some sofas, and a TV. I scanned the crowd of white faces, and it was easy to spot the tall brown guy with the big natural who was playing pool. I got a Coke and pulled a stool over to where I'd have a view of the table. Groups of guys and girls drank sodas and ate burgers or just stood around the table with their hands in their pockets. But all had their eyes on the game.

Was he just the smoothest man I had ever seen? JT moved about the table quiet and graceful as a big cat. He acted so casual, chuckling and chatting easily with the sandy-haired guy who was his opponent. Yet he hardly took his eyes from the table, and when he lined up his shots, his focus was complete. Almost every ball met its mark. I thought, *I bet that's how he plays basketball.* Maybe that's just how he plays everything, including me. Smooth.

Then it was JT's last shot, down the length of the table. His eyes traveled to the stick, to the cue ball, to the eight ball, to the pocket, and kept going straight up until they met mine. *Oh no*, I thought, *I'll break his concentration.* But a grin spread across his face, a look that said, *Watch this.* JT focused again and took his shot. The eight ball dropped and the cue ball stopped. There was a brief silence and then an eruption of laughter and cheers from the crowd.

"Way to go, JT!"

"Good game, man!"

"Another one, Johnny?" His opponent nearly ran around the table to shake his hand. "A rematch, whaddaya say?"

"Hey asshole, I'm next up!" shouted a burly guy.

JT carefully placed his stick back in the rack.

"No, man. I gotta go." He looked around at the other hopefuls. "Sorry, guys. Another time." And then he made his way over to me.

Oh, the frustration. I wanted to throw my arms around him.

To congratulate his victory with a sweet kiss. I was proud of him and I wanted to show it. This handsome man was mine. This talented man was mine. This man that everybody wanted was mine, mine, mine. I wanted to revel in it. I wanted it so bad.

Maybe JT wanted it, too. To reach out and smooth my shiny hair. To cup my face, his "tranquil sight for tired eyes." To pull me hungrily, happily into his arms. Maybe he wanted to claim this chick in her pretty paisley top for all the room to see.

But some of these guys were probably on the basketball team. And they knew coaches who knew other coaches. Coaches like my dad. I couldn't risk having anything spoil our precious four days.

JT's dancing eyes told me he understood it all.

"You want anything?" he asked.

"No, thanks. You?"

"I'm good now," he said softly. I slid off my stool and we walked nonchalantly out of the room.

♡

"I've been holding out on you," JT said, when we were in his dorm, and I was settled back into "my" spot on the bed, cigarette lit and boots off.

"Oh?" I took a drag, trying to appear unconcerned, but my heartbeat stuttered.

"Yeah. I wanted to tell you in my last letter, but I thought it might be better if I waited until I could do it in person." In person. I felt like I couldn't breathe. Had he been with someone in DC? Even worse, had he changed his mind about us?

JT held up an album with the most beautiful drawing on the cover. Album covers had become our generation's art—we looked forward to them almost as much as to the music. On this one, a handsome Aztec warrior held a languid black-haired maiden across his lap. The picture exuded a mood that I had no language for and yet somehow knew I had wanted all my life—peaceful ecstasy. "MALO" the title read. "Bad"? How could that be bad?

"I can't wait for you to hear this song. It's called "*Suavecito*." I haven't even heard much of the rest of the album, 'cuz I can't seem to stop playing this one song over and over again." JT laughed at himself. He hadn't changed his mind about us. And he hadn't been with anyone else, as far as I could know. All he'd withheld from me was a song, and now he couldn't wait to share it.

With the same manual dexterity that had run the pool table, JT rested the needle on the second track. Guitar and bass notes danced into the room to cha-cha with rhythmic timbales and congas, soon followed by exuberant horns, sweet piano, and masculine voices singing: "La la la . . . aa-aa-ah."

And then one sang about how he'd never met a girl like me.

I looked at JT. He was watching me. That dimpled grin spread across his face. I knew that the words were for me. I knew he felt that he had never met a girl like me in his life.

A girl like me. Who was that, exactly? It didn't matter. All that mattered was that he wanted her. He wanted me.

He came over to the bed and sat down, then slid his arm around my shoulders.

"This is fantastic," I murmured. I couldn't keep my hips from swiveling a little to the Latin rhythms.

"Just wait. It gets even better." JT tapped his fingers on my knee like it was a hand drum. He reminded me of a kid trying to contain his excitement on Christmas morning.

When I heard the chorus I learned why: "*Suavecito, mi linda! Suavecito!*"

They were singing my name. *Linda!* I looked at him, and I became the kid who just opened the big surprise package.

"It's for you! This is your song, Lynda."

And it was. Granted, *linda* in Spanish wouldn't be spelled like mine. But the sound was the same, it was my name, and in Spanish, my name meant "beautiful." I felt like I'd never heard anything quite so beautiful before.

"Who is it?" I asked.

"Well, that's crazy, too: Santana's younger brother is in Malo. Jorge Santana."

"You've gotta be kidding. I love Santana. *We* love Santana."

"I know," he said. "Since your last visit I've been having trouble listening to anything except that third album. Until this came along."

We finished listening to the happiest notes I'd ever heard. They were the outpouring of a young man in love, singing exuberantly to his *linda*.

Afterward I asked, "Do you know what *suavecito* means?" I'd had two years of Spanish, but only *-ito* rang a bell, "little one."

"I tried to look it up," JT said. "The closest I could come was *suave-* smooth and *ito-* little one. Like 'my smooth little one' or something. I'm not sure why it's not *ita*. But what I like to think is maybe she's gotten to him with her smooth little ways." He touched his index finger to the tip of my nose. "Which, by the way, also describes a certain other Lynda I know."

I couldn't help but smile at the thought of myself as smooth. I felt so un-smooth, so awkward much of the time. But if JT thought I was smooth, if he called me his little one, I'd revel in it.

And my insecurities would have to wait because now his mouth was on mine, and a new feeling had come over me.

I felt at peace, *and* I was in ecstasy.

♡

The next evening, I was washing the dishes after dinner. My sister was coloring at the kitchen table, and my mom was watching *All in the Family*. We'd often watched the show together, but I was in a hurry to clean up and get out of there. I had someplace to go!

Dad was pacing like he so often did, pantomiming a pitcher warming up to throw a ball. He did this frequently as an accompaniment to his old stories—Korea, playing ball, coaching ball —or when he baited me about civil rights or Vietnam.

This time it was about the first team he'd coached when we moved to Bethlehem. They were small-town boys—all white but one—who had grown up riding their bikes out country roads to fish and play in the creeks. Many of their opponents were black kids from inner-city schools, guys who had cut their teeth on the neighborhood basketball court. The locals who followed the high school team groused about how unfair that was, but it brought out the competitive spirit in Dad.

His team included this one white kid, Robin, who Dad would always say was his best player ever. Robin led his team of bumpkinish boys to win repeatedly over the stronger black competitors, until losing the final playoff game. Afterward, the league was redistributed so that small towns played other small towns, and Dad's teams wouldn't compete at that level again. It would be decades before I understood that or what it felt like to lose big, to have no hope for a rematch but still go on.

"Yeah, that Robin was something else." Dad swung his faux pitch. Suddenly, out of the blue, he asked, "Does Hannah know Jon Thomas?"

I froze. It sounded innocent enough, but why was he bringing up my JT?

"I dunno," I said. "Maybe. It's a small school. And he's pretty famous. Even I've heard of him."

"He sure is getting a lot of play in the newspapers." He ducked back for another throw. "More than he deserves, I think. Probably because he's black. I bet Robin would've run rings around that guy."

"Mmm," I said. I didn't want to engage on this subject.

"Well, I gotta go get ready. Hannah and I are going out." I hung the dish towel under the sink. "I'll see you later, Dad."

I wondered if he'd ever even seen JT play ball.

♡

"I started keeping a journal," JT said that night. He got up and went to his desk to retrieve it. It was a brown leather-bound book about half the size of a regular notebook. Malo was playing on the stereo, and he had set it to auto-repeat. When we were well into the third listen, he sat back down next to me and started thumbing through the pages. Basketball, classes, school committees, letters to me, and now a journal—did the man ever sleep?

"Wanna read something?" he asked. Of course I did. Anything that was a keyhole into the private world of JT/Jon/ Johnny T/Jonathan Thomas was a keyhole I wanted to peep through. He was quiet as he flipped through the entries. I was almost as intrigued by his fingers as by whatever he was about to let me read. They were long and lean just like everything about him. Strong enough to shoot a ball from center court or easily slide my hips underneath his. But there was a delicacy about them, too. The deliberate way they moved, like an artist playing an instrument. The way they played my body like an instrument.

"Here we go." JT handed the book to me, and I began reading about myself.

"What is it about this girl that has me so completely gone?" he wrote. "I truly have never met a girl like her. It's not that she's white. White girls never really interested me before. Yet I love the way she looks. Her long hair. Those dark brown eyes. That smile. And that warm body—it's so cool that she wants to share it with me."

I looked at him with glistening eyes. He blushed and smiled, nodded for me to keep reading.

"But the way I feel about her is so much more. Maybe the way she looks so innocent but she likes to talk a little tough? I dig that. If she was really tough, I wouldn't like it, but she isn't, so I do. I usually don't like it that much when girls curse, but she just makes it sound so cute. 'Fuck that shit!' she says, and blows smoke rings. And that's another thing, I usually don't like it when girls smoke either. But she makes everything look so damn sexy."

As was often the case, I had a cigarette in my hand. I winked at him, inhaled, and blew, one-two-three-four-five rings. Then my showing off made me gasp for air. He laughed so hard he fell over sideways on the bed.

I kept reading. "But this is what it really is: she's smart, and she's deep. We don't talk about race that much, but I still feel like she gets it. How could she get it? And why does she care? Maybe that's just what intelligence is, that you get it and you care. That's what I love most about her."

When I reached the bottom of the page, I looked up. JT gently took the book from my hands, got up and set it on the desk.

"That's enough for now," he said. "I shouldn't be telling you all my secrets." He laughed a little self-consciously. "Something must be wrong with me. I never do this."

He came back to the bed, and I slid my arms around his neck. He pulled me close, and we sat like that for the longest time. Just listening to each other breathe, feeling who each other was. Until Malo had finished its fourth replay.

Chapter 10

"THAT'S WHAT I LOVE," HIS JOURNAL SAID. HE'D SIGNED his letters "Love," too. But he had never spoken the words.

I'd said it to him the very first night. I'd heard "I love you" and wasn't even sure whose lips it came from until the fog lifted in the morning. Then, embarrassed, I'd tried to explain. But he had stopped me, said that he understood. That was the thing about him, he was so damn understanding. Maybe too understanding. Like why did he "understand" about my having another man? Why wasn't he jealous as shit? Why didn't he ask me to end it with Will?

I'd told him I loved him on my second visit, too. And again last night. And each time he'd pulled me a little bit closer, held me a little bit tighter but remained silent. Why wouldn't he say the words to me?

I was pondering this the next day as I got ready to meet Hannah. We were going over to Tuck's to pick up the acid he was fronting me to sell.

As usual, Tuck was friendly and laid back. He let us into the big old crash pad he rented where a few guys and occasional girl usually sat around watching TV or listening to music, cleaning their reefer, or smoking a joint. Back in his room, he motioned for us to join him on the bed. He had counted out one hundred orange tablets, each not much bigger than a pot seed but in the perfect shape of a tiny hatbox. It was disconcerting that something so small could be so powerful.

"Here it is, the orange 'Sunshine of your Love,' " he joked, riffing on the acid's street name and the Cream song. "Now you're gonna be really careful about this, right?" I nodded.

"You're not going to sell to anyone you don't know, right?" I shook my head.

"And if anything goes wrong, you have absolutely no idea where this came from, is that correct?"

I mimed my best confused look. "I have absolutely no idea where this came from, Mr., Mr.—what's your name again?"

Hannah chimed in with a song. "Tuck Tuck bo buck, banana fanna fo fuck, fee fy mo muck—Tuck!" We all laughed hearing the Shirley Bassey song from childhood.

"Hey, don't laugh," Tuck said. "I was the first kid I knew who could say 'fuck' to my parents without getting punished because it was my name in a song. I think they secretly thought it was funny."

He scooped the pills into a baggie, folded it, and handed it to me. I dug in my purse for a small velvet pouch where I usually kept jewelry and slipped the baggie inside.

"Thank you so much, Tuck," I said. "I was going crazy trying to figure out how to pay my girlfriend back the money she loaned me. I'm hoping I'll have yours by the next time I come home."

"That's cool," he said. "But go easy, OK? I'd rather you take a little longer and do it safely." He smiled amiably. Tuck was not very physically attractive, short and round and in his twenties already losing his hair. Hannah was so fetching, it was hard to imagine them in bed together. But I could certainly see why she liked him as a person.

Thanks to him, my new career as a drug pusher was about to begin.

♡

My treasure hunts for JT happened only on the first night; after that he was easy to find, either in his room or down the hall where male laughter wafted out of open doors. If he was in his room, he'd stop whatever he was doing and meet me at the door. If he was in another student's room, he'd get up, say, "Hey guys, this is Lynda. ("Hi, Lynda!" "Hi, guys!") OK, we'll see you later," and he'd escort me to his room. His room. "Our" room. I knew he had a roommate, but I'd met him only once. "Where does he sleep?" I asked JT. "Oh, he just crashes in someone else's room." I thought that was quite generous of him. Did everyone just curry JT's favor? I couldn't imagine that JT would expect, much less demand, that.

Once we were in our room, we followed our pattern. JT put on music and dimmed the lights. I kicked off my boots and settled into my spot on his bed. He slipped off his shoes, maybe took off his outer shirt, and joined me there. I'd smoke and we'd drink or get high, depending on who had what. We'd talk and touch and laugh, all the little rituals that helped us to fit ourselves back together after a day apart, after weeks spent so very far apart.

This night JT and I were especially eager for each other. Maybe because we'd had several nights together and now felt comfortable showing desire. Maybe because it was our last night until who knew when. We made out, stopping only long enough for him to change the song. Jesse Colin Young sang about his girl in the "Sunlight," and for some reason it made me think about what JT had written about me in his journal. He played Isaac, and we remembered that first time our love was so doggone good. He played Santana, and we knew that all too soon the time would pass so damn slowly without you.

After a while, he no longer got up to change the music. He left Malo on repeat, and each time "*Suavecito*" came on, I knew that nothing would ever make my heart, body, and soul feel so open. Like the petals of a flower awaiting her bumblebee, not that I wanted to get pollinated. (Thank goodness for birth control pills.)

Eventually our hips stopped rocking, and our pounding hearts slowed back to normal. That was usually when I was overcome with feelings for him. "I love you," I whispered into that soft whorl of hair behind his ear. JT shifted slightly, and I waited for the squeeze that usually followed. I was desperately hoping to hear those three words back to me. He pressed his lips to my cheek, but he said nothing.

Again, we fell asleep just like that, arms and legs a-jumble.

When I woke, it was dark outside. He was heavy on me, but I was grateful for the blanket he had pulled over us. I had absolutely no idea what time it was, and a touch of panic set in. Evening? Middle of the night? Or near dawn, when I should be getting up to go home? Oh God, what waited at home—not only my parents, but the trip back to school. The trip away from him. Panic led to despair.

Yet here he was, still sleeping soundly in my arms. Fuck panic. Fuck despair. I couldn't leave no matter what time it was. I would not leave. Yet I had to leave. Oh, why the fuck did it have to be like this?

JT stirred and his eyes opened. He smiled, as if seeing my face about an inch from his was the most natural thing in the world.

"Hey," he said softly. "I'm sorry. Am I too heavy?" He raised himself on one elbow. "No wonder I fall asleep on you. You're like the softest featherbed I've never had." He gently smoothed my hair from my face, still stuck where sweat and sleep had left it.

"You're OK. I'm happy to be your featherbed anytime," I said. "Good morning. Or should I say evening? I have no idea what time it is."

He craned his neck to look at an alarm clock I couldn't see. "It's ten thirty," he said. "And since it's dark outside, I assume it isn't ten thirty in the morning." Oh, that sounded so good. We still had hours before I'd have to go. He rolled over on his side next to me and pulled me up close.

"You know," JT said, "I never made it to dinner tonight." As if to prove it, his belly growled, and we both laughed. "How about I go over to the student center and get us something to eat before they close?"

"Sure. What are you hungry for?"

"Oh, maybe a grilled cheese or French fries. Or both?"

"Yum, that sounds good." We untangled and he got up. I pulled the blanket over my hip and watched him throw clothes on and take the needle off the album.

"You must be sick of this record. Put something else on if you want. Or I'll change it when I get back. But I gotta hurry. See ya in a minute," JT said, opening the door.

The door clicked shut.

That's when it happened. I didn't know why. I could have easily just dozed back to sleep or leaned over to slip another album on the turntable. Instead, I got up and moved across the room as if in a trance. It was like a beacon was drawing me over there.

On his desk lay his journal where he'd set it down the night before. I'd seen it and idly thought, "I wish I could read more of that." Then I forgot about it—at least on a conscious level. But as soon as he left, it seemed to light up in the corner. I moved toward it like a sleepwalker. I felt driven to see what he hadn't wanted me to see.

I leaned my bare hip against the desk and flipped through the pages, to the one that ended with what he loved most about me. I turned one more page, my pulse accelerating, and started to read.

But does she love me? She says so, but should I believe her? I don't think she's a liar. Everything about her seems authentic to me. But then why is there this other man? Is she just as real with him?

All I can think is that he must feel pretty confident about her to go off all the way overseas like that. Leaving her, expecting her to still be his when he comes back. I can't comprehend it. I'm afraid I'm going to love her and . . .

Click. The sound of a key in the lock, the door handle turning. I froze. There I stood naked beside JT's desk, his journal in my hands.

"I forgot my . . ." JT stopped short, and his eyes widened as he took in the sight before him.

"I . . . I . . ." I was speechless and motionless. Somehow it seemed so much worse that I had no clothes on. I had never felt so exposed, so ugly.

"Lynda, what's going on?" He closed the door and walked the few steps to me. He gently took the book from my suddenly meaty hands and set it back on the desk. I stood with ape arms hanging at my sides. He took me by my hunchback shoulders and guided me over to the bed. I pulled the blanket up, trying to cover my shame. But the shame was not about my body. The shame was inside me.

"I'm sorry," I finally said. "I don't know what came over me. It was just so interesting to read what you'd written. I wanted to see more."

"Why didn't you ask me, then?"

"I guess I thought you'd say no."

"Maybe I would have. But that's my right. And maybe I would have let you read it."

"I know. I'm so sorry, Jon," I said miserably. I felt like crying.

JT sat quietly. Then, "Well, I've gotta go if I'm going to get us that food." I thought I saw the slightest twinkle in his eyes. "Do I need to take my journal with me?"

"No, honestly. You can trust me." I heard how ridiculous that sounded, but still I added, "I won't ever touch it again unless you show it to me. I promise."

JT leaned over, put his hands over my hair, and kissed my forehead. He picked up the wallet he'd forgotten and left the room.

The journal still seemed to be pulsing softly from its place on his desk, but there was no way I would heed its siren call now. I'd seen what I needed to see, anyhow. JT loved me (hooray!) And he was also worried about Will (damn). Of course I wanted him to want me to choose him. But the thought of him worrying, about anything at all, was gut-wrenching.

Chapter 11

JT'S NEXT SIX-PAGE LETTER, WRITTEN JUST SHORTLY AFTER I'D left for school, was a stunner.

> *4/9/72*
> *Dear Featherbed.*

Not the greeting. That was our little private joke about falling asleep on each other. It was what came next:

> *I just don't know what to make of your little tale*
> *of another man and how long it took you to tell me*
> *about him.*

Wait, wait, wait! "How long it took," to tell him about Will? I remembered telling him the very first time we met—the dance, Hannah's introduction, our small talk that included my upcoming trip to see my boyfriend in England. And then I'd told him again the first night we got together. Hadn't I? I'd been so certain I had. Since he never asked for more, I figured he just didn't want to focus on it.

Yet his take was that I'd just told him on this visit. And he said that he had asked questions that I didn't want to answer. Friends always complimented my extraordinarily good memory, but I didn't remember him asking any questions.

He was playing "*Suavecito*" on the stereo as he wrote to me.

He said that getting his thoughts together had taken several hours.

And he continued a couple playful games that we'd started, me thinking that I was his "featherbed," and him pretending to be my "psychoanalyst." He prescribed my "treatment"—listening to the songs we love every day and seeing my therapist in my dreams every night. As if I didn't already.

All my love,
Jonathan

In the couple days that I'd been back at school, I'd been feeling happy. I replayed our scenes—the pool game, "*Suavecito*," even his catching me with the journal, his mischievous look. Most guys would be furious, maybe yell and stomp around. Instead, he'd touched me and talked to me kindly. That was my calm and understanding JT.

But now I could hear his hopelessness. And the puzzling question of whether I'd previously told him about Will. This time we'd just been talking a little about what would happen when school let out for the summer, and I mentioned that Will was coming home. Again, JT hadn't reacted, but then he'd written of his worry about Will in his journal. Now it sounded like this was the first he'd heard of Will. It was all so confusing.

I couldn't bear the thought of him sitting in his room, not doing anything, feeling *hollowed out*, he said. Mind full of worry and heart full of pain, and it was my fault.

Yet he was still writing to me. His sweet featherbed metaphors transported me right back into his arms. He wondered if anything notable happened after I left him. Oh JT, no, nothing; everything important that day was you.

All my love. There it was again. His love in writing. But not whispered in my ear when he had the chance.

♡

The mix-up turned my thoughts back to Will. I wondered about his holiday with Brenda, though in truth, I barely cared. I was being unfaithful, but now so was he. And he'd left me stuck with paying Colleen back. Maybe it was too hard for him to get a job there. But he didn't seem to be hurting for money now that he had Brenda. He could have even borrowed the money from her to give to me to pay Colleen back for my trip to see him. Man, that would be one convoluted arrangement.

Instead, I had to sell Tuck's acid. I began putting the word out as soon as I got back, after making it clear that I'd sell only to friends: "Don't send just anyone to my door, please."

Within a couple days I saw Ricardo walking across campus, and it reminded me that I wanted to see Linda. Something between us just seemed to click. When I got back to the dorm, I walked upstairs and knocked on her door. A different black girl answered.

"Yeah?"

"Is Linda here?"

"No, she's still at class. Who are you?"

"I'm Lynda, too. I live downstairs."

She said she was Linda's roommate and would tell Linda I stopped by.

About an hour later, Linda knocked on my door. I let her in and introduced her to Fran. Maybe because Fran was there, Linda invited me upstairs. Her roommate was gone.

We started getting to know each other. Now that I'd learned

some about what life was like for black men, I was curious to know about the experience of a black woman. Plus Linda was totally cute and seemed totally cool. She was mixed race, her father black and Irish and her mother Puerto Rican. Her dad was out of the picture and she lived with her single mom and a younger brother. She was the first in her family to go to college.

She came across as mellow, but I wasn't sure how she felt about interracial dating. I started by telling her about Will, and she was cool with it. She had a boyfriend back home with the odd name of Ditto. She showed me his picture, and he looked a lot like her—light-skinned with freckles and a big reddish-brown Afro. He could have been her brother, but they made a really cute couple. I didn't tell her about JT right away. While she might be OK with me dating a black man, she might not be so OK with me cheating on him—with another black man.

Soon it was commonplace for me to go up to Linda's room, especially if Fran was in class or across the hall with Pam or Cathy, or if Fran and I were getting on each other's nerves. Linda's roommate wasn't around much, and I got the feeling she wasn't interested in having a white friend. But Linda seemed as curious about me as I was about her. We shared music. I turned her on to Malo and she introduced me to Mandrille and El Chicano. We both liked the Latin rhythms. But our main topic was definitely men.

As I told her more about Will, a strange phenomenon occurred: I remembered what a good man he was, what he had overcome to get where he was, how much he loved me. I started to wonder why I had strayed from that love. I almost longed for the more innocent days when I didn't question who I wanted or where I belonged. These thoughts made me sad and added to my confusion.

Linda revealed more of herself, too. Ditto was very jealous, yet she'd been unfaithful to him with a few different black guys on campus, and she didn't have very good things to say about them.

"When they want some pussy, those brothers be like 'Yeah, sister, you're a black queen.' But the minute they get what they want, it's like you don't even exist."

I couldn't help but think about Curtis and how he'd so readily offered me to his friends for a gangbang. I thought it was because I was white. Linda wasn't describing a gangbang; she was simply talking about being treated callously at the hands of black men. But neither Will nor JT was like Curtis or those kinds of guys.

Linda also admitted that she wondered what it would be like to have sex with a white guy, which she'd never done. We both said "Mmm" about handsome South American Ricardo, then laughed as we both admitted we weren't sure if he counted as white. Her honesty spurred me to tell her about JT and my confusion about him and Will. Eventually she confessed something I wouldn't have imagined—that Ditto was a small-time pimp. This threw me, too. I didn't know much about pimps other than as fictional characters. I thought they dressed flamboyantly, but Ditto looked like a hippie. I'd also thought that all their girlfriends worked for them.

"Is he trying to get you to work for him?" I asked.

"No," she answered.

"Does he fuck his other girls?"

"Yes."

"So how can he be jealous of what you do?" I didn't understand it. She explained what he had told her—that fucking his girls was "work," just part of the job of keeping them in line and connected to him. She agreed that it didn't seem logical or fair, but it was the way it was.

I didn't think much of Ditto. What I disliked most was that he wanted Linda to quit college and come home. That reminded me of Fran's old boyfriend Fuckface. What was it with these men not wanting their women to be educated? I wondered how many women had dropped out or maybe not even started college because their boyfriends told them so. I was glad that neither Will nor JT was like that. Maybe the difference was that Will and JT were in college themselves, whereas Fuckface and Ditto were not, and seemed to feel threatened by their women being in a position they perceived as superior.

Linda and I dissected every aspect of our relationships. Both of us felt guilty for breaking our vows of monogamy, yet we were likely to keep doing it. It was the distance—the loneliness, the need to be held, and the desire to explore our burgeoning sexuality. It was the times—sex, drugs, and rock 'n' roll, free love, love the one you're with. We had no business making promises of fidelity in the face of what we were living with—hot hormones, long-distance love, and those free-wheeling times.

☮

Chapter 12

AFTER EVERYTHING THAT HAD HAPPENED OVER SPRING BREAK, my head was spinning. Front and center was JT. How did he not know about Will? The things he'd written in his journal were thrilling, but his worry about Will broke my heart. What was I going to do about Will, anyway? He certainly wasn't rushing to write to me about his spring break with Brenda.

Then I did hear from Will, and I couldn't believe the things he wrote, beginning with the fact that he'd been feeling resentful toward me because my mention of owing Colleen money made him feel guilty. *Please don't sell the acid*, he wrote but offered no other solution. He also chastised me for having gone out with a couple guys back when we were just getting to know each other. *What?* Why? We'd had no commitment then.

I guessed that Will was looking for excuses for what he'd done with Brenda. Yet he wrote that he didn't love her and couldn't forgive himself for letting me down. So, there it was, what I'd suspected: they had become lovers.

Did I care? I felt a pang. But there wasn't much I could say, considering that I had JT. I wasn't about to tell Will about JT, either. Maybe it wasn't fair since Will had confessed, but I felt that the truth about my stateside love life could only increase his misery. And I really didn't want to hear any more of his recriminations.

♡

JT's next letter stretched a record eleven pages.

4 / 13 / 72
Bonjour ma chére!

He was so happy to get my letter. And he was about to play Santana's "Taboo" until he read that I'd told him to put on "*Suavecito*" while reading it:

> *OK love, once again you get your way—your influence is incredible!*

I'd asked him to explain a previous reference to whether his mother and grandmother knew anything about me. He told me to picture these two conversations:

> *#1 Jon (to coach with mother in the next room):*
> *So Coach, I really dig this girl Lynda.*
> *Coach: OK, cool, but just don't let it interfere with your grades.*
>
> *#2 Mother (to grandmother): I heard Jon say he has a white girlfriend at the college.*

Jon's take?

> *It's nothing you need to worry about.*

I was glad of that, although I wasn't sure whether he was saying "don't worry because they wouldn't care" or "don't worry because it wouldn't bother me if they did care."

After a bit more chitchat, he said he had to go tuck in his roommate and have a discussion about the meaning of life, which I thought was cute. Then he went on:

> *OK, I'm here. We basically solved the state of the world's problems, among other things.*

But he had a bit of bad news, too: he'd carelessly thrown his key on the bed and accidentally scratched "*Suavecito*." This really aggravated him. That was *our* record.

Finally, he got down to the parts I always liked best, the personal thoughts about him and me. He noticed a pattern in our always having a theme record or song that captured the intensity of our meetings—first Isaac Hayes, second *Santana III*, third Malo, and:

> *I didn't intend to get so fucked up over you. The cataclysmic effect that you have had on my life can almost make me cry. Whatever happens in the future for you and me, these memories are going to stay with me forever, I'm sure of it.*
> *Bon soir, mi suavecito.*

I smiled when I read that he'd tucked his roommate in. And flinched about his scratching "*Suavecito*." Money was so tight, it sucked that he was going to have to buy it again (and I knew he would buy it again).

And if I could bring tears to *his* eyes, his last sentence made mine well up, too; yeah, the memories we'd already made in only three visits and some letters were intense, and forever—and I wanted more. It killed me that I had no idea when I would see him again. But I had mixed feelings that he was fucked up over me. Did I want that? Only in a good way. Unfortunately, the situation was much more complicated than that.

♡

There were less than two months left in the school year. After struggling for a year and a half to recover from the academic probation I'd earned in my first semester, I was now probably failing Advanced Rhetoric, which could land me right back in trouble.

I met with my "counselor," a short Humpty Dumpty of a man who clearly hated this part of his job. He had little time for me, and I had little respect for him. These were instructors who were assigned to advise undergraduate students, and input from mine was perfunctory at best. But in this meeting he had some disturbing news.

"Adding up the units you have, plus this semester, a full load in the fall, and then student teaching, it appears you still won't have enough credits to graduate."

"*What?* How did that happen?" I was stunned.

"Well, you failed a course." Why had I taken a goddamn eight a.m. judo class? "You never created a cushion of extra credits to make up the difference."

Cushion? This was the first I'd heard of the need for a cushion. I'd always been lackadaisical about school, and if anyone needed an attentive guidance counselor it was me. Trying to schedule classes at the start of a semester was daunting. But as with most of my life, I went day-to-day, giving little consideration to the big picture.

By the following year, my government benefits would run

out. I couldn't afford to not graduate on time. He suggested I take a summer course at a state university near my home, which I agreed I could do.

Then I had another subject to discuss.

"So, I've got this class, Advanced Rhetoric? I'm afraid I'm going to fail. I did well in Creative Writing, but this professor just seems to hate everything I do."

But by then my "advisor" had already turned his attention to other things.

"Just try to do your best," he said, looking down while shuffling papers on his desk. I wanted to say, "Help me, *please!*" But I sensed that even an impassioned request like that would clash with what I'd been taught all my life: never challenge a male authority figure. I sighed, got up, and walked out of his office.

The deadline for submitting a second round of writing in Advanced Rhetoric was coming up. But I hadn't gone back to that awful class since the instructor had humiliated me over my rhyming poetry, so I was far from prepared.

Back in my room, I looked over my writing. Almost nothing to show. I'd spent the semester mostly writing letters and a couple of other people's term papers. I had the poem I'd written for JT that didn't exactly rhyme, but that wouldn't be nearly enough. For the first time, I felt real fear about school. My parents would already be annoyed about having to come up with the money for one summer class; they'd be furious if they had to pay for two. I couldn't fail this class.

Then an idea came to me. Other people had passed classes using my writing; maybe I could "borrow" someone else's? But whose?

As usual, I was listening to music as I considered my options.

Late at night I would listen to my JT songs while responding to his letters, because it was the closest I could get to him. During the day or on party nights Fran and I had a different playlist from those. Jefferson Airplane's "Pretty as You Feel" had become the anthem for getting ready to go out, ever since the night we'd been putting on makeup while waiting for a tab of green mescaline—our favorite hallucinogen—to come on. The haunting harmonies of Grace Slick and Paul Kantner swirled around our room, trailing us like skeins of gilded ribbon. I'd looked at Fran and giggled. She was sitting at her desk dabbing mascara on one humongous eye magnified in her makeup mirror.

I turned back to my mirror. My own brown eyes didn't sparkle like Fran's, but they were deep and soulful. Usually I felt ambivalent about my face, but that night, as the drug and music filled me with self-love, I saw only beauty. My mother's high cheekbones and full lips, my father's dark coloring. I brushed my hair till it shimmered in the soft light. Yes, I was as pretty as I felt that night, and so was Fran.

We were proud that our eclectic musical tastes meant we owned some music that almost no one else had. We'd blast sexually suggestive Funkadelic out the window at students passing by: "If you will suck my soul, I will lick your funky emotions." Some stopped to listen and flash us a peace sign; others frowned and hurried away as we giggled like little girls.

Quicksilver Messenger Service's hippie boys brought tears to our eyes when they sang "Don't Cry My Lady Love." Steve Miller's "Jackson-Kent Blues" broke our hearts for the all too real event in which National Guardsmen had shot college students just like us not far away. Nobody else we knew listened to the Last Poets with their "Black Thighs." And there were so many more.

But when in doubt about what to play, the road to the stereo always led us back to Rodriguez. Later the documentary *Searching for Sugar Man* would declare that only six people in the United States had bought his first album; I was one of those six. But oh, his incredible lyrics. Pure poetry, cool, hip, urban, urbane. Like "Sugar Man," who brought you all the sweet things (drugs) you needed. Or the twisted imagery in "Inner City Blues," where madness passes by, she smiles hi, he nodded. His gritty voice was set to a folk-rock guitar that squealed its way into your soul. That was Rodriguez for us, our any-time, all-the-time choice in music.

As I struggled to figure out how to save my Advanced Rhetoric grade, Rodriguez's stirring music was playing on the stereo. I'd been toying with the idea of turning in plagiarized work, and then it hit me: almost nobody had heard of Rodriguez, much less would anyone likely recognize his lyrics. No matter how cool that obnoxious professor thought he was, he would never be the wiser, and I might still be able to get a passing grade.

I had a plan. An extremely high-risk plan, but a plan.

☮

Chapter 13

AFTER I SENT JT A FUN CARD THAT DESCRIBED THE CHARAC-teristics associated with our zodiac signs, he wrote back six pages.

4 / 20 / 72 (you don't want to know what time!)
Hello Libra Lady!

In comparing our signs, Libra (me) and Cancer (him), JT's conclusion was that he might not fare as well as I in this relationship. Moody Cancer retreats into his shell while charming Libra seeks to create balance. Whatever problem he saw in that, he took it in stride:

I can't help but be humbled next to your charms. But I
don't even care.

He then complained that I'd said I wrote my best friend, Colleen, a fifteen-page letter, while his had been only twelve. But it was a facetious complaint because his conclusion was that he'd just have to vie for my attention even harder. (Yes!) More believable was when he wondered what I tell my friends about him. Of course, who wouldn't wonder about that? If he only knew the way I gushed about him, going on and on and on to girlfriends who lapped up my stories of his constant attention, his romantic letters, his open-hearted confessions.

Next he teased me about using flattery to try to get my psychoanalyst to reduce his rates:

Sorry, Miss Smith, but my hourly fee is the same, with or without your darling adjectives. Though I do love your darling adjectives.

Then he wrote about his approach-avoidance conflict and his apprehension about how it was all going to turn out, but:

It's the thing I spend most of my time thinking about, other than just remembering what it feels like to hold/kiss/talk to/and sleep with . . . guess who, YOU. Which reminds me, it is going to be a very, very dreadful summer without you.

Love,

Johnny

P.S. I have a bunch of newspaper clippings I can send you if you're interested.

Of course, I wanted to see everything having to do with Jonathan Thomas. And he didn't know it, but not only did I love talking about him, he was also a major subject of my fifteen pages to Colleen.

I can't help but be humbled next to your charms. But I don't even care. How could I explain to anyone what those words meant to me? His facility with language, his willingness to lay down his pride for me. My heart just flipped when I read those things.

Yet, as he said, summer loomed. To JT it foretold a slump because we wouldn't see each other until fall. I dreaded that, too, but even worse, the impending return of Will felt like a meteor hurtling toward Earth.

My family was deep in the throes of planning their move to Texas. But this brought JT and me an unexpected bonus: rather than pick me up from school at the end of the year, my parents were going to give my grandfather's Chevy to me. I would go home soon to pick it up, and it would be mine from then on. So within the month, I'd get to see JT one more time—before summer vacation started, before Will came home, before whatever was going to happen that I couldn't bear to think about.

Meanwhile, the biggest rift so far took place between my roommate and me. For once, Fran was going out partying while I stayed in to study. In our dry county, certain stars had to align for us to get alcohol. Tonight, the stars were aligned, and oh, I wanted to go so bad.

But I had a project due in my Teaching of English class. My idea was to tape record and talk about different regional and cultural accents and idioms, only I hadn't finished the assignment by its due date. The prof, my favorite one so far, had given me a break on doing my project late. Now my second deadline was the following day, and I still had to prepare the lecture portion. Despite desperately wanting to party, I chose to be "good."

What I didn't expect was that a drunken Fran would holler up to me from outside our dorm. Or that she'd smash an empty wine bottle against the house mother's window. Or that I'd hear a rap on my door followed by the old biddy's accusation that I was covering up for my roommate. I played dumb and said that I'd been in bed.

The next day, as a massively hungover Fran groaned in her bed, I dashed to class to give my presentation. Like most introverts, I was terrified of speaking in class. But I was prepared. My classmates seemed interested in my talking points and chuckled as I demonstrated linguistic nuances by playing the parts of my geographically disparate friends. There was Pittsburgh Fran, who said "sar" for sour and called an asshole a "jag-off"; my black friend Double from "Cinci" who wanted to "chill" in his "crib"; and Colombian "R-r-r-icar-rdo" talking to his friend "Leenda." Afterward, the professor twinkled as he gave me verbal feedback, which included an A. Yay!

The speech may have been behind me, but the wine bottle incident wasn't. I was called to the college president's office and was expected to tell on Fran. He threatened me with "a demerit," which he described as "a black mark that will follow your entire college career."

I was furious as I rushed back to my room. If they thought Fran threw the wine bottle, why was I being punished? I figured my roomie would make things right. When I told her about the president's threat, I waited expectantly . . . and waited . . . and waited. But all I got was a rueful look and an "I'm sorry, Lynnie."

I began spending more time with Linda.

Chapter 14

I STILL HAD TO OFFSET THE DEBACLE OF ADVANCED RHETORIC, so I sat in my room, typing up my "Poem for JT" and playing the songs of Rodriguez, listening for the lyrics I liked the best. I was nervous—a touch guilty about using someone else's work and even more scared about getting caught. Professor Fake McCool couldn't possibly know Rodriguez, could he? *Nobody* knew Rodriguez. Still avoiding his class, I put a folder together and trooped it over to his office. Lucky for me he wasn't in, and I left it with the department secretary. Another task checked off.

Will wrote again, apologizing for the upsetting things he'd written in his previous letter: "I'm just going crazy over here," he wrote. He admitted he was still seeing Brenda but once again insisted that it was me that he loved.

And if I hadn't had JT, how the hell *would* I have felt? I thought about it, but not for long. It just didn't matter. I did have JT.

Will wrote that he finally had some money (from Brenda, or had a stipend come through?) but that he couldn't send it to me to give to Colleen because "I'll have to use it to get home." I thought, *why don't you just send me the money and stay yourself the fuck over there?* Then I felt guilty for thinking it. He wrote that he'd be home on June 22nd and couldn't wait to see me get off the bus in Philly on the 23rd. My stomach churned just thinking about it.

Letters between JT and me had dwindled a bit. We were both in the throes of catching up on work that we'd been pretty cavalier about. But the growing divide between us felt like more than dedication to a big semester finish. My feelings were still just as strong, but my confusion had gotten stronger. Every time I talked to Linda, I was reminded of how much Will and I had gone through to be together. And no matter what JT wrote in his journal and letters, he had still never said, "I love you."

♡

As if mirroring my uncertainty, JT's next letter was only one page.

> *5 / 14 / 72*
> *Hello there Missing Person,*
> *I guess I'm MIA as much as you, but it's not*
> *because I'm not thinking about you.*

He blamed it on schoolwork but also admitted that he felt insecure about where he stood with me. And ended by saying:

> *I just get that hollow feeling when there's less*
> *contact from you. Talk to me again about being a*
> *Cancer, maybe that's why.*
> *Avec amour, Jon*

God, it pulled my heartstrings to think that he was feeling so empty. Yet I was going through changes of my own. My mind felt like a rocket hurtling into space.

My grades and projects overwhelming me. And I was running low on speed!

Plagiarizing the obscure Rodriguez. But would I be caught? Then expelled?

Will and Brenda, sleeping together. June, going to Philly, how I'd feel when I saw him.

Colleen, needing her money. Selling acid, getting arres—*no, don't even think about it!*

My parents, Texas—relief they were leaving. Fear of being left, my little sister gone.

Fran. My roomie let me down. President's office, permanent mark on my record.

My new friend Linda, good talks about men and race. Would she disappoint me, too?

Summer coming. Time with old friends. A strange campus, no job yet, no money.

And worst of all: no JT, no JT, no JT.

What would happen to me? What would happen to all of us?

While I grappled with all this, Colleen had news: she had a steady boyfriend. Kenneth. In her letters she raved about him.

"Kenneth's tall with sandy hair and beautiful blue eyes. He's gorgeous!"

"Kenneth and I are engaged, although I don't have my ring yet. We've been working on graduating early so we can get on with our lives."

"Kenneth's family is from outside Philly. You'll probably meet him if we go to the shore this summer."

Kenneth and I, Kenneth and I . . .

I figured he was from one of the well-to-do suburbs. Colleen messed around with lots of different guys, but when it came to relationships she seemed upwardly mobile in the way that my mother wished I was. By contrast, I had not one but two boyfriends from poor families. But I didn't care. All I knew was that I would be seeing JT very soon, when I went home to collect the car. I wrote him that it would likely be the weekend before Memorial Day. I could barely stand to wait; we hadn't seen each other since spring break.

♡

5 / 19 / 72
Hello, woman (who? whom?) I am missing so
badly!

It was midnight, and as he wrote, he was also reading my most recent letter, which inadvertently had conveyed some wrong information. The plan with my parents had been that I'd go home to pick up the car, so of course I'd written to JT to tell him that I'd be seeing him shortly after. But my parents had called the night before to say that the car needed work and wouldn't be ready. Phone calls were too expensive for our budgets, and since our pay phones were on a dorm floor, chances were that he wouldn't get the message anyway.

I guess something happened, but I still kept thinking I'd see
your sweet face, up until about an hour ago. I just hope
that you are all right.

While writing to me, someone had called him, and he'd hoped it was me. Now I regretted that I hadn't at least tried to get that message to him.

I couldn't wait to get to that phone, because I thought it
was you telling me you were at Hannah's. But just let me
say, I will wait as long as I need to.

Then he said something out of the ordinary: he thought we should try to do more things together. Hmmm . . .

And the song he chose to write out this time? Marvin Gaye and Tammi Terrell saying that no mountain, river, or anything else could ever keep him from me.

So just for the record, I love you this big.
JT

And under his words he had drawn a sun, a moon, and many stars. In other words, a galaxy. I melted like a candy bar in summer.

But even his nine-page letter hadn't made up for the disappointment I felt when I found out I'd have to wait till the Memorial holiday to go get the car. At least then I'd have three nights at home instead of only two. But an extra week waiting to be with JT was excruciating. And there he'd been in his dorm room, excited, waiting for me, too—the me who didn't show up.

As much as I loved the cocoon of his room, the idea that he wanted us to do things together was extremely tempting. It was normal for couples to go out, like to parks or to dinner and a movie. But what could we do? The walls had ears, the trees had eyes, and I had nosy, racist parents.

With an unexpectedly empty weekend, I worked a little on my classes, hung out with Linda, spent time with Fran. Then Fran had an idea.

"Lynnie, why don't we live off campus for our last semester before student teaching?" As education majors, Fran would be required to do a stint in an elementary school, while I would go to a high school or junior high school. This assignment would take place in our last semester, spring of the next year. We'd requested placements at schools in Pittsburgh, and I was to live with her at her mom's house. But for our one remaining stint on campus, should we stay in the dorm or move?

We'd done OK in the dorm, but we were always a little envious of people who lived off-campus. They seemed so independent and cool, although we'd heard plenty of stories about nutty landlords and deadbeat housemates who didn't pay their share. After her "sorry," Fran and I hadn't talked any more about the wine bottle incident. I felt a little distant from her, but it wasn't enough to make me consider leaving my roomie.

Fran's friend Pam from across the hall had a car and drove us to see some student housing just outside of town. She was thinking about joining us in the rental. I would have liked to consider Linda, but her financial aid required that she live on campus.

The landlord let us into a sample apartment.

"Wow, Frannie, look at that." I was in awe of the apartment's one stylish feature, a black iron spiral staircase that led to the second floor.

"Stairway to Heaven," Fran laughed, playing on the Led Zeppelin song.

The downstairs had a living room, separated from the kitchen by a tiny bar, and one small bedroom in back. Between the staircase and the bar, whoever built the place sure had an eye for what would appeal to young college students.

"This is so cool," said Pam. "Imagine the parties we'd have!" We were all eager to take the next step toward adult independence. No nosy house mother. No shoe in the door. Just Blind Faith on the stereo and good-looking long-haired men bringing laughter and dope.

We circled up the spiral. The second floor consisted of one

large room with a tiny storage cubby on one side, plus the bathroom.

"How do you guys feel about sharing this room, since you're already roommates?" asked Pam. "Then I'd take the one downstairs." Since none of us had a local boyfriend, no one had special claim to the private space.

"Sure," said Fran. "And Lynnie, you can have that little cubbyhole. You can use it to write your letters late at night." She knew I liked dark cozy spaces.

The bathroom was utilitarian but still beat the dorm facility that had to accommodate up to fifteen girls at once. There'd be no more wearing flip-flops to avoid athlete's foot, no more carrying a bucket of toiletries down the hall.

We made arrangements with the landlord for fall. Our chance to cohabit off-campus was settled.

Then Linda told me that she didn't know if she was going to come back to school the next year.

"What? Why?" I couldn't believe it. Her grades were good. She had a scholarship and a work-study deal.

"Oh, you know . . ." she trailed off. I could tell that she was embarrassed. "It's Ditto. He's always bugging me to come home." She gave a sardonic laugh. "He doesn't like me being away from him, and he's worried about other men. He wants to get married."

"But Linda. You're still in college. You're too young to get married!"

"I know. That's what my mom says. But you know how it is. It's hard to say no to a man. Men control everything."

"But we don't have to let them. Look at the women's liberationists."

In truth, I didn't know much about feminism yet. It had followed on the heels of the civil rights movement, but a lot of peo-ple, even women, were still uncomfortable with it. "Women's libbers, bra burners, man haters, dykes," they were called. I had looked the term up in the dictionary: *Feminism: a belief in the social, economic, and political equality of women to men.* That sounded right to me, certainly nothing to be ashamed of. But for most young women, what their boyfriends had to say on the sub-ject carried a lot more weight than a dictionary.

"I ain't no man hater." With a leer, Linda pretended to be giving an exaggerated hand job. I knew she was half kidding. But only half.

"I'm not either. I love men—maybe a little too much." I grinned back and pantomimed an enthusiastic blow job. We cracked ourselves up, but soon our talk turned more serious. From what we could tell, white women were at the forefront of feminism, but black women faced a lot more resistance.

"'You gotta support yo' black bruh-thas in the struggle, sis-tuhs,'" Linda quoted, a touch bitterly. "And that's not just from the men but a lot of the women, too."

"Yeah, but you know what the feminists say, that men have done to us what whites have done to blacks. It's just a different kind of enslavement, keeping us under their control."

What should a black woman put first, her race or her sex? It was a problem with no easy solution. She shouldn't have to choose.

One thing I did know for sure: "I just hate to see you stop your education, Linda."

"Well, we'll see what happens this summer. Maybe I'll change my mind. You're gonna come down and visit and meet my mom after school's out, right?"

"Of course I will."

Come summer, I did visit Linda and her mom. And I met Ditto, too. Just like in his pictures, he looked like a freak, with his 'fro and sandals and overalls with bare chest underneath. But he also sported a big un-freak-like diamond pinky ring, and when he left, I knew he was off to do business that involved drugs, women, or both. I watched Linda's mom when he was there; her perpetual frown showed me that she and I felt the same about Ditto.

But come fall, Linda didn't return to college.

Chapter 15

THE CAR WAS FIXED AND IT WAS TIME TO HEAD HOME TO pick it up. Best of all, I knew I'd be in JT's bed by nightfall.

I spent most of the tedious bus ride watching the small Pennsylvania towns slide by. Many were blue collar neighborhoods with old brick row houses blackened by age and the soot from burning coal. The nicer porches offered wooden swings or wicker chairs dragged up from basements for summer. The change in seasons had added colorful flowerbeds and lush green to the trees where the exhaust-gray snowbanks had been.

To outsiders, these towns probably looked like quaint throwbacks to a simpler era. But the hardscrabble houses with faded aluminum siding, rusted bicycles, and dented plastic kiddie pools seemed as poor and provincial as the people themselves—farmers in their fields with blue eyes narrowed against the sun and any newcomers; tired housewives with overpermed blonde hair, lugging grocery bags while trying to direct their kids away from hippies and dark strangers.

I craved the big city with its noise, excitement, and diversity—a place that welcomed hippies and dark strangers and that cooked everything up in a big stewpot of art, music, language, and culture. Or so I imagined.

Finally, I arrived home. Dinner with the folks was predictable, but afterward my mom pulled me aside.

"You need to know about something."

I was annoyed that she was keeping me from getting ready to meet JT. "What, Mom?"

"Your dad just found out that when he comes back from Texas, his coaching job won't be waiting for him."

"What do you mean?" My stepdad had been a head basketball coach since he'd come into our lives, first in New Jersey and then here in Pennsylvania. He gave more time, effort, and passion to coaching than he ever gave to his teaching career or family.

"It means that the school found out about your boyfriend, Will. They told Dad that if he couldn't control his own daughter, then he couldn't run a basketball team, either. They fired him." She crossed her arms over her chest, her usually pouty lips pursed tight.

"Did they actually say that?" I was incredulous.

"Well, they said a lot of stuff. There was something about him letting his team take stuff from the other boys' lockers at an away game. You know damn well he would never do that. It was like they had to come up with other charges. But the real reason was you."

I was stunned. At first I thought I should feel sorry and apologize to my dad. But I hadn't done anything wrong. It was like when my grandfather died—it was his own prejudice that brought on his heart attack, not the fact that I had a black boyfriend. It wasn't my fault that these backward yokels thought there was a connection between my love life and my dad's coaching performance, which had always been very good. He didn't always have winning seasons, but that was par for the course in sports.

I had to wonder if my mom was even telling the truth. Was Dad really fired for something else, and she just saw this as an opportunity to lay guilt on me? I couldn't imagine what the something else would be; for all his flaws, my stepfather was a hard-working straight-shooter. I also couldn't figure out how someone in Bethlehem found out about Will.

After my shower, I retreated into my bedroom with Barbie to put on makeup together. She could tell that I was distracted.

"What's wrong, Sissie?" Her big hazel eyes that I'd ringed with brown liner showed her worry.

How could I explain such things to a child? Besides, part of the agreement I'd made when my parents let me come home after my grandpa's death was that I would not tell Barbie about Will.

"Nothing, baby. I'm just tired." I feathered a little blush onto my cheeks, then hers.

"Then why don't you stay home with me, Sissie?" She squeezed her hands into two excited little fists. "I know, we can play Mop-oly," as she called it.

Oh great, I thought, that's all I need. Monopoly takes hours and I can't wait to get to JT. But Barbie misses me so much when I'm gone.

"Aw, I'm sorry, honey, I don't really have time to play Mon-o-po-ly tonight because Hannah is waiting for me." I finished my makeup off with a little peach lip gloss and pressed my lips together. "But I promise, tomorrow we'll go to the mall." There was very little on earth more exciting to Barbie than going to the mall with her big sister. Her eyes lit up. My guilt was assuaged.

I glossed her miniature lips as well. "There, we're done. Take a look in the mirror, gorgeous!" She looked and preened, and my heart started to feel a little bit happy again.

The weather had warmed up since my visit in early April. On the bus I'd taken off my boots and had still been uncomfortably hot in my leotard and jeans. Now I changed the leotard for a loose cotton peasant top and decided just to go barefoot, which was how I'd been walking around campus for a couple of weeks. I smiled a little to myself, wondering what JT would think of my bare feet. Somehow I suspected that barefoot hippie girls were not what he was used to, but I had a feeling that he was still going to like this one.

As usual, I stopped to catch up with Hannah. A year older, she was graduating this year.

"Sooo, what are you gonna do when school is out?" I asked. Unlike Colleen, Hannah didn't write letters much, so I wasn't up on all her plans.

"I'll keep working at the hospital for now." It was a job she'd held since high school.

"You're still gonna keep the apartment, right?" With my family moving, I wouldn't have a home base anymore. Hannah had already assured me that I could stay at her place when I visited JT come senior year.

Of course, this assumed that JT and I would still be seeing each other. Will was coming home, and I didn't know what would happen there, but I couldn't imagine Jonathan and me not being together.

"Sure. But." Hannah's eyes twinkled. "I do have something new to tell you." She looked down at her hands, then back up at me. Serious, but then she couldn't stop the grin from spreading across her face.

"I'm having an affair with a married man."

What? Hannah was very cute, but guys seemed to treat her more like a sister. And compared to me, Hannah was a goody-two-shoes. I couldn't have been more shocked.

"Wow," I said, smiling a little, trying not to betray how I felt.

Then again, I didn't even know how I felt. What reaction was she hoping for? Approval? Judgment? Intrigue?

"And that's not all," she said. "Wait until you hear this." What else could there be? I waited.

"It's JT's coach. I'm going out with Roy Greene."

It took a moment for that to sink in.

"Holy shit, Hannah." Her grin grew even larger. I wasn't sure why. Did she think this was funny? Did she enjoy shocking *me* for a change? Or was she just happy in love?

She proceeded to tell me how their paths had crossed in the PE department and how a flirtation had turned into an affair.

"And you know what? He is sooo sexy, Lynda." She rolled her eyes and mimicked a swoon. "I've never felt this way about a guy before."

With her lack of experience, I could believe it. In pictures I'd seen, he was a good-looking man, but he had to be at least ten years older than us. I'd never been attracted to someone that age, so I couldn't relate. Listening to her gush, my heart fell; she might be into him, but he wasn't free to be into her.

"He's married though, Hannah. Is he gonna leave his wife?"

Her grin faded. "I don't know. We haven't talked about it. I don't think so, though." We just sat silent for a moment, contemplating how this was likely to end up. And what about his wife, how would she feel if she found out? I didn't think it was right, but then again, was I in a position to judge?

"I just don't want you to get hurt," I concluded.

"I know," she said. "I don't either. I'm going to have to keep my cool. There's something that might help, unfortunately—he's leaving to take another job."

"*What?*" My attention flew back to JT. His coach was leaving? The coach who had recruited, mentored, and tortured him

129

through three amazing years. Did JT know? And did he know about the affair?

Hannah wasn't sure what JT knew. When they saw each other around campus, they were friendly but usually didn't say more than, "Hi, Hannah," and, "Have fun with Lynda this weekend."

I wanted to get out of there and find JT. I really wanted to know what he knew. And as always, I was aching to see his face and feel him next to me.

"Have fun tonight." Hannah's grin came back. "And let me know if you find out anything about Roy."

I drove the two blocks to my usual parking place outside JT's dorm. I bounded up the stairs to his room and knocked, wondering where I'd eventually find him.

The door flew open. "Well, hello there," JT said with a grin.

Surprise! JT was home, waiting for me. Subtle as it was, it signified a change in our relationship. The hide-and-seek game might have been fun for a while, but now we couldn't afford to miss out on time together. Even before the door closed, he drew me into his arms. We stood still for a minute, just letting our bodies remember. Then he gently moved us into the center of the room and held me out in front of him.

"Let me look at you. Yep, it is you, all right. I just had to make sure, 'cuz I imagined this moment last week, and it turned out I was hallucinating or something." JT's beautiful dimples seemed to wink at me.

"I know. I'm so sorry. I thought for sure I was coming, but then that damn car problem." At least I'd had time to write an explanation and prepare him for my visit this weekend.

"It's OK," he said. "You're here now, and that's what counts." JT's eyes widened. "Hey, what happened to your shoes?"

I laughed. "It's been so hot out, I've been going barefoot at school. I have to admit the grass sure feels good."

"That just goes to show, you didn't grow up where I grew up. In the city, you would never go without your shoes."

"But I'm not in the city. I'm in JT's room. The coolest place on earth." I looked around. "It's pretty clean, too. I think bare feet are safe here."

He smiled happily. "Bare everything is safe here." And with that we moved to the bed so we could begin the night-long process of relearning each other.

"Cool, you're playing Isaac. Remember that first night?" *Our love so doggone good.*

"Remember it? How could I forget? I think about it every day. Well, maybe every third or fourth day."

"Fucker. Shut up!" I pretended to slap him, and he caught my hand mid-air and pressed my palm to his lips. His eyes held mine, telling me everything. But when would he say it with his voice?

"I feel deficient. I don't have a new song for you this time."

"That's OK. We have plenty of old songs to choose from." *Suavecito, mi linda. Suavecito!*

We talked about his coach leaving. He admitted that he was surprised and a little worried about how things would go for his senior year. I didn't say anything about Hannah and Roy. He didn't mention it, either. We had so much else to do.

♡

The next day, while I was getting Barbie and me ready to go to the mall, my mom drew me aside. *Now what*, I wondered.

"I wanna ask you something." She was twisting her wedding ring like she did when she was nervous. Yet she looked mad.

"OK?"

She hesitated, then blurted, "Are you going out with Jon Thomas?"

WHAT THE FUCK?

"What?" I didn't even have to pretend to be shocked. My heart was pounding. Fight or flight. I wanted to run away. "No. Why would you even say that?"

"Well, you've been seeing a lot of Hannah. I figured you two were spending time at the college, and I wondered why."

"It's her school, Mom. She knows people. Colleen is gone. Sharon has a steady boyfriend. Who else would I hang around with?" I started organizing things in my purse just to keep my hands from shaking.

"Does she know him? Have you met him?"

"Of course she knows him. Who at Moravian College doesn't know Jon Thomas? And yeah, I met him once. At a party or something. But that's it. We're not even friends."

I wanted to ask why she would think I was seeing Jon Thomas. Had she heard something from someone? But I knew too well how my mom's mind worked. My dad poked fun at her when she didn't know things, and that bothered me. Dad assumed that because she hadn't graduated college, she wasn't as smart as he was. It was true that she didn't have as much general knowledge as he or even I did, but she had a weird thing that we didn't have, a sixth sense, mostly of the suspicious kind and sometimes it was uncanny. Here it was again: she put Hannah and the college and all my nights out into her imaginary crystal ball, peered into it, and presto: out popped JT. I had to hand it to her. But I didn't have to like it. And I sure didn't have to admit to it.

♡

JT was waiting for me in his room the next two nights as well. We talked about Vietnam—when would the war be over? Also the election in the fall, the first time eighteen-year-olds would be allowed to vote—McGovern! On the last night, we talked about summer, which neither of us was looking forward to.

"I'll be teaching kids at basketball camps," said JT. "What about you?"

"I don't really know yet. My dad told me he couldn't get me my old playground job again." This was no big surprise, considering my past performance there. "I've gotta take a class up at Stroudsburg State to have enough credits to graduate. And I guess my parents will expect me to help them with packing and stuff. That's all I know right now."

Of course, I knew more than that. Will was coming home. He would expect me to be in Philly every weekend. But I didn't want to talk to JT about Will. And JT didn't ask.

The last ribbons of pink were still tying up the night sky as we lay back on his pillow. College bed, twin bed, one shared pillow—more than enough because it only kept us closer.

"I wish I could see you this summer," he murmured. "Those camps are OK, but I expect I'm gonna be pretty lonely this year."

"Me too," I said miserably. Will's return was less than a month away, and I was dreading it.

"At least we have Sharon to thank for letting me write to you at her house," JT added. He sounded sincerely grateful, but I winced inside. I was glad, too, but God, I hated that shit. Asking him to sneak letters to me through a friend. It must have been humiliating for him. And I was a grown adult. But I wasn't on my own yet. I could just imagine my parents' reaction if I suddenly started getting letters from Johnny Thomas or letters with no return name or address. My mother wasn't above opening and reading my mail, but soon my family would leave for Texas, and having to hide my relationship with JT would no longer be an issue. Would it?

It would probably be September before JT and I saw each other again. More than three months away. Already I was thinking about how unbearable that would seem. But I tried to focus on what we had right there in that moment, in his room, in his bed, the turntable stacked with songs that expressed our feelings for each other.

Daydreamin' and I'm thinking of you, sang Aretha, and he rolled me up on top of him. I let my hair fall over his face, and I heard him inhale the wonderful scent of my Breck shampoo. He pushed my hair to one side, and his eyes caressed my face. I pushed up on one elbow so that he could get a better look, and that gave him access to the little string tie that made my peasant top modest; he smiled as he undid it and revealed my not so modest cleavage. The tops of my breasts pressed against his chest, creating a fullness they didn't really have, and I knew that pleased us both.

I never met a girl like you in my life, Malo reminded me, and he raised my arms and lifted the blouse off over my head. It fell to the floor as the tips of his fingers traced the length of my hands, forearms, and shoulders, sending a tickle under my arms and down my sides. I giggled. He smiled and slid his arms around my back, pressing his palms against my wings, holding me reverently as if I might fly away. I wasn't flying anywhere, except in mind and body to that place he could take me, all smooth skin and strong bone and sighs.

Open your eyes, let it begin with me, crooned Santana, and he slid his hands down inside the back of my jeans, under my panties, to hold the curves of my ass. *Brand new day, fresh new way to live*, and I felt his sex against my pubis. I slowly rocked against it, watching his eyelids close. He rolled me to his side and unbuttoned my jeans. Isaac moaned, *I've got to know every time that you come, where it is that you're comin' from*, and we were rocking and rolling together, blood pulsing endorphins to every cell.

When our bodies quieted, the familiar phrase came whispering out over the beat of our still pounding hearts: "I love you." But this time there was no doubt that the words came from him.

He said it, he said it, *he said it.*

"Oh Jon, I love you, too," I whispered back.

☮

Chapter 16

ONE WEEK LATER, I STOPPED AT SHARON'S TO PICK UP MY first summer letter from JT. Ten pages.

> *6/2/72*
> *Hello My Love!*

He started off with a story about a chick named Sister who lived in his neighborhood—and who he had just had to talk out of stabbing him! Why? Because she wanted him, but he didn't want her. She was mentally unstable, but also:

> *As you know, there's no one who could hold a candle to you.*

His next story was sweet, too. His grandmother, getting the mail, called up to his window that he had a letter from Pennsylvania. He just about fell off the sill but instead played it cool, waiting five minutes to go get it. Then he flew down the stairs:

> *I couldn't believe you'd written so soon. I just about died of excitement!*

He sounded exuberant, but his mood changed as he talked about the summer without me and how much he already missed me every day. Then he answered my suggestion that we clarify what we meant to each other:

Either I'm crazy, or love has taken control of my heart. You aren't just a part of my life, you are all of it. (Oh. My. God.)

He finished by playing psychoanalyst, writing that an enforced summer absence from my therapist would give our heart rates a rest from exciting overactivity. And:

Now I'll close by sending an imaginary kiss across the miles. Your Jonathan

So, school was over for him, and he was at home. Sister! Who the fuck was Sister? But she didn't sound like any kind of threat—except for that knife business. I hadn't seen that side of him, the inner-city JT. But it sounded like it wasn't that different from the neighborhood Will came from, where women were named Sister and carried knives.

Then the part about trying to hide from his grandmother how excited he was about my letter. I pictured him waiting nonchalantly and then clattering down the stairs in his Converse All-Stars. That sounded like the JT I knew, the body of a man with the sweet heart of a boy.

But the *pièce de résistance* that would keep echoing through my mind as I finished my exams and packed to go home: "*You aren't just a part of my life, you are all of it.*"

Could that really be true? That of all the women he could have, he wanted me? Why did I have trouble accepting it? And what the hell was I supposed to do now?

For the first time, I drove home in my Grandpa's Chevy. Happy to have a car, but sad that nights with JT were no longer waiting at the end. I unpacked my suitcase into my old bedroom.

Wondered what we were having for dinner. Got through the night with my family. Let Barbie read bedtime stories to me for a change, in her halting second-grade reading level.

The next day I drove over to Stroudsburg State to register for a journalism class. On the way I heard a song that would haunt me all summer, "Where Is the Love" by Donny Hathaway and Roberta Flack. A lament from a man whose woman had two lovers, and when would she tell that other man good-bye? (And when would I?)

When I got back from registering, my dad was waiting with his big horsey grin. "Guess what? Thanks to yours truly, you have a job." He meant my previous job as a playground "director," which really wasn't the job for me; I wasn't athletic, and I didn't like to play games or do arts and crafts with the kids. I was a boring babysitter, counting the hours till I got off.

"So, all I'll require is a 10% finder's fee," he joked. Dad was nothing if not a jokester. He could be funny, but his humor often came at others' expense. I gave him a wan smile. "Thanks, Dad." I really was grateful that he'd made the effort on my behalf and glad that I'd have some spending money.

I waited anxiously to get my grades and to see what I'd gotten in Advanced Rhetoric. In my mind, that asshole teacher had all but forced me to cheat. Had he actually fallen for the idea that Rodriguez's wonderful lyrics were my own? Finally, the official notice came in the mail: I had gotten a C. No academic probation. I could still graduate on time. And I wouldn't be sent to the president's office for another "black mark," this time for plagiarism. Hooray!

Many years later I'd tell this story to a friend who was a fellow Rodriguez fan. "Oh my god, Rodriguez got a C," he laughed. I hadn't thought of it that way, but what a good point!

Rodriguez was obscure then but would go on to galvanize a movement and become an underground star, revered by millions. What an idiot that professor was.

I met up with Colleen, who was planning to do summer school at Pitt. Unlike me, she had that "cushion" of units, and just a few more would allow her to graduate early, along with her boyfriend Kenneth. It figured. I remembered her in eleventh grade, clutching a fistful of pencils, rushing up to me as I nuzzled a boyfriend in the hall: "Are you ready for the SAT? Where are your #2 pencils?" I had laughed and waved her off, blasé as usual.

Now I said, "Hey, I've got your money," and pulled out several twenties. The sale of the acid had gone according to plan. People I knew from the various movements. Freak friends of friends. Sorority girls in the hall. Luckily, I'd never had a nerve-wracking exchange.

"I'm really sorry this took so long, Colleen."

"That's OK. But it would've been hard for me this summer if I didn't have it. Have you paid Tuck back yet?"

"Not yet, but I've got it. He's been real patient about it." What a relief to think that I'd finally be square with everyone and not have to sell anymore. I changed the subject.

"So, when are we going to meet the famous Kenneth?" I teased. Hannah and I approved of Kenneth in theory, but we still wanted to see him for ourselves.

"Well, like I said before, Hannah can probably get her parents to let us use the camper again, right? We'll go to the shore and then stop at Kenneth's on the way home."

"That'll be cool. I could sure use a trip to the shore." It would be a treat to look forward to, because I wouldn't be seeing JT, and my feelings about seeing Will were ambivalent to say the least.

Chapter 17

JT WAS SUPPOSED TO SEND THE MAILING ADDRESS FOR HIS first basketball camp. One week passed and then two. I wondered miserably if he had just gotten tired of me and my complications. Finally, I wrote to him at home in DC. His return letter—six pages written over eight days—showed that we'd had an unfunny comedy of errors regarding where to send mail. To make things even more difficult, Mother Nature sent us all a hurricane.

> *6 / 13 / 72*
>
> *Dear Earthshaker,*
>
> *Yeah, "earthshaker," because you totally have shaken up my world. And it won't stop shaking until I can hold you in my arms—or at least get a letter from you.*

He went on to say he couldn't mail this letter until he heard from me, because he had forgotten Sharon's address at home. So he planned to just keep adding to it. What he added first was how, although he had enjoyed the summer basketball camps in the past:

> *This one already is sheer hell.*
>
> *Love, Nutty*
>
> *P.S. "Nutty" because only a crazy person would do these camps.*

6 / 13 / 72 (same day!)
Hey Love.

He said he just couldn't stop writing. Especially because he'd been hearing so many songs that reminded him of me, and he wanted to write them all out to me. But he was so tired, he'd get to one tomorrow:

Avec amour,
Mr. Lonely

6 / 14 / 72
Hey Baby.

He filled me in on the hot humid weather at the camp on the outskirts of Baltimore, plus the schedule of twice daily coaching sessions with the kids. Then the song he picked, Al Green's "Look What You Done for Me":

The best of my years will go to you
That's the only thing that I can do.

Oh my god, the best of his years. Coincidentally, I had written the same song out to him, he just hadn't gotten it yet.

6 / 14 / 72
Hello woman of my dreams.

He said he was exhausted but could always find some energy for me.

*Maybe I can't really see you, but there is a place I can kind
of see you. (The hint is in the greeting.)
Love,
"Bushed" (Do you know that word for tired? I just learned
it. But what does a bush have to do with anything?)*

*6 / 18 / 72
Hey Miss MIA.*

He wondered if he was ever going to hear from me. I sure
understood because I'd had to wait weeks before finally receiving this letter. And he said it was out of boredom, but he'd gone
out with another counselor and gotten drunk:

*So I woke up to face a hangover plus a head cold—feeling
pretty pitiful right now.*

He asked some questions about my life, whether I'd found
work and registered for a class. But I could feel the frustration in
his closing:

*Hey, I really want to get this goddamn letter in the mail,
but I need that address pronto!
Fumingly (is that a word?),
Mr. MIA (wait—am I MIA if I know where I am? Smile.)*

*6 / 19 / 72
Hi,
It's after midnight, but I'm pondering this song by the
Fleetwoods.*

The song asked whether my love was still warm or had it grown cold. (No JT, I could never be cold to you.) But he was worried enough to sign off as:

Mr. Sleepless

6 / 20 / 72
Dear Suavecito,

It's early morning but I've got to make sure that you understand what happened. It was all my fault. I forgot to take Sharon's address. And for some reason, it didn't sink in that you didn't have my address at camp either. All I could think about was that I wasn't hearing from you.

So, he had forgotten Sharon's address and couldn't send me his letter. And without his letter, I didn't have an address for him. How long could we have gone on, wondering why the other wasn't writing? I could hear his mood rocketing up, down, and around like a roller coaster.

I couldn't blame him. He was at a rural camp, playing ball and sweating in the heat, with not even a letter from me waiting on his bunk. He'd even gotten drunk. I had never seen JT drunk.

He explained his thought processes as he hadn't been hearing from me. Whether I'd been badly affected by the hurricane, or was out of town, or doing volunteer work, or just tired of JT, or was he just totally screwed up? He had resigned himself to never seeing me again, but he felt like crying just remembering what we were to each other. (Oh JT, my love.)

And then I went home, and there was your familiar envelope. All I can say is thank you sweetheart, for taking

the situation in hand. I will mail this epic immediately.
Love always,
JT

Wow. So there he was thinking I didn't want him anymore, and there I was thinking he didn't want me anymore. There was a synchronicity in that, and maybe a lesson. Because I was pretty sure we both did still want each other. Why was it so fucking hard to communicate?

Now Will was coming home from England, which was going to make my life very complicated.

♡

But before Will arrived, the hurricane did. Hurricane Agnes. "Agnes' Fury Tears Up Eastern Coast," read the newspaper headline. The papers would report that it was the costliest hurricane to hit the United States in recorded history, and Pennsylvania got it the worst. Torrential rains brought down trees and power lines, and the flooding was like none we'd ever seen.

By the time the squall spun off to the open sea, leaving behind a mellow summer drizzle, I was boarding a bus to Philly. June 23. I hadn't heard otherwise, so I assumed that Will's year as an exchange student was over.

I felt dispirited as I got ready to leave. I showered and washed my hair, threw on a tank top in deference to the humidity and wore boots with my jeans because of the rain. But I didn't have the energy to fuss over makeup or what to pack.

My mom pushed the bedroom door open, as usual without knocking.

"So, you're going then?" she asked.

"Yeah, Mom." She watched me quietly, then she just couldn't help herself, I guess.

"Don't you think it's about time he started contributing to your travel expenses?"

"Oh, Mom, please. You don't know what he does or doesn't contribute to."

Until he went to England, Will and I talked little about money. The way of our tribe was that we aimed to be egalitarian, but sometimes whoever had, paid. I took care of getting to him, whether by bus to Philly or advertising on a student bulletin board for a ride to Pitt ("Ass, gas, or grass" read a popular bumper sticker. I contributed to gas.) Then Will always made sure I was fed. But England had thrown two wrenches into the works: Will's scholarship stipend had been reduced (later I would realize it was probably the exchange rate, but we didn't understand that then), and then there had been my airfare at Christmas that neither of us could afford. My mom didn't know anything about my loan from Colleen, Tuck's "loan" of LSD, or the resentment it had created between Will and me.

"Bye, Mom. I'll be home Sunday." I brushed her tilted cheek with my lips as I moved past her.

"Bye, honey." She sighed and sounded sad, then added, "Be careful." I wondered what she pictured me walking, or busing, into. The "dangerous ghetto"? I knew it could be dangerous, but I was with Will. Mostly what I'd seen was people just trying to make it and have some joy along the way.

On the bus, I nervously chewed my cuticles. It had been six months since Will and I had seen each other, six months during which a lot had happened. What would he have to say about Brenda? Of course, I was still not planning to tell him about JT. Or was I?

When the bus squealed into the terminal, my stomach jumped when I saw that Will was waiting. His Afro was all picked out. He wore his customary T-shirt and jeans, lace-up suede moccasins, aviator sunglasses, and a big grin. Before I could say anything, he wrapped me so tightly in his arms that I could hardly breathe.

"Kitten, I can't believe today is finally here. I swear, I am never, ever going away from you again." I said nothing, just hugged him back. Will smelled like soap, but it was the wrong soap. When he kissed me, his lips didn't taste right. His body felt strange as well, too short, too compact. Where were JT's lanky limbs, sweet musk, and soft skin? Where was my *suavecito*?

Yet no matter where JT was, or whatever JT was doing, just like that my Philly weekends with Will resumed where they had left off. If I didn't come to see him, he would want to know why. I just couldn't face telling him yet. It was kind of like when he was in England, he was somewhat out of sight, out of mind. Now in a way I took the same attitude with JT. I wanted to be with JT, but I didn't know how to accomplish that. It me feel sick to think about it. So I got through my days by trying not to think about it.

☮

Chapter 18

7 / 1 / 72
Hey there lover of mine.

He described his happiness to once again come home to a letter from me. And that he knew what it meant: he was, without a doubt, head over heels in love with me. I silently thanked God.

From there he went on to talk about another synchronicity: that before I'd seen the Al Green lyrics he'd written to me, I'd written the same words to him. Our promises of the best rest of our lives had actually crossed in the mail!

And when he read of my worry about how he had fared in the big storm:

I was just mush after that, you incredible woman you.

The rain and floods had driven the camp counselors to take the kids to a local high school. Then a big truck had driven their belongings to them because the camp was obliterated. He knew it was bad where I was, too, from watching it on TV.

July 3
I can't believe it's taken hours till I could get back to your letter.

Apparently the camp was working the crap out of him. At least I didn't have that problem; I still just put in my hours at the playground, some of which were spent in reading and rereading JT's love songs. But for him:

Your letter makes up for everything. You know that, right?
JT

I knew his birthday was July 5th, oddly enough the same day as my stepdad's. The day after Independence Day, when the last thing I wanted was independence from JT. But we didn't have any choice.

July 6
Yesterday I became a man. Sort of. Because how can I be a man when my woman isn't here?

He said he would've done just about anything to be with me on his birthday. And that when we did finally see each other, he wanted us to celebrate, some way, somehow:

And I wonder when that might be because I need you so.
Birthday kisses from,
A Miserable Man

God, I really needed to see him, too. I so wanted to give him those birthday kisses. But instead, a girls' weekend at the shore came together. Hannah got the camper, Colleen took a weekend break from school, and I told Will that I wouldn't be coming down to Philly.

The Jersey shore was about a three-hour drive from our

hometown. The three of us shared the wide front seat of a pick-up truck that smelled like baked vinyl and carried the huge camper shell on its back. We traveled light, mostly bathing suits for the beach and something cute to wear out at night. While Hannah drove, we reminisced about past trips.

"Hey, Hannah," I said. "Remember that time right after I graduated? We shared a couple of cheap hotel rooms with a bunch of kids."

"Where was I?" asked Colleen.

"I don't know, but you weren't on that trip."

"What, Lynda doesn't remember?" Hannah teased. "You remember everything, even when it's not about you. Your brain is like our personal diary."

"Yeah," Colleen added. "I wouldn't remember half of high school if it wasn't for her."

Hannah went back to the original story—that I had made out with a guy, and when he came in his pants, it soaked through onto my jeans. We all started laughing.

"And I didn't have another clean pair to put on. I had to go to breakfast with a stiff white stain next to my crotch." We were all laughing now, but I'd been painfully embarrassed then.

"How about Mini Dick?" said Colleen with a sly smile. "I was there for that one."

We recalled that story: how we'd met three guys on the boardwalk and invited them back to our camper to make out. When my guy took my hand and forcefully pushed it down his pants, I said loudly, "Where is it? I can't find it!" The others all busted up laughing; the guys didn't stay long after that. I felt a little bad about humiliating him, but I thought he deserved it for being so aggressive. We girls had to do whatever was necessary to take care of ourselves.

Hannah gave Colleen an appraising sideways look. "OK, Colleen, are you going to turn into Colleen the Bitch on this trip?"

"Don't say that," protested Colleen. "I am not a bitch."

"Yes, you are," I said. "You just get so bossy sometimes. Remember the thing about the dishes last year?"

"I don't remember anything about any dishes," Colleen said petulantly.

"Let me remind you," I continued. "We'd just finished dinner and were having cocktails. Hannah and I wanted to get ready to go out, but you insisted we had to wash the dishes first. You had to have your way. That's when Hannah nicknamed you Colleen the Bitch."

"Well, my idea was just better," Colleen defended herself. "Then we didn't have to do them in the morning."

"So what? We'd just do them in the morning." Hannah paused, then added, "And why was it up to you, anyway? There were three of us. But you had to be in charge. Therefore, *voilá*, Colleen the Bitch." She and I laughed, and I was glad she had brought it up. I did get tired of Colleen's bossiness, and I wanted this weekend to go smoothly. Colleen was still pouting, so I thought of another story to lighten the mood.

"Hey, what about that time I got rescued by the lifeguard?"

"Yeah, he thought you were drowning, but a wave had just knocked your bathing suit top off," said Hannah.

"Luckily, you got it on before he got to you. He would have been in for a surprise," laughed Colleen. I remembered him dragging me into shore by the neck, which was even more embarrassing than losing my top.

Soon we were turning off the Jersey Turnpike onto the two-lane road toward the beach. "Ew, smell that?" Colleen turned up her nose at the sudden odor of saltwater, fish, and primeval marsh. To me those scents and the strident calls of gulls were always the first reminder: we're at the shore! We found the KOA campground and soon pulled into our spot.

Daytime was going to the beach in our bikinis and flip-flops. The crash of the ocean and the coconut scent of Hawaiian Tropic oil. Pointing out guys and having an occasional flirtatious exchange from our beach towels. Reading quietly when conversation lulled.

Late afternoon was a grossed-out shower in the group bathroom. Slathering lotion on tender skin and lolling around in the humid camper. Getting reinvigorated by a simple dinner, then the first round of cocktails while we got ready to go out—short dresses or tube tops and cutoff jeans, sandals, puka shell necklaces white against bronzed collar bones.

Nighttime was walking the boardwalk while carrying our bottle of booze in my purse. Giggling and bursting into the Drifters song, off-key and out of sync: "Under the boardwalk—boardwalk!" Being tipsy enough to flirt with guys but not so drunk that we invited them home. We weren't kids anymore. I was a college senior, Colleen was soon to graduate, and Hannah was a full-fledged working adult.

When the weekend was over, our trip had been a success—if success meant lots of laughs, hangovers, and first-degree sunburns. Colleen the Bitch hadn't really surfaced. Since all three of us were involved in relationships, we didn't go home with any make-out stories.

We did, however, stop off outside Philly to meet Colleen's guy, Kenneth.

Kenneth's family did live in an upscale suburb. He invited us in to use the bathroom and have a glass of water. As Colleen had described, he was a tall sandy-haired guy with a friendly smile. He seemed nice enough, but he didn't welcome her with any more warmth than he showed Hannah and me. Not a hug or kiss or even a private look passed between them. Was he just shy or was something else going on? Will would have swooped me into his arms. JT was reserved around others, but we'd had reason to be discreet. Kenneth's distance didn't seem to matter to Colleen; she talked about him all the way home. Tired, gritty, and eager for a hot bath, we hadn't stayed long.

♡

And then a miracle happened. It was late afternoon, and I'd just gotten home from my class when I got a call from Hannah.

"Guess what." I could hear the excitement in her voice.

"What?"

"JT's in town!"

"*What?*"

"Yes, and Roy, too. They came together for some basketball thing. They're at an apartment that Roy rents." I hadn't heard anything about an apartment. Surely it couldn't be where Roy lived with his wife. Was it a place he'd gotten to carry on his affair with Hannah, and maybe other women, too?

"OK," I said, "but I just got in, I've gotta go shower and get ready." My heart was on cloud nine, but I was all too aware that I hadn't shaved my legs in days—stubble, the brunettes' curse.

"No, there isn't time. They're only here for a couple hours, and then they're going back to DC or somewhere. We've gotta get over there. I'll pick you up in fifteen minutes."

Shit. I hadn't seen JT in over a month, and now there would be no time to prepare myself for him. But was I going to miss a chance to see my love over hairy legs or anything else? Hell, no! I took a wet washcloth to my armpits and between my thighs, brushed my hair, and put on a soft orange halter top with my jeans and Dr. Scholl's wood sandals.

Now what to tell my family? Barbie played on the floor with her dolls. My dad snored softly on the couch. Mom was making dinner sounds in the kitchen. I decided to take the path of least resistance.

"Mom, something's come up," I hollered on my way out. "I'm going to eat with Hannah. I'll see you later." I quickly pulled the front door closed behind me.

Hannah was already pulling up as I hurried to the curb. I thought, *she must be as excited as I am.* But how could that be possible? I felt like my heart was going to slam right out of my chest.

As she drove us to the apartment, Hannah explained that she'd been there with Roy a couple of times. It was nothing special, a one-bedroom walk-up on a busy street. There was only a small sofa and coffee table in the living room, plus stacks of moving boxes pushed up against the wall. Roy was clearly on his way out of town.

He met us at the door, and I found myself feeling suddenly shy. Here I was meeting JT's coach for the first time, and he was in the act of cheating on his wife with my girlfriend. Did he feel embarrassed? As hypocritical as it seemed, I disliked him for being unfaithful to his marriage. But could I judge him without also judging Hannah? And again, who was I to judge anyone?

Roy, though, seemed unabashed. In fact, he was effusive. "Lynda, hello. So nice to meet you." He took my hand between his and leveled his navy blues on me. With his tall frame and curly blond hair, I could see why Hannah found him so arresting.

It took only a minute for him to spirit her into the bedroom and close the door. That left me alone and still shy with JT. We had been so few places together, and this was a strange one. He walked over to look at a small record player, but if there had been any albums to go with it, they'd already been packed away. We perched on the couch, and it felt stiff and unnatural. With no words and only a look between us, we both scooted down to settle ourselves on the green shag carpet and lean back against the sofa.

Soft murmurs came from the bedroom. Again I wondered uneasily what JT thought of Roy and Hannah. Was he embarrassed for his coach? After all, he knew Roy's wife, too. Or did he just accept this kind of behavior? But judging Roy could just as well mean judging me. I didn't want to waste our precious time on that.

Because JT was *here*. With me! My leg was touching his, he was looking into my eyes, and we couldn't stop smiling. As usual, he took his time getting reacquainted with me. But the first thing he brought up made me uncomfortable anyway.

"So, how did you survive the hurricane? I heard you got hit pretty hard. Were you out there volunteering?" he asked.

"No, I wasn't," I answered, surprised. Why was he asking that? I felt ashamed to realize that it hadn't even occurred to me. I couldn't remember ever having seen anyone in my family volunteer. Maybe he had experienced volunteering through his grandmother's church? I pictured them, likely much poorer than we were and yet out helping others. The people I knew mostly just took care of ourselves, and suddenly it seemed so selfish that my cheeks burned with shame. I was glad there was only one dim light in the room.

"I guess my mom wanted me at home," I added, feeling so inadequate.

"Well, I'm just glad you were safe. You know what happened to me, taking the kids to the high school and all."

"Thank goodness you were all OK, too."

"Yeah. And then I didn't even have you to brighten up my boring birthday." My heart hurt for him. And I still had nothing to give him now. If only I'd known he was coming.

JT took my hands and gave me a mischievous smile. "Hey, this is our first time together since then. Are we gonna celebrate?"

I made a ring of my thumb and forefinger and encircled his long middle finger. "I guess we have to. After all, like you said, you have become . . ." I slowly slid the ring up and down, ending with a soft caress of the tip ". . . a man." He chuckled softly, closed his eyes, and pulled me against his chest.

"Ahhh," we both sighed at the same time and laughed.

We could hear soft talk coming from the bedroom and here and there a giggle, too. But soon they receded into the background.

In the foreground was the scratchy feel of the carpet under my hips (and the slight brush burn on my ass that would give me a smile the next day). The oppressive heat of a second-floor room on a humid night. Our combined sweat pooling in all my hollows. There was the catch in my breath when he moved inside me, the way my arms rested perfectly across his shoulders. A yearning feeling like walking at dusk along a dirt road toward home. His smell was the right scent in my nostrils, his lips left the right taste on my mouth. Mine were the ripples of pleasure that melted over him like sweet honey. Ours were the muffled cries into each other's neck.

Then "I love you," we both whispered, nose to nose, at the

same time, and again we giggled. Soon he lifted himself off, and I settled into the nook of his shoulder. We drifted into a peaceful nap, until we heard the bedroom door creak open, signaling the end of our midsummer miracle.

☮

Chapter 19

ONE WEEKEND I WAS LEAVING FOR PHILLY WHEN SHARON met me at the bus station to deliver not one but two letters from JT. I was a little nervous about carrying mail from him in my purse when I was on my way to see Will, but I just couldn't wait to read what JT had to say. The first one was four pages.

> 7/28/72
> *Dear Suavecito (yes I'm repeating myself, because it bears repeating).*

He had just gotten home from another camp, ecstatic to have a letter from me:

> *I couldn't wait because my grandmother had told me it was there.*

He complained about the camp and said that all he thought about were the times we had spent together. But then my last letter had bummed him out because I had told him of my confusion over the other man. I didn't want to bring Will up. But I thought I should. We wrote and wrote, yet our words ignored one of the central issues. Why? Shouldn't we be talking about it?

He said he almost cried to think of it because he felt that memories of me were all he was ever going to have. (That's so not true, JT. But I can understand how you feel that way.)

And then he blew my mind:

I love you so much that I don't want to put you through all this. So I think it's time for me to just quietly leave the scene and let you live your life.

Not because he wouldn't compete; he felt he was equal to anyone, but he just couldn't take how I'd said it was turning my head around. So he wanted to end things—not for himself, but for *me*.

My head was reeling. But I kept reading. About how his coach and his wife had told him I must really be something because they'd never heard him talk like that about any other girl. About how much he loved reading the words to Roberta Flack's "First Time Ever I Saw Your Face" that I had written to him, such a sweetly sensuous ode to love. About how he was listening to another song by her, "Do What You Gotta Do," a song about releasing your love when it's time to let go. About how he couldn't write out the words; in fact, he could hardly write at all.

That's when I noticed that a few of the words were smeared. Oh my god, had he actually cried while writing me this letter? Because I was crying, too. With that he signed off:

No matter what, I will still love you forever.
Jon

He'd love me forever. But *what the hell?* He felt he could vie with any man, but instead he'd bow out gracefully? How could I make sense of what he really felt, what he really wanted, when he wrote such contradictory things? And why didn't we talk about this face to face when we had the chance? Why was I so fucking tongue-tied around him? Was he just as tongue-tied around me?

I had no response to these questions except: I can't stand it, I can't stand it, *I fucking can't stand it.*

With an ache in my throat, I moved on to his second letter, six pages.

> *8 / 12 / 72*
> *Hey baby,*
> *I can only imagine what you must be thinking after*
> *reading my last letter. Strike that: I'm sure I can't imagine,*
> *but I only wish I knew.*

He wrote that he knew he hadn't lost me yet, but he figured it would probably happen. He wouldn't leave me willingly or let someone else push him away, but he couldn't stand the idea of me going through anguish. Then he wrote out the lyrics to "I'll Be Around," a Spinners song that spoke of a fork in the road and about choices and about bowing out gracefully. He said that it reminded him of our situation.

> *I especially like the line that says she knows he's fucked up*
> *over her, and he knows she knows, but he doesn't care; no*
> *matter what, he'll be there for her. That sure sounds right.*

And then he put me in my place regarding Will:

> *You say he deserves respect for having seniority. All I can*
> *say is that doesn't acknowledge our intensity. (Note red pen*
> *for intensity!)*

I was pretty sure that I was not gonna write again. But as usual your letter perked up my confidence. I love when you sign off with LOVE, Lynda.

So try to keep your love alive until I write again, and I will, too.

LOVE, (Note all caps for emphasis!)
Your JT

I saw his emotions swing from a perceived high road of wanting to bow out gracefully and maybe never even write to me again down to a resigned low of just sticking around and waiting for me to eventually lower the boom. And the sweet sadness with which he seemed to accept his plight. My only thought was, *I have to do it, I have to do it, I FUCKING HAVE TO DO IT.*

I had to tell Will it was over. That very weekend. It was going to hurt him, bad, but it had to be done. I couldn't let JT just bow out. Whether he was willing to back away to ease my confusion, to preserve his sanity, or for any of the countless other reasons it made sense for a man to extricate himself from a heart-wrenching mess like this one I'd caused, I wouldn't let him. After all, I was the one who was doing wrong. And I was in love with JT, not Will.

In less than an hour, I'd see Will. When would I tell him? At the station, he'd scoop me into his arms—not a good time to say, "Baby, I'm sorry but we're through." In his parents' house, the others would make a fuss over me—not a good time to say, "Sorry everyone, but I'm leaving your uncle/brother/son." Soon he'd motion me upstairs, ease me down onto the bed—not a good time to say, "Honey, enjoy it, because this will be your last."

Every scenario seemed unthinkable.

What if I just got off the bus now and wrote him a letter

when I got home? No, that was cowardly. Will deserved to have me face him.

If he asked about another man, would I tell him? Would any good be served by that? And was I concerned about good, or did I just not want to admit the bad of what I'd done?

There was no getting around it: what I was doing was terrible. I hadn't set out to create this mess. But I hadn't stopped it, either. I fucking had to fix this. I would do it immediately, before I lost my courage.

When the bus squealed and sighed to a stop, I saw Will waiting in his usual spot. I expected him to snatch me up with an exuberant grin, but instead he just hugged me, a long, quiet hug that felt full of meaning. I searched his face for a sign of something, anything.

His eyes looked so sad. For a moment I had a crazy guilty notion: could he know about JT, the letters in my purse? No, of course he couldn't.

"What's wrong?" I asked.

"Oh, Kitten," he sighed, "it's nothing. I'll tell you when we get home." He picked up my bag with one arm and ushered me though the crowd with the other. I was silenced by his unusual mood.

On the subway, he held my hand but didn't speak. He only smiled sadly now and then as we rocketed through the noisy tunnel.

Will's mom and the younger sisters were the only ones at the house. "Hey, Lynda," they greeted me, but everyone was subdued, and all eyes stayed on the TV. I wondered where Joe was. Will discouraged any further communication by shepherding me upstairs. We sat on his bed. I knew this was not the time to tell him we were over.

"What's going on, Will? Is everyone OK?"

He sighed and took my hand. "I don't even want to tell you about this," he started. "It's so embarrassing."

"Well, you have to tell me now." I figured it might involve Joe drinking, especially since he wasn't home in front of the TV as he would usually be on a Friday night.

"So, Joe's been drinking a lot." He stroked my hand absently.

"Yeah, I kind of figured. And it sucks, but it's not that unusual, right?"

"It's worse this time. And something got said . . ."

Turned out one of his sisters had invited a friend to spend the night. That was new. I'd been seeing how insular the family tended to be, with only relatives and almost no friends allowed in. I figured maybe it was shame, not wanting outsiders to see what went on behind closed doors. Then again, my family never invited people over either. Why was that?

"God, this is so hard." Will put his head in his hands. I had a feeling I knew what was coming. "She said that Joe came to the bed and touched her while he thought she was asleep."

The girl was fifteen. If it happened, it was wrong. But nothing would be done because the girl didn't want to press charges. Yet there was Will, totally embarrassed again by his father. I gently took his hands away from his face.

"Baby, listen to me. Whether he did it or not, it has nothing to do with you. You're not the one who did it. You're not that kind of man. And I don't think less of you because of whatever kind of man your father is."

He turned and took me in his arms with a muffled sob. I thought about all the years of suffering that he'd weathered in this family. Poverty, alcoholism, abuse, shame. Will's escape into karate and school, and finally, me.

"Kitten, I don't know what I'd do without you. You're the only thing that makes it all worth living."

I smoothed his hair, squeezed his shoulder. I felt his sweat through his shirt. Suddenly my eyes were hot with tears, too. I loved JT, but I didn't see how I could tell Will I was leaving. Not now. Maybe not ever.

☮

Chapter 20

SUDDENLY, FALL AND ALL ITS CHANGES WERE RIGHT AROUND the corner. My parents' house had been sold. The things they were taking to Texas were stacked by the front door. My mom put in an address change so that my government benefits would be sent to my new apartment, and I would open a checking account. They had pre-paid my tuition for the year, so all I'd be responsible for was living expenses—apartment, food, car, and the required textbooks.

I was getting rid of stuff and packing up the rest to take with me—clothes, records, books, and a box marked "Very Important" that held report cards, pictures, birth certificate, high school diploma, my writings, my poetry award, and of course, JT's letters. Now that I was an adult, I was responsible for all of it.

I wanted a little private time with my baby sister before we separated, so I took her out for a special dinner at a "real" Italian restaurant with dim lighting and tablecloths, a much fancier place than our local pizza joint. She dressed up, and I put on my one cute little non-hippie dress, a silky navy mini from high school.

Our waiter brought menus and lit a candle even though it was only four p.m. I ordered lasagna and salad; she wanted pizza. (Pizza?) We chatted while we sipped our Cokes.

"Are you going back to college when we leave, Sissie?" Barbie asked, her mouth pursed in a Betty Boop bow over her straw.

"Yeah, baby. It's my last year, finally."

"I'm gonna be in third grade in Taxes. What's third grade like?"

"It's a little harder than second grade. But you'll be OK, you're one smart chick." I ran my hand through her hair, and she beamed.

Then her expression turned cloudy. "How long till you come to visit, Sissie?" she asked.

I explained that it would be from September to December, about three months.

"That sounds too long," she pouted.

"I know, honey. But remember you'll have school, and you'll make friends. It'll go so fast."

Our food came, and for a while the only sounds at the table were from her blowing on the pizza or gurgling the bottom of her soda glass and both of us taking turns saying, "Mmm. This is good. Want a bite? Yeah!"

As the meal wound down, I came to a decision I'd been considering. "Baby, there's one more thing about Texas that I want to tell you."

"What, Sissie?" Her eyes were two frisbees.

"Some of the people there think differently than we do."

"What do you mean?"

"Well, you know how I'm always saying that we have to treat everybody the same? Whether they're white, black, Spanish, or whatever?"

"Yeah, Sissie, I remember."

"So, some people in Texas—not all, but some—don't believe that. They think white people are better. They don't always treat black people very nicely." She watched me seriously, and I saw her little brain processing what I was telling her. I tried to choose my words carefully.

"You're gonna hear people say bad things about black people sometimes. Like 'nigger' is a bad word, remember?" She nodded. "And I just want you to know that it's OK for you to keep thinking the way *we* do. You don't have to change your mind to make them happy. Do you think you can remember that?"

"I think so."

"And you don't have to fight with them over it." God knew I did not want my baby sister getting her little ass kicked by third-grade crackers. "It's OK to have your own opinion and keep it to yourself if you want to. But it's also OK to stand up for someone if you want to. It's your choice. Do you understand?"

"I do, Sissie. I can keep quiet or stand up. It's my choice." She swallowed her last bite. "Hey, can we get ice cream?"

"Sure, baby." I figured that meant the conversation was over, and I hoped that my message had gotten through.

♡

Soon I hugged my family good-bye next to their overstuffed Ford station wagon, while my sister held onto my arm and cried. Then I climbed behind the wheel of my packed Chevy. I desperately wished that I could hang around until JT arrived to register for classes, but I had to get back to school for my own registration hell. This time I was going to the apartment I'd be sharing with Fran and Pam. We were in for a transition.

Things had become strained between my roomie Fran and me before school let out in spring, mostly due to the big event involving the crashed wine bottle and my "black mark." Now a third roommate, Pam, would add another dimension. But we were all looking forward to a fresh start with our new off-campus lifestyle.

In some ways, the apartment wasn't even as nice as our dorm rooms. It was sparsely furnished—bean bags in the living room, twin mattresses in the sleeping areas, and a cheap kitchen dinette with four chairs. But who cared? It was ours. No dorm mother. And that fabulous, sexy, sophisticated staircase.

Upstairs, Fran put her things on one side of the bigger bedroom and stuck by her promise to let me have the attached crawlspace. I set up a small footlocker as a little desk/vanity and curtained off the cubby with the life-size American flag that had been draped across my father's casket years before. Downstairs, we had Fran's stereo and Pam's color television. After a trip to the local head shop, we added a couple of inexpensive Indian batik bedspreads, plus the posters from our old room—Sly Stone, Jerry Rubin, and "I get by with a little help from my friends," the Beatles. Our decorating was done.

Next, we had our first of many trips to the grocery store. We knew we needed staples, but putting together dinner menus was a little more challenging.

"How about eggplant?" Fran asked. She had the most cooking experience and would likely be our head chef.

"Oh, I love fried eggplant," I exclaimed.

"Ugh, I hate eggplant," Pam grimaced. Further negotiations were needed.

We settled on dishes like spaghetti, baked chicken, and fried pork chops—and eventually Pam even tried eggplant, pronouncing it, "Not bad."

Soon we had issues about division of labor. As expected, Fran cooked our main course while Pam and I set the table, made salad, buttered vegetables, and poured drinks. The conflict arose when Fran felt that, as head cook, she should not have to wash dishes, whereas we felt she could pitch in sometimes. A stalemate ensued, while stuff piled up in the kitchen sink. It was amazing how many dirty dishes three girls could produce in two days.

The fact that we soon ran out of plates got Pam and me to clean up, but not without grumbling.

"I can't believe that little bitch doesn't think she should have to do a single dish," I complained, up to my elbows in suds.

"I know," agreed Pam, furiously toweling the plate I handed her. "And yes, she does cook for us, and yes, she is a good cook. But it's not like we just sit on our asses. We help, too."

Ironically, though, we kept our voices down; a stalemate was one thing, but we didn't want our chef to institute a strike.

I had passed my summer course and scheduled a full load for fall, so I was on track to do student teaching in the spring and then graduate. My first government benefit checks came, and I opened a bank account.

Will was back at Pitt for two quarters before student teaching in late spring. Now that I had a car, he expected me to visit every weekend. But I didn't always want to. There were frequent parties in our apartment complex, and one weekend my roommates and I decided that it was our turn to host. We watched the guests mingling, putting on albums, toking, and laughing. We felt so grown up.

JT was back at school at Moravian in Bethlehem. With my parents gone, it would be much easier to see him. I was looking forward to going back for Sharon's wedding. She had asked me to be her maid of honor. I was honored, but I didn't know what to wear.

"It's a simple wedding," she wrote. "Just any dress that you think is pretty will do."

I considered the blue mini—too school-girlish. I also had a long South American alpaca skirt—too warm for September, and the tribal pattern didn't feel right for a wedding. The rest of my clothes were jeans and leotards, a few other tops, and my one pair of hot pants. The single local dress store carried only old lady clothes.

I figured I'd check out the head shop just because it was in town. Their small selection of clothing was all freak wear, so I didn't expect to find something appropriate for a wedding. But I was wrong. They had added a couple of maxi-dresses, and the one I tried on was just what I was looking for. It had a scoop neck and empire waist, a soft peach and sage green flower pattern, and it clung to me in all the right places. I still needed shoes, but I couldn't wait to wear it.

While waiting, I got a shock in the mail from Colleen.

"Kenneth broke up with me," she wrote. "I can't believe it. I'm devastated."

I was speechless. How had this happened so quickly? Why had she no inkling? I thought back to his polite distance the day we stopped to meet him. I knew that she could be pushy ("Colleen the Bitch"). Had she pressured him into an engagement he didn't want? Was that why she had no ring?

Now she was at home while, except for Hannah, her friends were still away at school. No fiancé, no wedding, no plan.

But Colleen wasn't one to go without a plan for long.

"Here's what I'm going to do," her letter continued. "I got a job in the cocktail lounge at Hotel Bethlehem. The tips are really good there. I'm going to live at home, save money, and apply to work on a cruise ship. Since I'm not getting married, I might as well travel the world for free."

It sounded like as good a plan as any.

♡

When I'd moved to Bethlehem years before, I'd dreaded it. I was entering sixth grade without a clique, without anything familiar to help me feel grounded or accepted. In time, the girl across the street became my best friend, but then her family moved away, which left me to enter high school completely alone. Until Colleen reached out to me. She was the girl from the better side of town who had gone to the better junior high. Our last names placed us next to each other in several classes, and even though I was shy and quiet, her curious, intelligent eyes kept turning to me. Soon we were calling each other at home. I needed her help in advanced math, and she needed . . . well, I'm not sure I ever knew what, but something.

Colleen tried to bring me into her foursome of well-off girls, but in no time it was clear that I didn't fit. Once they invited me to go shopping "in Philadelphia," which actually meant that they were planning to shop in a rich suburb—the city itself was too rough. One of the girls' mothers drove us to stores like Bonwit Teller and Lord and Taylor, and later we ended up at an expensive boutique.

"What do you girls think of this outfit?" asked one, sashaying out of a dressing room in a knit skirt and top. Villager, $120. "I'll take it," she exclaimed.

"I'm thinking about this leather jacket," said Colleen. It was a beautiful jacket, copper-colored, buttery soft. She twirled in front of the mirror and looked back over her shoulder. $375 marked down to $250 because of a tiny stain. "I can live with that," she laughed.

Meanwhile, I had $20 in my wallet. What had my mother thought I could buy, some stupid old lady scarf? When I got home, my mom asked with barely concealed excitement how it had gone; she loved it when "rich girls" invited me out. I went to my room without answering and cried myself to sleep.

For whatever reason, Colleen gravitated toward me and soon left her group behind. As she told me later, those girls were smart but predictable. I was smart and interesting. She was drawn to me. By the time we eventually had that conversation, I was more confident. I thought, *finally someone appreciates me.*

But back in tenth grade, I wasn't confident. I was flattered by her attention. We talked on the phone most nights and went to our school's sports events and the local YMCA dances. She asked non-stop questions and seemed to want to soak up something I didn't even know I had.

People around her were always laughing. She clowned a lot, but whether they laughed with her or at her, I couldn't always tell. She talked about how she was going to enter the Miss Lehigh County pageant in our senior year. Her skinny body was topped by what she herself called a "tiny ant head." The way she moved reminded me of a daddy long leg spider, herky jerky. When she talked about the pageant, other girls would laugh or cut their eyes at me, like *really?* We'd been raised on busty, beautiful Miss Americas. Colleen did make it into the pageant, though.

While I was uncomfortable in the limelight, Colleen loved it there. She tried out for musicals and cheerleading and sometimes was chosen. She got attention by teasing, talking, laughing, poking, showing off. She'd gain even more attention by bringing up sex, especially later, especially to boys. Always moving, her awkward spidery dance. But she was fun. And she was intelligent. She made people think. She made me think. She brought me off the sidelines and into the game.

Yet we were so different. "Placid," she called me. Placid like a lake, calm, unruffled by hidden currents. To me it sounded bovine, placid like a cow chewing its cud. I never complained, though. A calm demeanor was something I cultivated to hide my shyness and anxieties. If people believed it, all the better.

Boys were a big part of nearly every conversation we had. No detail was too small—what we hoped for and how far we'd gone. We were both virgins who planned to keep our virginity until marriage. While I tended to settle into going steady with boyfriends from our school (roughly one per year), she had crushes, dates, or make-out sessions, often with boys from other schools.

One day during the summer after high school, Colleen and I went swimming at a local quarry, and we ended up on a lake float with a guy we didn't know.

"Let's play Truth or Dare," he suggested, "but only the Truth part."

"What do you mean?" I asked.

"You know, we'll each tell something we've never told any-one before." He admitted that he'd tried to cheat on the SAT and had gotten caught. I told them about my one and only drinking party senior year, when some kids brought alcohol stolen from a house break-in; everyone in attendance was questioned by po-lice in the principal's office the next school day, and I didn't know whether to feel cool or embarrassed. Colleen already knew about that situation, but I couldn't think of anything I hadn't already told her.

When it was Colleen's turn, she confessed with a sly smile that she had let her prom date finger her. I was stunned because in all of our talks about boys and sex, she had never told me this. I looked at her with newly appraising eyes.

I wondered what else she had held back, when I thought we were sharing everything.

☮

Chapter 21

WEDDING BELLS WERE RINGING! AND I WAS ON MY WAY to Bethlehem—to Hannah's apartment (where I'd be staying now that my parents were gone), to take part in Sharon's wedding, and best of all, to see JT. But no more taking the bus because now I had my own car.

When I arrived at Hannah's, Colleen was already there, after working her shift at the hotel. She had cut her hair into one of the cute shags that had become stylish, and she was wearing the still-enviable leather jacket. I noticed that Hannah was slipping into a new brown leather jacket, too. Was I the only one still wearing my beloved army fatigue?

Our plan was to catch up over a bite at the mall, after which they'd help me look for a pair of shoes for Sharon's wedding. Then I'd be going over to JT's room.

While waiting for our food, Hannah and I asked Colleen, as delicately as we could, about her break-up with Kenneth.

"Oh, God, it was horrible. Just horrible," she repeated, shaking her head in disbelief. She described the final scene at Pitt. Sitting on a bench outside her dorm he'd told her, "I don't want to marry you, I don't even want to be together anymore." Then he'd turned and tried to quickly walk away. Something came over Colleen, and she flung herself at him, wouldn't let him leave.

"I was hanging onto his leg and crying, 'Please don't leave me, please don't leave,' and he was trying to shake me off," she said. Hannah and I exchanged glances. This was a Colleen we'd never seen.

"Every time he got away, I grabbed him again," she continued, "until he was practically dragging me along on the ground." Her eyes brimmed, and a tear slowly made its way down her face and clung to the tip of her chin. "But finally, I just had to let him go."

We allowed a respectful moment of silence for the enormity of what she'd just depicted. Then I asked tentatively, "And, so, how are you doing now?"

"Oh, I'm just devastated," she said. "After I told everybody we were getting married? How could he lead me on like that and then just dump me? It's so humiliating." She used her napkin to wipe her chin and blot her eyes, then covered her face with her hands. She hunched over and her body shuddered. Hannah and I watched, not knowing what to say. I laid a sympathetic hand on her shoulder. Then, just as quickly as it had started, her crying stopped. She sat up straight and eased her arm out from under mine.

"That's why I've gotta do something," she said firmly. "I can't just hang around here, pining for a future I'm not going to have. I've got to make my own future. So, I'm applying to get a job on a cruise ship."

While we ate, we asked her about what that would entail. Then Hannah caught us up on her news. Roy Greene had indeed taken a coaching job in Chicago. She'd expected it and claimed not to be upset about it. She admitted that maybe her spirits were lifted a bit by the fact that she'd already met someone else. Jamie was a local guy, and although things were still very new, she had a good feeling about him.

We went out into the mall, which I knew from experience might not have what I was looking for. Instead, I made yet another serendipitous discovery for the wedding—a pair of suede sling-back sandals, rust-colored with chunky heels, the perfect complement to my slinky flowered maxi.

"Well, that's it for Lynda," said Hannah, laughing, while I paid the cashier. "I suspect we're now going to get ditched for a certain basketball player. And I've gotta get home, too . . ." she batted her long eyelashes ". . . cuz guess who's coming over."

"I am so jealous. I hate you bitches!" said Colleen. "But just wait, my time is gonna come."

"Don't worry, I'm sure it will," I reassured her. I had every reason to believe that it was true.

♡

A short while later, I was lighting a cigarette in my usual spot on JT's bed. "Wanna go to a wedding tomorrow?" I asked him.

In spite of the struggle inside him over whether to fight for me or give up gracefully, here we were, and at least one thing was not in question anymore: on a night when I was due to visit, JT would be waiting in his room. This was our first time together since our impromptu summer rendezvous.

It was also the first time either of us had ever invited the other somewhere. Hadn't he written last spring that he thought we should do more things together?

"I don't think so," JT said. "I won't know anyone. And I've already got a short paper due Monday." He poured two little plastic cups of wine. "You go have a good time, and I'll catch you when you get back."

I was disappointed, but I didn't think much of it. Besides being her maid of honor, I wanted to be there for Sharon. She was marrying a black man, and her family didn't approve. They might not even attend, which I knew would be terribly painful for her. Afterward, I would still have all night with JT.

His new circumstances made our visits easier than ever. For senior year, he'd earned the respected position of Resident Advisor—assigned to watch over the students on his floor and give advice as needed. The job included a dorm room all to himself. It was perfect.

JT couldn't wait to share another piece of new music—an album by a singer-songwriter named Bobby Womack. I didn't know Bobby's songs, but they'd soon be added to my favorites.

"Listen to this first track," JT exhorted, "it's called 'I Can Understand It.' " Wow, the energy that poured out of the speakers. A rocking guitar that reached all the way down to my gut and a gritty blues voice that squeezed my heart. In that song, Bobby sang out his misery to the love who seemed to be leaving him:

> "When I try my best to make you happy
> And I wake up early one morning and find you packing..."

Once again, JT's music had me dancing in place on the bed, while he kept the beat on his knee.

"That's a boss cut," I agreed. As he played it again and again, I couldn't help but wonder if JT loved it in part because of how it sang to our situation. He was certainly working hard—at basketball, at school, at me. Did he fear that, like Bobby, he would soon find me packing? We didn't live together, so I couldn't "pack." But I could just not come back: I could leave him for Will.

I did my best to show JT that I had no intention of leaving.

♡

176

Saturday dawned a beautiful Indian-summer day just right for a country wedding. After getting ready at Hannah's, I hummed along to the radio as I maneuvered a sun-dappled highway out of town. When I arrived at the small church she'd chosen, Sharon gave her stamp of approval to my outfit. Her long blonde hair and sunshine smile always reminded me of Peggy Lipton on Mod Squad. I complimented her wedding dress, a soft flowing white cotton gown, handmade. It was simple and beautiful.

"Is your family here?" I asked.

"Just my mom and sister." It turned out that her brother had to be away on business, but her father had refused to come. She grimaced. "As far as he's concerned, it's as if I'm dead."

"I'm so sorry, hon," I said. I had a pretty good idea of what she was going through. Her groom seemed nice enough, if a little overwhelmed.

This was the first service I'd participated in, and I was relieved that my role was a small one. Afterward, we went to the groom's mother's house for sandwiches, cake, and champagne. Besides our initial hugs and greetings, my main communication with Sharon was a wry smile or an eye roll as some relative bent her ear or tried to make small talk with me. Soon I was yearning to go to JT.

I thought about surprising him in my maid of honor dress, something other than my usual jeans, but then I'd have to leave his dorm still dressed up the next day. So, I went ahead with the plan to go change back at Hannah's and call him. The pay phone on his floor was right outside his RA room. While it rang, I pictured JT stepping out to answer it with his usual happy smile, and waited for his low, sexy murmur.

Instead, he answered in a high, shrill voice I'd never heard before.

"Guess who's here!" he chirped.

I didn't have to guess. Whether due to her aggressive manner, her selfishness, or the way I had seen her eyes on him, I knew immediately. Before I could answer, he handed the phone over to her.

"I hope you don't mind that I came here," said Colleen.

I paused for a second while my heart rate slowed from a possible actual heart attack to mere palpitations. Then I answered with a coldness that I hadn't intended but couldn't help.

"That depends on why you did."

"Well!" she sputtered. "I can't believe . . . how could you . . ." I couldn't make out full sentences due to the ocean of blood that had rushed into my head. ". . . I would never . . . you should . . ."

"Tell Jonathan I'm on my way," I ended her bluster by hanging up.

By the time I got there, she was gone. I wondered what conversation had taken place between them after my call.

"She just showed up here," he said. "I didn't know what to do. She's your best friend, after all."

"What did she say?" I asked.

"At first I thought you'd told her to come over . . ."

"I wouldn't do that without asking you," I interrupted.

"I know," he said, starting to roll a joint. "It was just my first thought. Like maybe you wanted to hang out with the two of us after the wedding. But then she said that she just knew we were both at loose ends waiting for you, and she thought we could keep each other company. She brought this," he added, indicating the baggie that he was now emptying of its last vestiges of dried leaves.

When he lit up, I took a hit. I exhaled, leaned back, and tried to relax. But I was uneasy. Why would she come here? Did I dare tell him I didn't want him spending time with my friend again? That would be rich, what with me having another boyfriend. Besides, JT was a man, a local celebrity, and independent—I suspected that he wouldn't take kindly to being told what to do. I didn't even know for sure whether he ever saw other women. I thought not, but like Crosby, Stills & Nash sang, we were living in the era of "love the one you're with." So, my friend who had just been dumped had come by to share some reefer and chitchat with the most interesting man around? I started to feel like I was overreacting, when I should have been sympathetic and generous. I was the one he wanted to have in his bed, and now I was here.

Bobby Womack was crooning one of his sweet songs, about how much a woman needs it. JT's dancing eyes told me that he agreed.

♡

JT usually introduced me to new music, but the next morning, it was my turn to share an album with him by Gil Scott-Heron.

Will had been the one to turn me on to Gil and actually knew him personally; they had both been part of a summer program for high school students at a black university. For some reason, even though he liked Gil's music and poetry about the black experience, Will didn't sound too fond of Gil. When I asked him why, he said that he thought Gil was kind of phony.

"The guy is not from the ghetto," Will had said. "He's middle-class. What does he know about the struggles in the 'hood?"

"Well, you treat me like I understand, and I'm a white woman. I haven't lived any of it."

"Yeah, but you're different, Kitten. You just have so much compassion."

"Even so, at least Gil is black."

"I s'pose," Will conceded grudgingly. I'd wondered if there were more behind his reluctance to fully embrace Gil.

Now I played Gil for JT, who had no preconceived notions about him. One song in particular grabbed us from the first two soft repetitive piano notes, like a mourning dove. Then:

"Did you hear what they said?"

The song built tension as Gil told the story of a brother who was killed in service to his country. A flute went as crazy as the world had become, and Gil's voice rose to a wail of agony, asking a mother to imagine if her only son was dead but couldn't be buried.

Finally, softer again:

"This can't be real."

When the last note ended, our locked eyes were shiny with tears. There was still a war on. JT was of draft age. He had a mother and grandmother who would cry and cry if told their boy was dead. But JT had a college deferment. Unlike so many others—young boys sent to battle, many of them black because what the hell else were they going to do—JT was alive, and here. His hand sought mine, and we sat in grateful silence.

Later, another song caught our attention, "The King Alfred Plan." It was a spoken word piece that told of a concentration camp being readied for black people. In Pennsylvania, what the hell? And where was Allenwood, PA? We agreed that we'd do some research and find out more.

I also shared for the first time my recently developed atheist belief system. I'd been thinking about it ever since Fran and I took our ill-fated Intro to Bio course. Although I'd missed a lot

OUR SONG

of those eight a.m. class sessions, I'd made some of them, and I
was absolutely astounded at what I learned. Evolution, the Big
Bang Theory—why had I never heard about these ideas before?
My high school education was not religious, but I started to feel
like it was an indoctrination that left out many possible truths.

Jonathan listened to me seriously, like he always did, although a little smile played about the corners of his mouth. I was
puffed up with righteous indignation about how there was no
God.

It wasn't quite so difficult to say good-bye this time, because
we would see each other again in a couple weeks; I would come
back for my birthday, plus a dentist appointment (one of my
excuses for not seeing Will, like Sharon's wedding had been).
The sky looked ominous, and it was already drizzling when JT
walked me to my car. He leaned down over the open door to
block it with his windbreaker. That teasing smile came back.

"Now you be careful out there. Because if I'm not around,
and there's no God looking out for you either, then I don't know
who is."

"Even if there was a god, I think he—or she (I added point-
edly)—would have better things to do than follow me back to
school." I smiled back. "Don't worry, Jonathan. Now go inside
before you get soaked." He shut the door, waved one last time,
then pulled his jacket up over his head and broke into a run.

By the time I was on the highway, the rain had become so
bad that my windshield wipers could barely keep the glass clear
enough to see. Technically it was still daylight, but the sky was
so black that it might as well have been night. The dark was broken up only by flashes of lightning, followed by booming thunder. Thick fog rolled in and surrounded me, blocking my vision
of other cars and the scary big trucks that traversed the state. I

181

gave in to common sense and pulled off the road to wait out the worst of the storm.

I entertained a funny thought: what if there really was a God, and He was angry at my having forsaken Him? Wasn't the Bible full of warnings like that? For just a moment I wondered if I had made a terrible mistake, and now God was going to take His retribution with this horrific storm.

Then I had a mental laugh at myself. Brainwashing ran deep. Like I'd told JT, even if there were a god, he (or she) would be way too busy to torture me. And anyway, I did not believe any of those things.

Soon the rain slowed and the fog cleared enough for me to see. I pulled back onto the highway, still safe, my belief system intact. What was a storm anyway? Storms were just part of life.

Chapter 22

BACK AT SCHOOL, I HAD A LOT TO THINK ABOUT. ESPECIALLY after I got my next letter from Colleen.

"JT and I went shopping for your birthday present," she wrote. "Goddamn, that man is so fucking charming!" The two of them shopping for my gift? How did *that* come about? I couldn't imagine that he had sought her out. So, she must have gone over there again. And how many times? Where was this leading? What did she want? I felt like I knew all too well what she wanted. Why didn't I have the nerve to confront it? Again, I felt guilty because I had Will. I felt that my complaining would be unfair and would appear very uncool, especially if everyone's motives were innocent. I wanted to look cool to JT. And I did *not* want to remind him of Will.

Later I'd learn that Colleen had made it her mission to remind JT of Will.

Fran, Pam, and I celebrated my twenty-first birthday at the apartment. Fran made my favorite eggplant dinner and gave me a pair of gypsy filigree earrings. Pam had made the trip to the next county to buy us some rum and Coke. A few people in the apartment complex stopped by. It was a mellow celebration made all the better by a card from JT that arrived in the mail that very day. "I can't wait to celebrate your birthday my way," he wrote. My mind was already on my upcoming weekend with him. The next day, I bid my roommates good-bye and eagerly started the long drive.

When I arrived at Hannah's, she greeted me with, "Guess what, Colleen wants us all to go out for pizza for your birthday." By "all" she meant the three of us and JT. I had mixed feelings. Sure, it was nice of my friends to want to celebrate with me. But we three girls could have gone out for lunch the following day, so did Colleen just want to butt in on my time alone with JT? Still, I couldn't think of a reason to say no. I called JT (who already seemed to know about the plan), and soon Colleen came bouncing through the door, talking a mile a minute like usual. We three swung by JT's dorm and then walked the couple blocks to the restaurant. JT and I were behind my friends, but Colleen kept turning around to talk to us, and most of her comments included eyes directly on him.

It was a brisk fall night, and the pizza shop felt warm and welcoming. The lights were so low that we all stood still at the entrance while our eyes adjusted. The place was full, so for a second it seemed that we might not find a table. Then Colleen was striding toward the back of the room, talking loudly enough over her shoulder to JT that people looked up from their meals.

"Haha, don't wait for these sheep to get moving," she laughed. "I bet you're like me, JT—you like to take charge and get things done." As she whooshed between tables with us walking behind her, I wondered what the hell she was talking about. JT had been standing there for a moment just like Hannah and me. He hadn't acted like we were moving too slow. We slid into our seats, me next to him, Hannah across from me, and Colleen across from JT. Colleen grabbed a menu and started talking to him as if Hannah and I weren't there.

"What do you like, JT? Pepperoni?"

"No, just cheese for me. But should we get a pitcher of beer?"

"I might need one all to myself if I'm not getting any pep-peroni," Hannah joked.

"I don't need pepperoni," I said, "but I'd love some beer." Hopefully beer would help ease the awkwardness I was feeling. Colleen had said, "these sheep"; why was she trying to portray Hannah and me in an unflattering light? And "I bet you're like me, JT"? What was *that* about?

Or was I just imagining things? Maybe I was losing my mind.

JT gave the waitress our order—half plain, half pepperoni, plus the beer. When the pitcher came, he poured.

"Here's to the birthday girl," he said with a big smile at me, and we all clinked glasses.

"Cheers, Lynda," said Hannah, taking a big gulp.

"Happy birthday," said Colleen. "Mine was in May, JT, so I'll always be older and wiser than Lynda." She took a sip and looked at me. "Speaking of wise, have you seen this guy play bas-ketball yet?" She tipped her head toward JT. I was sure she knew that I hadn't. I shook my head, mouth still full of beer.

"Well, you should. He's uh-mazing. I didn't have anything to do this week, so I went to the game. You demolished that other team, didn't you, JT?"

He frowned and looked uncomfortable. "It's a group effort," he said.

"I want to see him play," I said, looking at him. "There's just never been a home game when I'm here." I didn't add that JT had discouraged me from attending games that were away at other schools, worried about my being on the road in bad weather.

But again, I felt unsettled. Jealous even. Why had Colleen gone to his game? Was that normal? And had JT known that she went? I was hours away, and she was right fucking there. In spite of the beer, I found myself turning inward. Maybe JT noticed, or maybe he saw how Colleen was trying to get his attention. By the time our food arrived, he'd turned his body toward me and away from her.

"So how was your trip?" JT asked quietly. He made it clear this conversation was just between us, his brown eyes and secret smile enveloping me like a warm cloak. Maybe I wasn't going crazy.

"It was long, but otherwise fine. No big storm that made me wonder if I should start saying my prayers," I teased, also keeping my voice low and smiling back. JT continued talking to me while Hannah and Colleen had their own conversation. I started to feel more relaxed, whether from his attention, a couple glasses of beer, or both. Soon I got them all laughing with the story of a god punishing an atheist with a storm. Colleen was laughing, too, but she seemed more subdued. She didn't make any more attempts to monopolize JT.

Alone together finally back in his room, JT gave me my birthday present, wrapped in tissue paper. It was about eighteen inches square and one-half inch thick.

I shook it. "Gee, I wonder what this is," I joked.

"I know," JT said. "Do you think it's a new car? Maybe the Hope diamond?"

"I don't need diamonds or cars. I've got my chariot downstairs. And look at my new earrings that Fran gave me." I shook my head, and the blue stones dangled in their lacy settings.

"Nice ones," he said, reaching out to finger the stones, and then trailing his hand across my cheek. It was his first intimate touch of the evening and sent a shiver down the back of my neck. Slyly he asked, "OK, so what *do* you need?"

"Just you," I said, giving my hair a little unconcerned toss, "and maybe a really fine record album." I pulled apart the tissue paper.

"Oh my god," I said when I saw the cover. "Bobby Womack? You couldn't have made a better choice."

"You sure you didn't run out and buy it as soon as you got back to school?" he asked. "I was worried about that."

"No, the head shop doesn't have much of a selection. Come on, let's put it on."

"You save yours," JT said. "We'll play mine since it's already open."

Like we always did, we played it. And played it again. And played.

☮

Chapter 23

I WAS HEADED BACK TO SCHOOL AFTER MY BIRTHDAY WEEKEND, but on the way I had a mission: a side trip to Allenwood, PA, to check out Gil Scott-Heron's "King Alfred Plan." JT didn't want me to go.

"I really wish you would rethink this," he'd said, as we lay side by side in his bed that morning. We were turned toward each other in a nearly mirror image, with twin bent elbows and heads propped up on our hands. The narrow mattress kept us so close that I could almost feel his body hair reaching out like the tentacles of an undersea plant, our magnetic attraction. The only parts that were actually touching were our feet; he massaged my arch with his toes.

"I know you do," I said, "but I just feel like I have to."

"Why?" he asked. "This isn't your battle."

"If it affects people I care about, then maybe it is my battle." I shifted my feet so his toes could take up their massage on the other side. "Besides, who better to go than an innocent-looking white girl? You with your brown skin and big Afro?"

"I have to admit I'm curious," JT said. We'd both done research on Gil's song. Allenwood was right off the highway that I took to get to and from school. It held a prison that had been used as a Japanese internment camp during World War II. Supposedly it sat empty now, but according to Gil it was one of several sites being quietly readied to serve as concentration camps for black people.

"And you're right," JT continued, "I don't think it would be a good idea for me to go there. But I don't think it's a good idea for you to go, either. You don't know what you're going to run into."

"I promise I'll be careful," I said, adding the famous last words of many a naïve young person: "Don't worry, nothing bad is going to happen to me."

With no parents expecting me home anymore, I could have stayed with JT as long as I wanted, but this time I felt I should get on the road early. I didn't know what it would take to find Allenwood or the prison or how long I might want to poke around there.

At my car, he held me close, and my chilly hands found the inside of his jacket pockets. JT always looked sad when I was leaving, trying but failing to cover it with a joke and a smile. This time there was no joke, no smile. He held on tight and didn't seem to want to let me go.

"If you get into any trouble, call," he said. That was new. Long distance calls were so expensive that poor college students like us seldom made them. I made local calls to JT only after I arrived at Hannah's. Everything else took place through letters.

The day was autumn crisp but clear as I drove north and then west. I was buzzing with nerves and excitement about doing something mysterious yet meaningful. My first spy assignment, self-directed. I smiled, thinking back to the James Bond movies I'd seen, the sexual innuendos that, at thirteen years old, I hadn't fully comprehended, starting with Goldfinger and Pussy Galore. My mother had taken me to movies that my friends' parents would not allow them to see, and for a moment I felt sad, missing the mom I'd had before she started trying to control my life.

"Your mission, should you choose to accept it," I said in a

fake British accent to the empty car. Oh wait, was that Bond or *Mission Impossible*? Either way, I answered myself back in a deeper, sexier voice: "I'll have a vodka martini, shaken not stirred." I wasn't even sure what a vodka martini was.

I pulled off the highway into a tiny town like hundreds of other small Pennsylvania villages. I drove around, not sure what to look for. I couldn't exactly stop and ask someone, "Can you tell me where the concentration camp for black people is?" Steering toward the outskirts, I found myself on a paved, potholed road that wound through some corn fields. There was a dark sedan up ahead. As the road took a sharp turn, I lost sight of the sedan but expected to catch up to it after I rounded the curve. Instead, the road came to a dead end in front of a gate next to a small empty-looking clapboard house. There was no sign of the other car.

I stopped at the padlocked gate and sat still for a minute. *What the hell?* There wouldn't have been time for that driver to stop the car, unlock the gate, drive through, lock it again, and drive on. I looked at the narrow old three-story frame house; maybe it had a garage entrance around back, but it was still hard to imagine that someone could have concealed a car so quickly. Already, this was weird.

Nonetheless, I got out of the car. I left my things inside, with the exception of a small Kodak Instamatic camera, and locked the doors. The gate was attached on both sides to a chain link fence, and on the other side was a small graveyard. I followed along the fence for a bit and found an opening large enough to step through.

The cemetery was charming, shielded from the elements by low-hanging trees. I walked among the old headstones. Did anyone ever come here? Did someone live in the house? I looked inside a trash barrel and was surprised to see crumpled bags from McDonald's. Someone had been here recently. I snapped some pictures.

The rough asphalt became a dirt road. After a turn and slight grade, I could see smoke from a chimney off in a valley. Then up ahead some odd round structures caught my eye. They reminded me of igloos, and I walked toward them.

What strange igloos! There were several spaced widely apart on either side of the road. They were taller than a man and built out of dirt, with only a wood plank door and a small window-like opening near the top. They looked military, and the word "bunker" came to mind. I could easily imagine some kind of weapon being pointed out of the high window holes. I wanted to take pictures, but for the first time, I was scared. What if someone were watching me through one of those openings?

Yet wasn't this what I had come for, to investigate and bear witness? With shaking hands, I raised the camera and took a few more snapshots.

That's when I heard them: a pack of barking dogs. A big pack. Of loud barking dogs. Coming toward me.

I looked around desperately for a safe place. There were no trees. I was pretty sure dogs could follow me up one of the bunkers if I could even climb it. They were getting closer. I knew you weren't supposed to run from dogs, but what else could I do? The barking grew louder, I could make out growling and snarling, and just as I had decided that turning and running was my only option, the barking stopped. Just like that. Like someone had called them back? Or like someone had turned on a tape of barking dogs and then switched it off again?

Or like maybe I had triggered a tape that stopped playing.

Either way, I was shaken, enough to jog back down the road,

slip through the fence, and lock myself in my car. Maybe I wasn't cut out for this espionage stuff. The worst thing I'd imagined was being stopped and questioned by a guard. I hadn't imagined cars that disappeared into thin air, war-time bunkers, and vicious attack dogs.

I felt ashamed, though. Here I was running from what might not even be real dogs. Dogs were used to break up demonstrations; I'd seen pictures in magazines of human flesh captured between their jaws. And dogs weren't even the worst of it, what about the people who had been lynched, or shot? What about the college students in Ohio, just like me and not even very far away from me, who had been gunned down while protesting the wrongs of our government? The shocking story was immortalized by Crosby, Stills, Nash & Young about soldiers shooting us down, and:

"What if you knew her and
found her dead on the ground?"

Could someone like me end up dead at the hands of an American soldier? Could people like JT, Will, or Linda be rounded up into concentration camps? It wasn't as if it hadn't happened before.

These thoughts plagued me as I made my way back to the highway toward school. I wondered what JT would say. And was I even going to tell Will?

♡

10 / 20 / 72
My Dear Lynda.
Oh, that's just way too stuffy.
Hey Lover!
That's more like it!

He was sipping a vodka drink on a Friday night while writing to his coach, his mother, and me:

Three of the people I care so much about.

He said he had decided not to refer to any of our previous letters, but instead to treat things like we were starting over. I wasn't quite sure what he meant, and the tone was subdued, but at least he wasn't talking about breaking up. He recounted his busy week, and how much he missed me when I wasn't there, and ended with:

Time for bed and dreams of guess who, the woman I love.
J.

His after-my-birthday letter. Only one page. And here he was, already sounding so down, and only a few days after seeing me. Could I blame him? Because in spite of Sharon's wedding and my birthday, two visits in close proximity, he probably wondered if my other weekends were spent with Will, and he must have wondered when I would come back to him. My parents were gone and things could have been different; I could have driven to see him every weekend. But I still had two lovers and now my other lover expected me, too; there had been no resolution.

For his part, Will was impatient with my weekends away. He too was going through some changes.

A mix-up in red tape had resulted in Will's not being able to get a dorm assignment. Scrambling to find housing for the fall of his senior year, he was referred to three black women who were seeking a fourth roommate to share an apartment.

When I first arrived at the apartment and met his roommates, I definitely felt a vibe. They were polite on the surface, but I saw how stiff their politeness was—not like Will's sisters, who teased me so playfully. I never saw Will's sisters cut their eyes at each other when they thought I wasn't looking.

Will felt the vibe, too, and didn't like it. He didn't last long there. Soon he was invited to stay with "Dr. Frank," one of Will's past U Pitt history professors who had kept up with Will's progress. Dr. Frank's wife, a union organizer, looked at her husband like she still found him sexy, which I thought was romantic. They lived in the suburbs of the university and had three children who idolized Will. As a math major he was happy to help them with their math homework, and they were thrilled when he showed them some karate moves. To accommodate Will, Dr. Frank's teenage son had vacated his waterbed in their converted basement, and I was welcome to come stay any time.

Theirs was a busy household, but we'd meet up for a family dinner or all go out together for McDonald's. It felt like being part of the kind of family I wished I had. A family that welcomed a black student in need and "of course" were going to vote for McGovern. The only hard part for me about weekends there, aside from missing my little sister, so far away in "Taxes," was that I knew I'd rather be with JT.

♡

A new development had taken place in our cheapo apartment: Pam's scream pierced every corner of the place after she found a radish-sized spider inside the paper towel roll. Fran was the daughter of a widow who, unlike most women of the time, was not used to waiting for a man to deal with household emergencies. She carefully carried the roll outside, slammed it against the ground, and crushed the spider under her shoe.

We thought it was an anomaly until we heard a news report about a species of poisonous South American spider that had made its way as far north as Pennsylvania. Aaiieee!

Fran had the next encounter while studying on a bean bag. She noticed one crawling up the side of the bean bag and quickly bashed it with her textbook. From then on, we were constantly looking over our shoulders and under our belongings. I expected to be next and couldn't go to bed at night without shaking out my blankets. But I wasn't next.

Pam was in her downstairs room when a movement along the edge of the carpet caught her eye. She shrieked, and we came running. Fran grabbed a dustpan and used it to lift the carpet, then sever the wretched beast against the baseboard. But if only the spider was the worst thing we saw. Under the carpet there was no floor, just dirt. And in the dirt was a dank pool of black water. It was easy to imagine all manner of smelly prehistoric life crawling out of that hole. Pam shivered in revulsion.

"That's it," she said, "I can't live like this." Pam packed her things that very night and drove to her parents' house in a nearby town. She would finish out her last year of school from home.

We understood, but it left Fran and me wondering how to afford the missing third of the rent for the next two months. Luckily, we got wind of a guy whose rented farmhouse had burned down. Andrew was a tall hippie dude with long straw-colored hair, a beard, an earring, and a ready grin. He moved into Pam's room, sinkhole and all, and it wasn't long before Fran started spending most of her time down there with him.

☮

Chapter 24

10 / ~~29~~ 30 / 72
Hey Lover,
I've been so busy that my letters have slowed down a bit, so
I imagine you're wondering whether I'm missing you. The
answer? Fuck, yeah.

(Oh, Jonathan, me too. Fuck, yeah.)

Then he made me smile by referring to my last letter as full of drama, adventure, and amour. He was quite impressed with my account of my trip to Allenwood. And he agreed that an innocent-looking white girl (beautiful white girl, he said) was a good candidate for doing an investigation, but:

You really blew it with the camera, baby. Hard to appear
innocent when you're documenting with pictures!

Still, he said he couldn't wait to hear the story all over again from me in person. Which I could hardly wait to tell him. Then he asked if, now that he and Colleen were hanging around together, she had delivered any "interesting tidbits" about him:

I'm wondering what her view of the relationship (J&C) is.

I'd told him that I re-read all of his letters from the beginning till now. He said how tedious and tiring that must have been. Was he just being modest, or did he really have no idea how utterly charming I found them and him? I could only hope he did, as he then wrote out all the words to a very long song by Syreeta Wright and her husband Stevie Wonder, "To Know You Is to Love You."

He wrapped it up by calling me his natural high. And then:

Whatever is on your mind, remember, both sides have to be taken into account.

Undying love for always,
Jon

I felt queasy when I finished reading, and I wasn't even sure why. "Hello Love," "Undying love for always," plus he missed me and wanted me there—yeah, all that. But what was this J&C relationship? What "interesting tidbits" might Colleen deliver? Most confusing of all, what did he mean by "remember both sides have to be taken into account"? His and Will's? His and Colleen's? Hers and mine? Mine and his? And why was I afraid to rock the boat and ask? Because I was shy and the stakes were high, that's why.

I really didn't want to go see Will that weekend. JT was a magnet pulling at my core. But I had told Will I would, and something, my history with him I guessed, made me keep going back to him like a robot. On Friday I put my things in the car and got on the road to Pitt. At Dr. Frank's, we sat around eating and talking with the family until bedtime.

"Lynda!" The next morning I was awakened by one of the kids calling down the stairs to me. "You have a phone call."

What? Who even knew I was there? Much less had the number? The waterbed was soft and toasty, and I didn't want to leave it. But I threw on yesterday's jeans and top and ran barefoot up to the kitchen, where Dr. Frank's teenage son was holding the receiver of the wall phone. "It's a woman," he whispered. I just hoped nothing was wrong back at my apartment.

"Hello?" I stepped from one foot to the other, trying to escape the cold floor.

"Lynda. It's Colleen." It took a second to sink in, but then I realized: of course she knew I was there, and she probably knew Dr. Frank's last name.

"Hey, Colleen. What's up?"

"I'm coming out to Pittsburgh today. I have to take care of something. I thought maybe I could stop by and visit for a little while."

"Uh, OK. I guess." It felt a little weird to invite company, but I couldn't think of any reason why Will or the family would mind. "Sure. What do you have to do?" I figured it was something about her early graduation from U Pitt.

"Great. I'll tell you later. I'll be there around four. What's the address?"

Will and I spent the day watching TV and playing ping-pong with the kids. We both had homework, but neither of us was in the mood. I was on edge waiting for Colleen. When the doorbell rang, I went to answer it, and the family followed to meet my friend.

"Hey, what a great house," was the first thing she said when I introduced her around. "Hi, everyone. Hi, Will."

"Hi, Colleen," said Will. "What's going on?"

"Oh, not much. Feels kinda funny to be back here without

being a student." Colleen looked at the family. "I just graduated this summer," she explained.

"Man, I can't wait until I can say that, too," laughed Will. We continued chatting for a few minutes, and then the others wandered off to their own pursuits.

"Lynda, how about we take a walk and have a little 'us' time." Colleen looked at Will. "You don't mind, do you, Will?"

"No. Not at all. You girls go on."

"Women!" we both shouted in unison, and he laughed because he knew we would. He turned back downstairs.

I'd felt the chill air when I opened the door, so I got my jacket, scarf, and gloves.

"They seem nice," Colleen said as we walked toward the sidewalk. "And so is this neighborhood."

"It is. And they are. Will's really lucky to be here."

We ambled quietly down the street for a minute. "Boy, it almost looks like it's going to snow," I said. "Did you get your business taken care of? What was it anyway?" I was thinking about her drive home, and my drive back to school tomorrow if there was an early winter storm.

"Well, actually, this is my business. I came to see you," she said. She stopped and turned to me. I looked at her, confused.

"Lynda, I've been seeing Johnny."

"I know. You guys went shopping for my present together."

"No, I mean, I'm 'seeing' him. We're together."

"You mean . . . you fucked him?"

"Yeah, we're fucking. But it's more than that. We're together. As a couple."

"I . . . you . . ."

I couldn't speak. I felt like a snow shovel had just gone WOMP in my face. Like a plow had just pushed me under a mountain of ice. Like I had fallen through a hole in a frozen lake and murderous water was rushing into my lungs. I could see a blurry Colleen, her lips moving, but I couldn't make out the words. What was she saying? *My best friend.*

"And like I told him, I can't give him up for you and never you for him."

I felt like a wet, leaden snow suit was dragging my arms and legs under the ice. I was drowning.

"So, what I'm gonna do," she continued, "is when you come home to see him, I'll leave town. That way there's no conflict. When it's my time, it's my time, and when it's your time, it's your time."

My time, your time? What were these concepts? Time had stopped for me. *Oh JT, my love.*

Finally, I found some words. "Why did you do this?"

"I didn't 'do' it. It just happened."

It *just happened.* I didn't believe in that shit. People picked up a phone, wrote a letter, went to someone's dorm room. I had done it and so had she. It wasn't fate. It wasn't an accident.

"It didn't just happen, Colleen. You went there to go after him."

"So what if I did? You already had a boyfriend and I didn't. Should you have two boyfriends while I have none?" I stared at her in disbelief. What kind of bullshit arithmetic was this? These weren't apples and oranges, add two, take away one.

I shook my head. "You know I'm in love with Jon, not Will. I've been trying to leave Will."

"You haven't been trying very hard. How do you think Johnny feels, knowing you're here with Will every weekend?"

"I haven't been here every weekend. I've already been home twice just since school started."

"Nonetheless, you're here more than there. You're here now, and Johnny knows it."

I felt sick to my stomach. "If he knows it, it's because you told him, Colleen."

"Yes, I told him. He knows I'm here talking to you. I told him you need to know. And I told him what else I think, too: that you're going to marry Will, and he'll be left all alone."

There it was. After all my effort to be discreet about Will, to not openly discuss the relationship with JT because I didn't want him to feel like he was second best or to think that he couldn't have me. All my silences, while I tried to figure things out, and because I truly didn't want to hurt anyone. She had opened her big mouth, her Colleen the Bitch fucking big mouth, that I thought was just a joke among girlfriends, her personality quirk, nothing to ever really worry about because friends were loyal. Instead, she had betrayed me royally, broken my silence without asking, spoken for me when she didn't truly know my heart, or knew it and didn't care—all to serve her needs and pull JT into her web.

And so, when I finally heard the news that would turn my life upside down, I was standing on a sidewalk on a cold fall day, when all the trees were bare of leaves and the sky was an ominous gray. "I have to go back," I said, and started walking. She followed behind in silence. At the front door I didn't stop or turn.

"I'll write you," she said. I didn't answer. I went inside and locked myself in the bathroom to cry.

♡

"What did Colleen want?" Will asked when I came out. I had splashed cold water on my face and hoped he wouldn't notice my red swollen eyes. How was I going to hide my heavy heart?

"Nothing. Some school thing like she said. Just wanted to stop and say hi."

It was a McDonald's night. Usually I loved that—there was no McDonald's in my college town—but tonight I dreaded it, having to sit and make conversation and pretend that my world hadn't just imploded. I begged off with a stomachache.

"You're not pregnant, are you?" Will teased. He probably wouldn't mind if I were. I gave him a weak smile.

"No, just queasy. Maybe something I ate earlier? I just want to lie down for a while."

When the house was quiet, I got under the covers in the waterbed. I wanted something soft and warm and safe to cradle me like a womb. I stayed that way the rest of the night, and Will ended up eating the burger and fries they brought home for me.

The next day I hung around as long as I could stand it, putting on a happy face. But after a while I just had to get out of there. Will took me in his arms and I felt his urgency. I knew he was thinking about how we hadn't had sex since I'd arrived. It was unusual for us. Not that I really wanted to anymore; since he had come back from England, I'd learned how to move my body while my heart remained stoic. I had returned to the lost art of the faked orgasm.

"I'll make it up to you," was all I could say, even though I wasn't sure I ever could.

On the highway back to school my thoughts turned 'round and around with the repetitive churning of the car's wheels against the asphalt.

JT had fucked her. He and I had no commitment, but she was my best friend.

"Love the one you're with."

She had chased him. She knew about Will. And she had used that knowledge against me.

"Pass so slowly, time without you."

I'm wondering what her view of the relationship (J&C) is. Was JT trying to find out if I knew about them? Or was he using me to get information about her feelings for him?

When exactly had it happened? Surely not before my birthday? The thought sickened me, the idea that maybe we'd sat there in the pizza shop and they'd both known. Whenever it was, she'd gone to his room. She had taken some pot. They had toked up, listening to music. Was it "*Suavecito*"? "I Can Understand It"? "Sunlight"?

Was it "Your Love Is so Doggone Good"? *Please, no.*

How did it start? I knew she would have made the first move. But he hadn't stopped it. They'd taken their clothes off, lain naked in our bed. Was his heart happy or heavy?

Obviously, his dick got hard. How did he feel when he came? Did they fall into a peaceful sleep with him still on her, arms and legs braided, like we did? Or was he eager to climb off?

Ugh, now I really felt like puking.

I remembered a summer night in Colleen's backyard, hanging out with a guy from our high school class after we'd all graduated. We were lying on a blanket with Tim in the middle, looking up at the stars, when Colleen proposed that we have a kissing contest. Always so goddamn competitive. But it sounded like fun, so why not? Three minutes each, we decided.

"Me first," she said and leaned over him. I could see the outlines of their faces moving, hear a couple of guttural "mmfph" sounds until I called time. They laughed and then he turned toward me. His arm pulled me in, and I felt his soft lips against mine. He was a good kisser. Not closed-mouth but not fully open either, more lips than tongue. I knew she was watching, but she wouldn't see much. His back was to her and our heads were barely moving.

"Time!" said Colleen.

"Mmmm," he murmured and we separated.

"OK, Tim, what do you say?" She couldn't give him a minute to catch his breath. He sat up.

"Well, you both kiss very different," he started. "Colleen is more animalistic and Lynda is more refined."

"But which did you like better?" Colleen insisted.

"They both have their merits. But I guess if I had to choose, I like refined."

I smiled inside. I liked refined, too. It seemed much sexier than just diving into someone's molars. I guessed she thought her way was passionate. Now I wondered, what did Jonathan prefer? I would have said slow and sensual because that was the way we kissed, the way we did everything. If so, was he taken aback by her aggression? Or did it turn him on in a way I didn't?

No matter how he felt about it, he/she/they had done it again. And again.

"We're together," she'd said. "A couple. I told him you're going to marry Will."

Remember, both sides have to be taken into account.

When I got to the apartment, the first thing I did was search the kitchen cupboards. Ah yes, there it was, the big bottle of rum leftover from my birthday. I could hear the muffled voices and laughter from Fran and Andrew in Andrew's bedroom. I poured a Coke over ice and carried it all to my little cubby upstairs. I got out my pen and writing paper.

"Dear Jonathan.
Hi JT.
Hello my love.
You motherfucker."

I couldn't even get started. I poured the rum, took a big swallow, and added more. And then did it again.

After a while I heard Fran coming up the spiral staircase. "Lynnie? You OK in there?"

"No," I snuffled. She pushed the American flag door aside.

"What's wrong?"

"Colleen and JT are fuh-fucking," I sobbed, taking a big gulp of my drink. I sloshed some rum and Coke on myself and wiped it with my sleeve.

Fran sat down on the floor. "What? How do you know?"

"She came out to Pitt to tell me."

"Oh my god, what a bitch she is! I'm so sorry." She handed me a tissue. "What are you gonna do?"

"I don't know," I cried. "She actually has a sharing plan! She was talking about how she could leave when I come home so I could still have my weekends with him."

"What, is she nuts? Like it's all her decision to make? Besides, she still has all the weekdays plus the weekends you don't go home."

"She has everything," I sniffed. "How can I even go there now? How can I be with him, knowing he's just been with her?"

"I know you probably don't want to hear this right now, Lyn, but how has JT dealt with knowing that you're still seeing Will?"

"I don't know," I started crying again. "You're right, but how did it go this far, Frannie? How did I let it? I care about

Will, but I just love Jon so much!" I felt like my heart was going to explode, but from guilt or pain, or jealousy? All of them.

I started to get up, forcing her to move, too. "'Scuse me, Frannie, I'm gonna go call him." The nearest phone was the pay phone at the grocery store, about a mile away.

"Lynda," she called me by my first name in her best I'm-your-mother voice. "Do not go out now." She eyed the near-empty bottle. "How much of that stuff have you had?"

I belched. "Not enough. But I have to go, Fran. I just have to talk to him. Let me out, please."

What was she going to do, restrain me like the time she wanted to wash my smelly smoker's top? I grabbed my keys and purse, started the car, and pulled out on the road. I made it to the phone booth and dialed. It took all my change just to get a dial tone. Then it rang and rang until finally a strange voice answered.

"Hello?"

"Is Jon Thomas there?"

I heard the footsteps, the knock on his door. The voice returned.

"Sorry, he doesn't answer."

"Would you tell him that Lynda called, please?"

I hung up the phone. Did he know that I knew? Was she already back there with him, telling him, right now? Or had they already moved on to other things?

The drive back to the apartment was the loneliest ride of my life.

☮

Chapter 25

JT'S NEXT ENVELOPE FELT ALMOST EMPTY. OH MY GOD, OH MY GOD.

11 / 6 / 72

Hello Lovely.

I got your message last night, and Colleen thought I should write you right away. I guess after hearing from her you need to know my take.

This might surprise you, but I just don't think that this change is all that significant. I mean a person can have more than one friend, right? The difference here is that the two friends are close, too. I guess the only problem is confidentiality, or rather, the perception of a lack thereof. I think a conscious respect for privacy can go a long way.

Yes, I'm simplifying or maybe even minimizing. I just don't think anyone needs or wants unnecessary stress.

I do want you to know that I missed you like crazy this weekend.

Sorry this is so short, but I have exams every day this week. I'll write again soon, and just remember that this guy loves you.

Jon

Where to begin? It was only one page, but it sure packed a punch.

Colleen told him to write me? *She* was calling the shots now?

Not that "significant"? After all the "I love you," the angst of our summer separation, the agonizing questions I still asked myself every day, and maybe he did, too? Or had he stopped asking questions? Were he and she not that "significant"? Or were he and I not that "significant"?

And a person can have more than one "friend"? Is that what she was, his "friend"? Did he usually fuck his "friend"? Was that what I was too, his "friend"? And did he usually fall in love with his "friend"?

"Confidentiality." That's what he was worried about? That I'd hear about their trysts or vice versa?

Oh, but he missed me "like crazy" this weekend. Really? Wasn't she there? Didn't he fuck her Friday night when she came to him, told him that I was with Will in Pittsburgh, convinced him that she should come out and tell me about them herself? That long drive just to assert her dominance because that's what an alpha monkey does? And did she go to him Saturday night, screeching about her success, her crooked yellow grin telegraphing her glee, aggressive and ugly, because that's what an alpha monkey is? Why did he let her in, why didn't he see what she was doing, why didn't he banish her to the tall treetops, separate from other females where she belongs because she will try to hurt them—hurt me? Why did he join her in hurting me?

Remember that this guy loves you.

Oh, JT, if only you had remembered.

Chapter 26

"Colleen kept her promise," Hannah said when she let me in.

"Huh! Which promise is that?"

"She's left town. She wanted me to tell you."

"How did she know I was coming?" I hadn't answered her letter.

"I guess JT told her. She said she was gonna go visit some friends at Pitt."

"She has friends? Imagine that. Hmm, maybe she'll go seduce Will while she's at it." I felt so bitter. "Hannah, what do you think about all this?"

"Jesus, of course I think it's wrong. I mean, out of all the men in the world, she had to go after the one you love?" She made a face like she smelled something bad. "Plus, I just don't see her with JT. She just isn't . . . cool enough, or something." Then she grinned. "Lynda, you're one cool chick. That's why I picked you for him. I didn't pick her."

I had to smile. "Thank you for that. But I just don't know what's going to happen now." In spite of Hannah's compliment, I could see that she felt sorry for me. I felt sorry for me, too.

"So, not to change the subject, but have you heard anything from JT's coach?"

"No," she said. "But I didn't expect to. And now things are getting pretty serious with this Jamie guy." She smiled. "I don't miss Roy at all. Is that terrible?"

"Not at all. It's a lot better than if you were crying your eyes out over him."

"I guess he was just an exciting fling," Hannah said.

I wondered if that's what I'd thought about JT when I met him, too. An irresistible desire to experience a high-octane man. But instead he had flung something on me: I fell in love. I sighed and started getting ready to go see him.

I wanted everything to feel the same. But everything felt different now. I parked my car where I usually did. Is that where she parked? I passed a girl coming down the dorm stairs, was she staring at me? A guy in the hall was on the phone, was it my imagination, or did he give me a pitying glance? Or was I paranoid?

JT opened his door. I'd written that I was coming, and he was there. Just like the old days, the days when he'd stopped running and let me catch him. He smiled at me the same. He took me in his arms the same. But nothing was the same. She'd been there.

Did she sit on my spot on the bed?

Were those albums stacked by the stereo the ones he'd planned for me or the ones he'd played for her?

We tried to act normal. I re-told the story of Allenwood. Then JT asked me a question that made my cheeks flush with embarrassment.

"So, dang it," he said, "McGovern lost. You voted for him, right?"

This election was the first time that eighteen-to-twenty-year-olds had the right to vote. It was an important step, finally allowing young people to vote for or against the politicians who would send them off to war. Being twenty-one, I could have voted for my first time anyway, but thanks to the change, youth were expected to turn out in droves—to get Tricky Dick out of office and finally end Vietnam.

Only, I hadn't voted. And for such a stupid reason: I didn't know how. Maybe because I wasn't on campus as much, I hadn't seen a recruitment table on the quad, and no one had approached me with registration papers as I hurried to a class. I didn't know how to register, and I was too shy to ask someone. Now I was too ashamed to admit it to JT. I hoped he couldn't see it on my face.

"Oh, of course I was for McGovern," I hedged, feeling stupid. "How did this happen—that Nixon is so unpopular, and yet he won?"

"He isn't unpopular with everyone. I guess the economy is pretty strong, and whether he caused that or not, he gets credit for it. Apparently, war is good for business," JT grimaced. "Plus, some say McGovern is just too left-wing. Which of course," he cupped my face in his hands and smiled, "is why people like you and me wanted him to win."

I wanted McGovern to win, but I had done nothing to make it happen. I'd wanted to win JT, and once I had him, I'd done little to keep him. Why was I so passive? I felt like I was shrinking inside myself, the wicked witch melting. Only I wasn't wicked, I was just . . . inept.

"What are you doing for the holidays?" JT asked next.

"My parents want me to come to Texas for Christmas. I'm mixed about it, but my little sister is missing me, bad. I miss her, too." He reminded me of a previous joke we'd shared about Texas, that I should check to see if the phone number for the KKK and the Police Department were one and the same. We laughed like we had the first time. For a moment, it almost felt like the old days.

But only for a moment. Because then we were listening to a Bobby Womack song. Jonathan raised a quizzical eyebrow as he sang one of the lines, about how my friend Annie Mae told me all she sees:

"Have you ever thought maybe
she was trying to get next to me?"

I couldn't look away, my throat constricted. Was he telling me something that I should have known?

With a big gulp, I forced myself to try to bring up my friend Annie Mae.

"Can we talk about Colleen?" I asked him.

"Lynda." JT frowned. "You know I can't talk about her to you." My heart felt like lead in my chest. What had happened to his declaration on our very first night, "You can always talk to me about anything"? For some reason, that rejection continued my silence about Will as well. How could I tell him that I didn't plan to marry Will when he was "a couple" now with Colleen? And were those the words he would use, too?

A couple of times I wondered, how does Colleen feel out at Pitt? Was it her turn to be eaten up by jealousy? Was I a terrible person for wanting that? It didn't matter because soon he'd be hers again.

Whatever he felt, JT didn't seem like himself. He seemed down.

Later I tried to remember everything, as always playing it over and over in my mind. But this visit had felt surreal, like a dream.

We had made love, but it was almost as if there were two ghosts in bed with us. The ghosts of Will and Colleen.

♡

After I left JT for school, he wrote to me that same night.

11 / 20 / 72
Oh my love.

He described feeling restless, starting out for the library and turning back, trying to sleep and giving up. Only writing to me felt like what he really wanted to do.

He wrote about why he had seemed depressed and didn't want to talk about things when I was there. He didn't want to hurt me. (Too late, Johnny.) But then wasn't it too late for me to not hurt him? Because he admitted:

I knew you had hurt me.

And then came the earth-shaking lines, the "significant" lines.

I guess without even knowing it, I engaged in Newton's
Law: For every action, there is an equal and opposite
reaction. Or something like that. In other words,
reciprocity and showing my unhappiness to you, and I guess
it did what it was supposed to.

Wow. I knew what he meant. And I'd have to think long and hard about all the implications of what he said. I felt sick.

In a wounded rant after learning about him and Colleen, I had written of how frustrated I was that, in only a few weeks, she had managed to accomplish what it had taken me months to do, meaning get close to him. JT denied it:

Nobody, but nobody, can ever do what you do.

Then he said he'd better change the subject before he got in hot water. He was listening to Traffic, "The Low Spark of High Heeled Boys." He wrote a couple lines about how if he gave me everything would I take him for a ride and take his pride. And he was going to sign off, but then he wrote out another song—a long one, every lyric and every backup lyric—from Bobby Womack, "(If You Don't Want My Love) Give It Back." It was a song about how Bobby's woman had two men, and he had tried his hardest, but if that wasn't good enough, he would have to give his love to someone else.

Someone else. Annie Mae. Colleen.

Altogether, he had spent over five hours on this letter, signed simply:

Love,
Jonathan

So there it was, lurking in JT's seven-pager: Newton's Law, an equal and opposite reaction. For my having hurt him, I knew. But I also knew JT was not a vindictive person. Had I stripped him of his pride? I was sure some would say yes. What would he say? I knew he was frustrated, yet he'd hung in with me, led me to believe that he was handling it. Instead, his unhappiness over Will had finally boiled over, and now I had gotten burned too.

When I read my own words written back to me—how easily she had accomplished what it had taken me months to do—I felt ashamed; it sounded so childish. I meant the time it had taken for him to trust me; the way I had to search for him on campus until he finally felt safe enough to like being caught. But he had let her right in. The poisonous spider.

The Bobby song was complex, and he'd included every note, syllable, background line, and repeat chorus. What was he trying to tell me? Did he want his love back? Was it so that he could give it to someone else? Or was my indecision just tearing him up? So much that he had to do something this extreme to get my attention. (Oh, JT. I'm so, so sorry.)

But if he was that unhappy, why hadn't he asked me to change something?

☮

Chapter 27

IF I'D FELT CONFUSED BEFORE, NOW I WAS A BASKET CASE. I was still using speed, staying up late into the night. I was still listening to "our" music, but it all seemed tainted now. Of the many things that were troubling me, one—no matter how trivial it seemed—was that Colleen had seen him play ball and I never had. I decided that on my next trip I had to go to his game, my last chance before the Christmas break.

It all went wrong from the start.

After my hours on the interstate, I rested on Hannah's couch. I was on the phone with JT, letting him know that I'd be over soon. There was a knock at the door. Hannah opened it and I couldn't believe my eyes: Colleen! Why hadn't she gone away like she had promised? I knew why, because Colleen did what Colleen wanted.

And it was about to get worse.

"Is that JT?" she asked, over my phone call. I nodded. "Let me talk to him." I looked at Hannah, whose eyebrows shot up. What nerve Colleen had!

Why did I hand the phone over? Why didn't I say, "No, you've had your time, now this is my time"? I guess because nerve wasn't my strong suit. I'd been raised to accommodate people. No wonder Colleen liked how "placid" I was, that word she sometimes called me. I barely heard what she said to him thanks to the rush of blood inside my head.

Colleen handed the phone back. "I'll be over soon," I told JT and hung up, still in shock.

I turned to her. "I thought you were going to leave town."

"Oh, I know. I intended to," Colleen said and shrugged. "But there was nowhere I wanted to go. Don't worry, I won't infringe on your time," she said. Ignoring the fact that she already had.

She continued. "I do have a little favor to ask, though." What, that maybe I should leave town instead of her? How the fuck could she ask me for a favor?

"Johnny has gotten behind in school this semester. I told him I'd write one of his papers. But you know me, I'm not that great a writer. I was hoping that maybe you'd do it for him." She flashed a smile that I guess she thought was winsome. Apparently she didn't know that it's hard to appear winsome when you're acting like a shark.

Wow. I couldn't believe her gall. So why did I ultimately say yes? This was a responsibility that she took on, not me. And was he behind in his schoolwork because of the time he was spending with her? Just the idea of it made me boil. The bottom line, though, was that I didn't want JT's grades to suffer. I'd always known him to be honest to a fault, so I suspected that for him to ask her to help him cheat meant he was already suffering. By contrast, my academic ethics were flexible, and writing a paper for someone else was easy for me.

She pulled a paperback book and typed instruction sheet out of her purse. "It's just an analysis of this book," she said. "It's so boring, I couldn't even start it." So, it wasn't just a paper but also some historical book to read? Jesus. Still, I knew I could skim it and probably do a decent job. Maybe my own ego played a role, too.

That night I took a bottle of sloe gin to JT's room. I didn't intend to get drunk, but he also had some pot. While I knew that for me those two were a dangerous combination, there I was, about to combine them again, because I had stopped caring. I wanted to enjoy my time with him, but thoughts and images of the two of them swirled in my head. Pretty soon I was on that merry-go-round that I couldn't stop. As I spun faster, JT tried to gentle me off the runaway horse, playing one of our favorite Scott-Heron songs, about the restorative effect of letting the sun shine through in beautiful music like "Lady Day and John Coltrane."

But it was too late for me. There was no sun on a night like this. Just like during our first time together, rancid liquid came roiling up and out of my mouth. Only this time I didn't make it to the bathroom; sloe-gin-red vomit landed on the bed, the floor, JT's sneakers, and some of his albums. I knew I should offer to clean it up, but that would only make me throw up again. I sat at his desk naked, holding my head in my hands while he changed the sheets.

"Here, just get in bed," he coaxed. "I'll take care of it."

I passed out immediately. So I didn't see JT down on his knees. Cleaning up the spoils of all our mistakes.

The next day he was kind, but distant. It added to my sadness, but I couldn't blame him. He was already dressed and ready to head out to campus to run errands and then attend some pre-game strategy meeting when I dragged myself out of bed and started putting my clothes on.

In spite of my sore heart and pounding head, I wanted to connect with JT.

"I'm looking forward to finally go see you play tonight."

"Yeah, it should be a good game." He was distracted, putting albums in their covers, tidying up—or was he just avoiding me?

"What time will you get back?" I asked him. The game was out of town, but not terribly far.

"Could be ten or eleven, depending on overtime and stuff. I'll call you at Hannah's when I get in."

I hated to bring it up, but I had to. "I'm really sorry about getting sick last night, Jon," I said miserably. The smell of vomit still permeated the room.

"It's OK. It happens. Come here." JT grasped the opening of my jacket in his hands and gently pulled me toward him. He kissed my forehead. He kissed each of my cheeks in turn. But he did not kiss my sour lips like he had that first time.

♡

Colleen was right. The book for JT's paper was boring. I tried to read it, but after taking a couple of aspirin I fell asleep on Hannah's couch. She was at work and the apartment was quiet. When I woke up, I felt a little better and was able to at least begin perusing the book.

Hannah came home with a pizza for our dinner, a perfect antidote for a hangover, and by the time we finished it, I was almost back to normal. I told her about what had happened at JT's and how humiliated I felt.

"God, who can blame you, Lynda? Look at what's going on." Hannah made a face. "And can you believe she asked you to let her talk to him? What a bitch."

This couldn't have been easy for Hannah because she'd been a friend of Colleen's since before I'd met either of them. But Hannah seemed to share my view of the situation.

"I know," I said, "I was kind of speechless."

"And now she wants you to write this paper for her? Are you sure you want to do that?"

"I don't know, Hannah. Of course I don't want to do it for her. But I guess I want to do it for him."

We moved on to talking about what we were going to wear to the game; or, more specifically, what I was going to wear, since her new sweetie wouldn't be there. I decided on the alpaca skirt I'd found the year before at the head shop. JT had never seen it. In fact, I'd hardly worn it at all. It was a beautiful long, soft, fuzzy A-line. Beige, brown, and black fibers wove tribal designs in the soft wool. A snug black dance leotard and brown boots would complete the outfit, and my waist-length sheath of brown hair would top it off. It was a simple yet dramatic look, but one thing posed a problem: the skirt hugged my waist and hips like a second skin, yet it had no zipper or buttons. Getting it on and over my shoulders took quite a bit of wriggling and a little sweat; getting it off seemed to require an assistant. Even when I'd tried it on in the store, I'd needed Fran to help me out of it.

"I can help you get it on now if you need me," Hannah said, "but how are you going to get it off?"

"Well, hopefully JT might still enjoy helping me out of my clothes." That process would be more awkward than sexy, but I still wanted to wear the skirt. I wanted to look good for him in something he'd never seen, and yeah, maybe for anyone else who might be watching—JT's teammates, anybody who had seen him with me, anybody who had seen him with Colleen.

Hannah drove us to the game, an away game for which JT usually didn't want me to risk the winter weather. That night the weather was cold but clear, and the roads had been plowed. We found seats about halfway up the bleachers at center court;

it was a great spot from which to view all the action. I was buzzing with excitement to see JT play.

The home team ran out one by one to the expected roar of their fans. Then it was the challengers' turn to enter the floor —and there he was! My JT looking so tall, dark, and handsome. They received a lot of cheers, too, including mine. I'd thought I'd be too cool to scream, but I just couldn't hold back. From the noise, it was obvious that a lot of the followers JT and his team had garnered had also made the drive to support their heroes. And why not? These guys had put their little college on the sports map.

The teams warmed up, and I saw for the first time how the natural grace I'd observed—whether playing pool, putting the stereo needle on an album, tracing my cheek with one long finger, or sliding his body into mine—extended to the basketball court. I didn't know if he saw me in the stands. But it didn't matter. I saw him and he was a work of art. He was a poem written by the human body. And his team won! A "tsumani," one newspaper would call them. "Like wildfire" was how they described Johnny Thomas scoring twenty-eight points.

I rode back to Hannah's on a natural high. I couldn't wait to hold him in my arms, tell him how incredible he had been. I wanted him to slip his hands under my skirt and up my thighs, lift the wool that had started to feel a bit scratchy over and off my shoulders. I wanted him to put me naked into the cocoon of his bed and help me figure out how to banish the ghosts forever.

While I waited for his call, I finished skimming the book and made some notes for his paper. The apartment was warm. I started to think that maybe I should have had Hannah help me out of my skirt. But she'd gone out right after we got home.

When the doorbell rang I thought, oh, she's back—I'll ask her to help me now.

Instead, I opened the door to Colleen.

She looked as surprised as I felt. "Oh, you're here?" she said. "I thought you'd be with Johnny."

"I'm just waiting for him to get back," I said.

"Is Hannah here? That's why I stopped by."

"No, she went out."

"Oh. OK. Well, I'll just go on home then."

Colleen didn't move, and I knew that she wanted me to say no, stay and talk to me. In the past it wouldn't have been in question. After all, she had been my best friend for over six years. But I didn't want to talk to her now.

"OK. G'night." I closed the door. And waited for his call.

And waited for his call.

The call that never came.

Hannah got home at about one in the morning. She wasn't surprised to see me. She wasn't smiling, either.

"Lynda, I've gotta tell you something."

I froze. Please, please—god that I do not believe in—please do not let him be with Colleen.

"I just saw JT at a party," Hannah said.

It took a second to sink in. He was at a party?

"Was she there?" I had to ask.

"No."

"What was he doing?"

"Just drinking beer and talking."

There was nothing else to think but that he was standing me up, while I sat there like a fool, waiting and writing his paper.

"Hannah, can you help me out of this skirt? It itches like hell." I thought about how excited I'd been to wear it for JT.

Then I pictured his beautiful lips pulling at a cold bottle of beer. I imagined him feeling elated about his big win but still humble as he accepted the kudos. I saw his dancing eyes, eyes that weren't dancing home to me anymore.

Hannah went to bed, but I stayed up all night. I finished writing the paper and typed it at her kitchen table. At five a.m. I wrote two notes and gathered up my things. The good-bye note with instructions to Hannah to give to Colleen I left next to JT's book and paper. The other one I took to JT's dorm.

The first hint of light was rising in the sky as I drove into the parking lot. I climbed the stairs to his room as I had done before, always with a happy heart, but this morning my heart was as frozen as the winter ground, and the December cold made ice of my runny nose, my tears. I stood outside his door, wanting with everything inside me to knock and then fall into his warmth and be made unbroken. Instead, I taped my note to his door and slipped quietly back outside.

I'd be on the highway by the time JT awoke to read my final words of love:

Chapter 28

FROM THAT MOMENT ON, I BECAME A ZOMBIE. I SLEEP-walked through my days as if I were OK. How could I be both numb and yet in such terrible pain? When a letter from Colleen arrived, I didn't read it. And there were no more letters from JT to decide whether to read.

My mom wrote that she had arranged for me to visit the family in Texas over the Christmas holidays. I didn't want to go to Texas. But then I didn't want to be in Pennsylvania either, or anywhere else, so what did it matter?

Barbie loved seeing me. I tried to keep from her the truth that her Sissie had become a zombie. At my grandfather's restaurants, I ate as much fried chicken and okra, or enchiladas, rice, and beans as I wanted. I wondered how a zombie could still be hungry, how food could still taste good.

My uncle and his wife took me shopping in Amarillo, their closest "big city." I found a chic forest-green velour jumpsuit that represented how styles were changing, less countercultural and more sophisticated. Also a plaid jersey dress (clingy yet demure, for student teaching) and a cool velvet hat. I wished that I'd be wearing those things with JT, but I would not.

After the holidays, I had only a couple weeks to finish classes and take finals. Next up I would be going to Pittsburgh to student teach and live with Fran at her mom's. Between our classes and her romance with Andrew, I didn't see much of Fran. Our community dinners had stopped, and our contacts became hit or miss. Then came another big hit.

At the start of finals week, Fran came to me. "Lynda, I've got something to tell you."

Studying for an exam, I was distracted and barely looked up. "Yeah, Frannie?"

"It's really hard to say this, but . . . you can't stay at my mom's house for student teaching."

"What? Why not?" This had been our plan from the beginning. She had my full attention now.

"I just don't think it would be fair to my mother."

"What do you mean, fair?"

"You know, you and Will," Fran said. "Him being black. My mom's not very modern that way."

"But it's not like he would come to her house. Why would she even have to know?"

"Lynda, she already knows you're seeing him. And there would be phone calls or something."

"Did she say I can't come?" Even I heard the plaintive note in my voice.

"No. But I just think this will be better for everyone."

I was stunned. I didn't see how it could be better for me. How long had Fran been thinking this way?

"Why didn't you tell me sooner? It's so late now. I don't know what I'm gonna do." I felt like crying, but zombies don't cry.

"I just couldn't bring myself to tell you. I'm sorry, Lynnie." Fran looked sad, but I could tell from the finality of her tone that there was no use in arguing. And what had happened to two for one and one for all, roomies to the end?

There was no way I could postpone my student teaching. I

had to be registered with the college because after that semester my government benefits would end, and so would our apartment lease. I couldn't just foist myself on Will and Dr. Frank's family, and I was afraid to be in Pittsburgh by myself. So the next day I went to the student teaching office. I asked if they could assign me to a smaller town closer to school. They said they would try but couldn't guarantee anything.

For the first time, I missed my parents. Not the childhood parents I occasionally had fond memories of or the fantasy parents I wished I had. Real parents, because I knew that my mother could at least take charge of this situation and get me where I needed to be. I was an adult—sort of—but I felt like a motherless child.

I called Will and we made an emergency plan: he would take the bus to me (first time coming to my campus—it hadn't made sense when I couldn't have a man in my dorm room) and drive me and my things to his parents' place in Philly. Then I'd go from there to whatever town I got assigned to, hoping that I could then find a place to live. When it came to why Fran didn't want me at her mom's, he sighed. I was sure that rejection was nothing new to him.

Soon Will was there in the apartment with Fran, Andrew, and me. He brought his textbooks so he could read ahead. I felt bad that Will's last quarter (before his student teaching started in Philly) was getting off to such a discombobulated start. But it got worse.

After my last final, I came home to find Will sitting on my bed and glaring at me. His face was gray and angry as a thunderhead.

"What's wrong?" I asked.

"These are what's wrong." He held up a paper bag. Inside

were twenty-two letters from JT, plus a birthday card, photos, and newspaper clippings.

Good thing I had no more finals because I knew where this night was going.

"You saw him while I was gone? And you kept on even after I got back?" Will asked incredulously. It was a rhetorical question. All the letters were dated and inside their postmarked envelopes.

"I'm not seeing him anymore," was all I could offer, weakly.

"And you gave me shit about Brenda? Who I *left* to come back to you?"

"I'm sorry, Will," was all I could say. And the pain I'd been suffering for weeks dug in even deeper. But was I hurting for him or for me? I felt dirty with self-disgust.

I wanted to ask how he found the letters. The bag had been tucked in a corner of my cubby, concealed by the footlocker. But it didn't feel right to accuse him in the face of my great lie. I figured that he must have suspected something and gone looking for evidence. How much time had he spent digging through my personal business when I thought he was reading his textbooks?

Still, could I blame him?

Will and I spent the night in anger, accusations, tears. "How could you do this to me, Kitten?" he asked again and again. Each time I felt sicker because I knew about all the hurts and horrors he had experienced in his life, and now I had added more. This could have been my chance to tell him the whole truth: that I hadn't meant to hurt him, that I was in love with JT and wanted to be with him. But JT was with Colleen now. JT had hurt me and didn't seem to care. Would I leave a man who, in spite of everything, still wanted me? To go to a man who no longer did?

Instead I said, "I guess I was just lonely." At least that was true.

Finally, near dawn, both of us drained physically and emotionally, Will had an ultimatum.

"I want you to tear up those letters," he said.

It felt as if he were asking me to tear out my own heart. JT's letters, sexy and lyrical, quirky and cute, his one-of-a-kind and just-for-me words on paper, so full of his late-night love. But I felt I had no choice.

We sat at the kitchen table. One by one, I removed each letter from its envelope. I wanted so badly to re-read them, to mourn and say good-bye. Instead, I tore each one into strips and put them in a paper bag. Then I ripped up the newspapers and photographs. When I was finished, the bag was full. I stuffed the bag and all the empty envelopes into the kitchen trash.

We went up to bed. Will fell into an exhausted sleep. I lay awake for hours staring at the ceiling.

Then I eased out of the covers, padded down the spiral stairs, pulled the paper bag out of the trash, and hid it behind a bean bag chair. I carried the garbage bag out to the dumpster, hoping that Will, if he even noticed, would think Fran had emptied it. Then I crawled back into bed, hoping that Will wouldn't be awakened by the thumping of my telltale heart.

The next morning, while packing and carting stuff to the car, I slipped my booty into a suitcase full of school papers.

I was a zombie, and I hated myself, but I had to keep JT's letters.

♡

I also kept a letter I'd received from Gil Scott-Heron after I'd written him at his record label about my trip to Allenwood. "I would very much like to hear about it and see your photos," he wrote back. Short on funds as usual, I hadn't developed the film yet, so I planned to do it while Will and I were at his parents. But where was it? Everything I owned I had brought with me, and now the film was nowhere to be found. I was mad at myself for not being more careful with the only real evidence of what I'd seen at the prison and for disappointing Gil. Could I not do *anything* right?

Within a few days, though, I had something else to focus on. The mailman delivered a notice that I was assigned to a senior high English class. Soon I re-packed the car with basics, said good-bye to Will, and started driving there with one goal: find the school and a place to live.

The high school was in a small town near my college. I easily located the school on the outskirts and then bought a newspaper so I could start the hunt for an apartment rental. But without roommates, most apartments were out of my reach. Plus landlords wanted proof of employment, and I had neither proof nor employment.

Near the end of the day, tired and discouraged, I ended up in a small real estate office. The older woman who greeted me tapped a pencil against her cheek.

"I might know just what you're looking for," she said. "I live in an upstairs apartment in an old, renovated Victorian. Vicky, the woman downstairs, is looking for someone to rent a room."

"Really? Here in town?" Suddenly things were looking up.

It turned out that Vicky worked as a cocktail waitress at a bar-and-grill nearby. The realtor sent me there and called ahead. Vicky was a pretty but tired-looking woman in her early thirties.

"I need the extra rent," she explained, "but I've been nervous about having a stranger in the house with my two girls. A college student is perfect." Before I left, we shook hands on our deal.

Besides my room, I was welcome to have dinner with them and eat anything else I liked. The amount she wanted for rent and food was almost the same price I'd paid for rent alone at the apartment with Fran.

The old house was beautiful and tastefully furnished. Vicky's six- and nine-year-old daughters were excited about having a new roommate, and because Vicky sometimes worked nights, she asked if I'd mind being home alone with the girls. I said I didn't mind at all because I'd be working on lesson plans. "Plus, I go see my boyfriend most weekends, so you'll have privacy then."

"There's not much privacy when you have two kids," Vicky laughed. "But I know what you mean."

I seemed normal. They didn't know that a zombie was moving into their home. But I would be a harmless zombie and maybe even a helpful one.

On the first day of school, I was jittery with nerves. I wore the plaid jersey dress I'd bought in Texas, along with pantyhose and my suede wedding sandals. The front office directed me to the teachers' lounge: "Mr. Reynolds has a free period now." How odd it felt to be looking for the teachers' private lair instead of a classroom. In the lounge sat my supervisor, Reynolds, with a cup of a coffee and a cigarette, holding forth to another man.

"Mr. Reynolds? I'm Lynda Smith, your student teacher." He smiled and mumbled an aside to the other man that I couldn't hear.

"Here, sit down, Lynda. Let's have a little chat about what to expect." Reynolds took a drag off his cigarette. "But first, what brings you to our fine school?" His tone was sarcastic.

"Well, I had to find a placement at the last minute, and you guys had an opening, so here I am." I smiled my fake zombie smile.

"I'm glad you're here. Because otherwise I would actually have to work," he said, looking at the other man, who laughed. It soon became clear that he didn't plan to work much at all. After observing for this first week, Reynolds told me, I'd be teaching all his classes. *What?* During teacher training, I'd heard that I'd start with one class, then two, and build gradually until all five were added, around week six or seven. Should I complain? No. I couldn't risk not having a placement.

"Mr. Reynolds, what are the students like?"

"You can call me Bob. And basically, the kids here are studying auto mechanics, hairdressing, and the like." He leaned forward, like we were sharing a secret. "Not exactly the cream of the crop, if you know what I mean. Especially in English class." He grimaced, and the other man nodded in sympathy.

I wasn't thrilled with "Rah Rah" Reynolds, which I later learned was the kids' nickname for him because he'd dismissively reply, "Rah rah rah" when a student brought up something controversial, like marijuana or Vietnam.

Soon I was off to observe him and got another surprise: I would be teaching Victorian literature to these future auto mechanics and hairdressers. Why weren't they studying something more contemporary? And how in the hell was I going to make authors like Dickens and Tennyson interesting to them?

By the time the day was over, I'd found the cafeteria and watched Rah Rah's other four classes. On my way home, I stopped at the local library to look for reference materials. And discovered that a zombie could be utterly exhausted.

♡

My days fell into a routine. I was lonely. Fran and I were estranged, Colleen and I were estranged, and worst of all, I had no JT or even just his letters to look forward to. But I did enjoy evening dinners with Vicky's little family, dinners often made of Hamburger Helper, which I loved. After homework and baths, the girls were allowed some time to hang out in my room before they were shooed off to bed.

As soon as I started teaching, my workload became intense. I began to use my diet pills to control my sleep/work schedule. At about eleven p.m. I'd take a pill, go to sleep, and then shoot up wide awake within a couple hours. Then I'd spend the rest of the night working on lesson plans. I knew I wasn't getting enough sleep, but I didn't see another way. Shy by nature, I found it nerve-wracking to be up in front of the class. Lazy by nature, Rah Rah rarely stopped by after my first week in charge.

I even came up with a few strategies that seemed to interest the kids. I showed them differences in the Victorians' styles and messages and compared them to more current writers—hoping that they would relate and maybe, just maybe, keep reading. We studied Robert Browning through his tale of the Pied Piper, which paralleled modern day ethnic strife. It also helped when one issue of their *Weekly Reader* periodical featured Sigmund Freud, which gave me an opportunity to introduce them to psychology, and hinting at sex always got their attention.

The kids were seniors, looking forward to graduation in a few months and more interested in each other than in me. One exception was a young man who clearly had a crush on me. The weird thing was, I found him kind of cute, too. He had longish hair, round John Lennon spectacles, and a hippie demeanor. Only a few years younger than I, he gave me something to look forward to in last period, but there were two barriers to anything more:

1. He was a student. I was his teacher.
2. I was a zombie. He was not.

Chapter 29

WHEN SCHOOL LET OUT FOR THE WEEK, I GOT INTO MY already-packed Chevy and drove to see Will at Pitt. After the tearful night when he had me rip up JT's letters, and after my promise that JT and I were through, Will and I had resumed as we'd been before. He had left Dr. Frank's to move into an apartment with a guy from his karate club. Friday nights were set because a friend of Will's had a band that played near the campus. The bar was far-out: stiff sixty-cent shots, stuffed sixty-cent egg rolls, and a mixed crowd that was there to get down. I'd traded my baggy patched hip-huggers for some fitted jeans, and Vicky liked to loan me some of her sexy little sweaters.

I might have been a zombie, but after a week fueled by speed, anxiety, adrenaline, and exhaustion, I was still ready to cut loose—hip-shaking my sadness away with booze and blues.

And then it happened: the US announced plans to withdraw from Vietnam. On a Saturday night when I was at Pitt, the students took to the streets.

"Let's go out, Will!" I begged. "This is historic. This is what we've been waiting for." I leaned out the window to watch the cheering waves of young people move through the night. I wanted to join my tribe in celebrating what our generation had been marching, protesting, and in some cases, even dying for.

"Kitten, no," Will said. "There could be fights or riots or some shit. I don't wanna get involved in anything like that."

"Why would there be riots when it's a happy occasion?" And

where has my ardent revolutionary gone, I wanted to add. I pouted, but he was unmoved and I was too weary to face the tide alone.

Later, when I told Vicky about it, she sighed, "I wish I'd been there. I'd have gone." We were having one of our increasingly intimate talks. She sipped a glass of wine.

"Being a wife and then a mother, I never had a chance to be just myself. And I never expected to be doing this alone."

"Does the kids' father help you?" So far I had seen no sign of him.

"No," she made a face. "He's a total prick. I don't even know where he is, and that's just fine."

She confided that at one time her depression got so bad that she'd tried to take her life. I told her that my mother had confessed the same thing about her early years as a single mom.

"I'm in a better place now," Vicky went on. "I decided that my girls deserve more."

"You're giving them more, Vicky. You're a good mom."

"Thanks," she shrugged. "But I still wish I'd gone to college and all that stuff."

"Well, it can sometimes be confusing and overwhelming." I decided to confide in her, too, which I hoped wasn't a mistake.

"Like, you know I go to see my boyfriend, right? But you probably don't know that he's black. My family hates him, but they've never even met him." I told her how my family had kicked me out. I hoped that Vicky wouldn't kick me out, too.

"That just sucks." Vicky's face flushed. "I don't know why people can't live and let live. Is he good to you?"

"Yeah. He's a really decent guy," I said.

"That's all that matters then." But was it? Didn't it matter whether I loved Will?

Eventually I told her about JT, too, and she sympathized with the dilemma I'd been in, a dilemma that was now over (the zombie took a little silver bullet to the head).

One day Vicky brought home the first issue of *Ms.* magazine. It was becoming clearer that the struggles for rights had so far left out how the female sex was often the butt of everything from jokes to job discrimination to violence. But we had reason to be hopeful because the light of social change had turned on another bright bulb: the Women's Movement.

I felt safe at Vicky's. The only worrisome event took place one windy night when she was at work and the girls came running to my room.

"Lynda," whispered the youngest. "We think we heard someone outside."

I put down my book and walked with them through the house, peering out between the silky curtains. The streetlights cast moving shadows as wind tossed through the trees.

"Hear that wind?" They nodded solemnly. "Did it sound like that?"

"No," Vicky's older girl answered softly. "It sounded like footsteps. Like shoes on the porch."

Fuck. What was I to do? I didn't want to bother Vicky when she was working. Should I call the police? It seemed silly when I hadn't seen or heard anything.

I got the girls into bed and promised I would work in the living room, keeping eyes and ears open. Nothing happened. But what would I have done if something had? It was beginning to sink in just how little I knew about how to handle the problems of real life. And I had thought that I knew so much.

♡

It was all the talk in the teachers' lounge: Watergate. When other teachers asked me occasionally what I thought, I didn't know what to say. I'd never really been politically informed; instead, I'd followed the leadership of my hippie tribe. Hate was wrong, love was right. War was wrong, peace was right. Tricky Dick was a warmonger, therefore he was wrong. When Vietnam vets like John Kerry, who spoke at the big DC peace march I'd been part of two years before, came home and said that the war was so wrong, I knew that they had to be so right.

But this Watergate thing was confusing. So Nixon had ordered a break-in to sabotage the Democrats? Plus there were so many details and so many names—Nixon and Agnew sure, but also Woodward and Bernstein the reporters who "scooped" the story, the mysterious "Deep Throat" who informed to them, Nixon's advisors, FBI and CIA personnel, and more—and I had no tribe to interpret them for me.

Of course, the televised hearings would result in many charges and convictions and would ultimately bring down Richard Nixon, who resigned to avoid being impeached. Sources in the White House reported that Nixon became extremely paranoid during the Watergate investigation, and there was real concern that he might press the "red button" that would initiate nuclear war with Russia.

One revelation about Watergate that would personally touch me later was when several of the guilty parties were sentenced to Federal Prison—at Allenwood, PA! The newspapers called Allenwood a "country club prison," meaning it offered an extra-comfy sentence for "white collar" criminals. What I'd seen at Allenwood wasn't exactly a country club, it looked like a place readying for war. I wondered if Gil Scott-Heron's song had frightened officials into changing the public face of the prison to conceal what else was going on, but did white authorities even know about Gil? It seemed unlikely. I felt a wave of guilt all over again remembering that I'd lost the film I'd shot at Allenwood, the film that Gil had wanted to see.

The one other thing that the teachers liked to talk about—the male teachers anyway—brought the *Ms.* magazine articles closer to home: they'd banter about which of their female students was the most sexy. I couldn't believe they were so gross about it in front of me.

"Did'ja see what Hotsy Totsy had on today?" Rah Rah might ask. "Whew, those tight pants!" He'd shake his hand as if he'd just burned himself on her, and other men in the room would grin. Apparently, they all knew who Hotsy Totsy was.

I wondered if that compared to my little crush in sixth period. But these men were in their late thirties and forties, while I was only four years older than my cute student. And I certainly didn't talk about him that way.

I also wondered uneasily if the men said anything about me when I left the room.

When Will moved home to Philly for student teaching, it made my weekend drives longer, but I had my thoughts, my cigarettes, and the radio. My mind still swirled like a Texas tornado, and sometimes the radio whipped up the deadly winds of memory.

The Doobie Brothers sang about where you'd be without love. I joined them, asking JT, where would *you* (rather) be? The unspoken answer: with Colleen, apparently.

Rod Stewart cried, "Ohh noo, not my baby," over how his baby wouldn't let him down. But I had to face facts: oh yes, my baby had. Baby who was no longer mine.

The Temps bragged that there was no woman like the one

they got, and a dark cloud dropped over me, because the woman JT got wasn't me. Was Colleen now his "sight for sore eyes to see"? Wasn't that what he had called me?

The worst of all was when, lost in thought, I was sleep-driving to the radio, only to be awakened by the song about the best girl of his life, "*Suavecito, mi linda—suavecito!*" My own sudden storm of gasping and crying could even force me to pull over till it passed.

I'd bisect the long drive with a stop at Hannah's for a bathroom break and some girl talk.

"How are things with you and Jamie?" I'd ask her.

"Great. We're gonna move in together as soon as my lease is up." That was less than two months away.

It sickened me to ask, but I had to. "Hannah, do you hear anything about Colleen and JT?"

"Not a lot. Just that they're seeing each other. She stops in sometimes but doesn't say much about him. She knows you come by on your way to Philly."

Then we'd talk about my student teaching, my chauvinist pig supervisor, Rah Rah, and Will. Pretty standard stuff.

Until it wasn't. Until the night I walked in and Hannah said, "I have a message for you."

Bump, bump, bump went my heart. I could imagine only one sender.

"JT wanted me to ask if you'd stop by on your way through."

ACK! "Did he say why?"

"No, just to give you that message."

Well, here I was, on my way through. But I was unprepared—should I wait until the next weekend? Oh, fuck it, I knew I couldn't wait. I went to Hannah's mirror and took a quick inventory.

Like Colleen and many other females our age, I had gotten my hair cut into a shag. I thought it would make me look older to my students. I was wearing the same navy and orange plaid dress that I'd bought in Texas and worn on my first day at the school. It was a wraparound with a V-neck, not low-cut, but with my bra (bra—JT'd never seen me in a bra!) there was a hint of cleavage. The jersey hugged my waist and draped across the curve of my butt. I was also wearing the chunky sling-back heels which made my long legs look even longer. I'd painted my fingers and toes a similar rusty red color and wore matching lipstick. A dress, heels, polish, lipstick! JT had never seen any of these things on his barefoot hippie chick before. I decided that my appearance could pass a test. Was this a test?

"You look good, woman," was Hannah's appraisal.

Next, I took a quick measure of my heart. Did I really want to see JT? Of course I did, and especially since he'd been the one to ask. Why hadn't he written me? But he had no idea where I was living. Most importantly, though, what did JT want? I knew what I wanted him to want, but I didn't know whether he wanted it.

"Good luck," said Hannah, giving me a hug for courage.

It had only been a few months since my last drive to JT's dorm, but everything looked subtly different. Of course, that was in winter, and now it was spring. But maybe it was me that had changed.

JT was waiting. Did he know that I would come tonight or was he just hoping? Of all the times I had felt nervous or awkward (although excited) standing at his door, this was the worst; I didn't know what my role was. His eyes widened when he saw me, just like that first night when Hannah, Colleen, and I had shown up with wine and trivia. Then he smiled and waved me in.

Everything was as I remembered. Especially the scent of his room, not dirty or funky but that masculine clean sweat smell. I sat on his bed and closed my eyes, just inhaling it for a moment. I wanted him to touch me.

"How you been?" JT asked. *Where was Colleen? Was she coming later? Would I, should I, still be here?*

"Not bad." I shrugged. "And you?"

"OK. Getting by." Getting by. Did that mean he wasn't happy?

JT gestured toward my outfit. "You look very teacherly, Miss Smith." It sounded like he approved. I lit a cigarette, crossing my legs and letting my skirt ride up a little. (Remember these, JT? Oh, so what—Colleen had nice legs, too.)

"Thank you," I said.

"So, I guess you're wondering why I've called this meeting," he teased. I remained silent, hiding my feelings behind the same mysterious smile I'd given him on that first night.

JT cocked his head. "And I guess I wouldn't be me if I didn't think a song could express it better than I could."

I inhaled and blew a couple of smoke rings through my shiny red lips while he selected a record, put it on the turntable, and gently set the needle down. There was a slight crackle. JT watched me. I watched him back. And then came the opening notes of "Hello Stranger." Barbara Lewis sang about how good it is to see you, and please don't tease me because "I still love you so."

When the song ended, I looked down. I was in shock. JT still loved me so! But where was, "Lynda, I'm sorry"? Why wasn't he saying, "Lynda, I want you back"? How could he not say, "Give him up, and I'll give her up"?

I wasn't hearing what I needed to hear. But I could have said those things to him, too. In spite of everything I'd handled wrongly about Will, my stupid pride over JT going with Colleen was still so hurt, I couldn't see that maybe it took guts for him to invite me here. I just knew that I needed him to fix things without my having to ask.

I looked up, impassive. JT's face, too, was a mask. If he was disappointed in my lack of reaction, he didn't show it. We talked of other, safer things: basketball, Texas, student teaching, Watergate.

I wanted JT to play our old songs. I thought that if he did, he'd have no choice but to take me in his arms. Maybe the right healing words would have come from one of us, or both of us. But he didn't and they didn't. After a while I said, "Well, I guess I'd better be going." I gathered up my things, and he walked me to the door.

"Bye. Thanks for stopping by." JT gave a wan smile.

"See ya. Good luck with everything." I flashed a fake grin.

As I walked away, I wondered if he could hear my heels click smartly down the hall. I wondered how he could not hear the scream echoing in my head, the cries choking in my throat. I wondered if this would be the last time I'd ever see him.

☮

Chapter 30

A MONTH LATER, STUDENT TEACHING WAS OVER. I PACKED up my things at Vicky's and loaded them into the car. Vicky watched with one daughter wrapped around each hip. All four of us had wet eyes.

"We are sure gonna miss you, Lynda," Vicky gave a big sigh and then handed me my favorite top of hers, a navy blue midriff sweater with a zillion tiny buttons.

"Wow, Vicky, thanks. I'm sorry I didn't think of a little something for you." At least I had let the girls rummage through my meager belongings for keepsakes to remember me by.

"That's OK. You really helped me out here. Between the rent and the free babysitting, I'm back on track now." We were both grateful that our union had worked out so well.

During my pit stop at Hannah's, I stepped into a living room full of boxes, some stacked, others still half packed. Hannah was giving up her apartment.

"Whoa, look at this," I said, as I wound my way through the rubble.

Hannah was sweating in the heat, her black hair tied up in a loose ponytail. She brushed some loose strands off her face with the back of one hand.

"I know, isn't it crazy? I can't believe I'm finally leaving this place." She threw an armful of bedding into a box.

I felt melancholy watching Hannah say good-bye to her home, which had been a place of respite for me, too. It signified how much things were changing. We talked about me going to

Philly to Will's parents, her moving in with Jamie. But there wasn't much time to wax sentimental. Already the sky was looking like it might storm, and Will was expecting me.

"Sorry Hannah, this'll have to be a quick stop. I gotta use the bathroom, and then I better get—"

"Hel-lo-o!" a voice called out, interrupting. Not just A voice: THE voice. JT. Oh my god, JT was here! Hannah and I looked at each other, wide-eyed, as he pushed the door open. She shook her head to let me know she had no idea he was coming.

"Well, my, my, my—look who's here," JT said. "I came to say good-bye to Hannah, but I didn't expect to find you, too."

Hannah filled in for my shocked silence. "Where you heading, Jon?"

"Back to DC first. Then hopefully on the road playing basketball. But not till tomorrow. I have a few things to wrap up, and the dorm is closing. I'm spending the night over at Harvey House." He gestured in the general direction of the house, as if it mattered. I wondered if JT was as nervous as I was.

I knew Harvey House. It was an old three-story that had been turned into student quarters. I had visited it once when I briefly dated a guy who had a room there.

"How about you, Hannah?" JT asked.

Hannah gave him her wide Cheshire Cat face. "I've got a man, JT." His mouth made an O, with a fake shocked look. "Yeah. We're moving in together."

"Wow. Congratulations! I'm so happy for you." He crossed the room to give her a hug. I knew he really liked Hannah.

"And you, Lynda?" JT let go and faced me, cocked his head to one side. "What are you doing?"

Oh, dangerous territory, JT. "I'm on my way to Philly," I said. "I'll be looking for a teaching job."

He nodded. "Well, don't let those kids drive you crazy. Hannah, good luck, I'm glad I got to say good-bye. If I ever come back this way for anything, I'll look you up." He paused, then:

"Lynda, would you walk me out to my car?" So smooth, just like that first time when he'd asked me to come back to his room. I gave Hannah a good-bye look. We both knew I wouldn't be coming back.

When we got outside, JT asked, "Can I borrow a little of your time?" I nodded. He ushered me to my Chevy and then slid into a big white car that I hadn't seen before. I followed him to Harvey House just a few blocks away. Fat raindrops were already plopping on the windshield.

All the windows of the house were dark. No one else seemed to be there. JT guided me by the elbow to an upstairs bedroom without turning on any lights. I guessed that he didn't want to break the mood. Maybe in the light one of us would think, what the fuck am I doing? But we didn't need light: the glow of a streetlamp filtered through the leaves of a big maple tree and into a window, bathing everything in gold.

We sat on the edge of the bed. I was still as a statue while JT smoothed my hair, cupped my cheeks. He turned my chin toward the window so that he could study my profile in the streetlight. I could make out the outline of his brow, his nose. I wondered if he were thinking what I was thinking: this really is the last time I'm going to gaze upon this face.

JT ran his hands down my arms and then pressed my palms together inside his—this is the church, this is the steeple. He brought the steeple to his lips and prayed to it with a kiss.

He loosened my top from the waistband of my jeans and lifted it up over my head. I wished I had on Vicky's blue sweater with the tiny fancy buttons. I would have held my breath while he held my gaze, making an art form of slipping each one open. But I hadn't known to wear it; instead, just a plain old tank top came off in his hands. He pulled his own T-shirt off, and his long arms drew me in. My breath caught in my throat from the sudden shock of his bare chest, the slight scratch of his body hair between my breasts. I felt the pulse of a heartbeat, but I couldn't tell whose it was.

We stood and dropped our jeans. JT pulled the sheet back on the bed.

"Which side do you want?" he asked. As if we were going to sleep.

"The bottom," I answered.

He chuckled, and for a second the spell was interrupted. But it didn't take long to be re-cast. His capable warlock hands took me by the shoulders and guided me down. *Double double, toil and trouble; make me yours.*

I knew we would have sex. I also knew this wasn't about sex. My heart had never felt so full, or so empty.

A wind picked up, turning the streetlight into a kaleidoscope of leaf patterns flickering across the walls. Thunder cracked, and lightning suddenly lit up the room, showing only a spare college desk and chair. Shiny linoleum floor. Our jeans in a pile on top of our shoes.

Rain started coming down in sheets. Another flash of light revealed the cotton candy of his hair. His broad, bony shoulders. A sheen of sweat. His eyes, not dancing.

One of the bolts of lightning seemed to strike so close, I wondered if it would come in the window and electrocute the iron bed. For a second, I thought about Will and Colleen, if they'd find out that I had died in JT's arms. A part of me wanted to die right there in JT's arms.

We had no stereo, but there was music of another sort: the rain against the window, the squeaking metal springs of the bed, booms of thunder, the wheels of a passing car on wet pavement. My quickening breath into his mouth, his soft moan against my ear as he came. The tears that rained down my cheeks made no sound at all.

We didn't talk much. What was there to say, if the big words were not going to be spoken?

☮

PART THREE

—————

2014

Chapter 31

FORTY-ONE YEARS LATER, A WILDFIRE WAS RAGING THROUGH the Southern California foothills. Having lived by these hills for fourteen years, I'd survived many near misses and one conflagration that burned into my front yard. I'd done a lot to protect important belongings. But I hadn't taken special care with the bins of mementos stashed in my garage. The bag of JT's letters should be in one of them. But what if it wasn't? Years of moving to new apartments and houses meant that things got lost sometimes.

When I found them, I was overcome. I wanted to sit and read them all in order, pull each one out of its envelope, scotch-taped together all those years ago, the ink beginning to smear under the tape. I wanted to consume each letter and relive that entire year of him. But I didn't want a fire to consume me, so I had to continue preparing to evacuate. As I worked, emptying my safe, packing the car with the contents and the bins, I made two promises to myself: I would have JT's letters digitized so I could never truly lose them, and I'd start writing a book about the year I spent loving him. In truth, it was much longer than a year. In truth, my love for JT had never ended.

Soon, the big wildfire was contained—this time. I began the process of keeping both those vows. I wrote the first chapter of this book. And I scanned JT's letters onto a flash drive.

Then something arrived in the mail that caused me to conceive one more promise to myself:

> 🙢
>
> *You are cordially invited to the*
> *Class of 1969*
>
> 45TH HIGH SCHOOL REUNION
>
> *June 21, 2014*
>
> BEAUTIFUL HOTEL BETHLEHEM
>
> *Bethlehem, Pennsylvania*

I would be going to the East Coast. JT was in DC. I knew I would try to see him one last time.

♡

I already had the date in my calendar. Colleen and I had remained friends; she lived in our hometown and always gave me plenty of notice. Our high school class held a reunion every five years, and I'd never missed one. In the past, I'd always stayed with Colleen. This year I had reason to consider a hotel.

Miraculously, Colleen and I had survived the betrayal over JT. In fact, she and I had lasted decades longer than she and JT, decades longer than Will and I.

Will and I had moved to Philly and gotten married. I

couldn't help but remember Colleen's prediction to JT: Lynda's going to marry Will and leave you behind. She was right about the marriage. But I never would have married Will if JT and I had lasted. Will was a good man, but I knew from the first day of marriage to him that I shouldn't have done it. I did it for him, not for myself, which was a terrible reason considering that JT still owned my heart.

I spent too many nights (after Will had gone to sleep) crying, taping JT's ripped-up letters and pictures back together, and wondering how things had gotten so fucked up. I was teaching, junior high reading which was not what I trained for, and not enjoying that either. Something had to change, but what?

After Will and I visited my early childhood city of Los Angeles, I knew I wanted to move back there. Besides my other sources of unhappiness, I'd never grown to love the rain and snow and humidity of the East Coast. I wanted California sun. That's how I eventually came to leave the marriage. I told Will I wanted to move and asked him to come with me, but he said no.

"That was a vacation, not our real life, Kitten," he said.

"But that's the point. I want it to be my real life," I told him.

So, I ended up moving and within a year I'd gotten a divorce. I knew Will had a rough few years after the breakup, but I still believed I had done the right thing. He deserved real love just like I did. He went on to marry again and have kids and apparently live a fulfilling life.

After cruise ship training, Colleen had moved to Baltimore to work out of the port and be closer to Jonathan in DC. We had slowly resumed writing and talking without ever bringing up what had happened with him. She was still seeing him, and it was painful to listen to her talk about her and JT. I didn't tell her that. I didn't say so many things. Eventually she told me that they broke up because JT was hardly coming around to see her anymore. I didn't hate hearing that.

Once I'd even had an opportunity for revenge. After JT and she broke up, Colleen fell for a Baltimore attorney.

"Lynda, I am so crazy about this Rich," she told me over the phone. "He's tall, dark, and handsome. Smart and funny. Beautiful manners, too."

"Wow," I said, with just a drop of sarcasm, "he sounds a lot like JT. You were crazy about him, too, right?"

She was silent, but only for a second. "Well, JT. You know what the problem was there. I hated the way he always talked in circles. And all those songs—what the hell was he trying to say?"

That made me go silent. I had so loved JT's sweet and sexy word play, how he spoke to me through music. Did I hate *anything* about him? Only that he had ever fucked her.

She wanted a favor: when Rich came to Philly on business, would I have dinner with him and see if I could find out how he felt about her? Sure, I said, why not.

Though not my type, Rich was quite charming. I tried to bring Colleen into the conversation, but, "Yeah, she's a nice girl," was all he'd say. After a couple of cocktails, the talk became more intimate. He put his elbows on the table and rested his chin on his fists.

"You know what I really want, Lynda?" he asked in a wistful tone.

"No, Rich," I said with an indulgent smile, "what do you really want?"

"I want to fall crazy, madly in love with a woman who is crazy, madly in love with me."

Rich's eyes met mine over the top of my glass. I had two simultaneous realizations: Colleen was not going to be that woman, and now Rich was flirting with me.

I knew I could take him from her, at least for now.

But I didn't want this man, and revenge wouldn't bring back what I'd lost. At my door I thanked him with a hug. I told Colleen that I had a nice evening but couldn't really get any information out of Rich.

She and I only ever had one fight about JT. We were packing her up to move to California (she had fallen in love—again—and moved there even before me). Still unhappily married to Will, and after sharing a bottle of wine, I'd let slip my frustration over her interfering between me and JT, and for what? Because now she hadn't even ended up with him. It devolved into yelling, then crying, and finally she apologized for the first and only time.

"I know I hurt you," Colleen wailed. "I'm sorry! But I can promise you, it will never happen again."

And "it" never did happen again, with me.

♡

So, in the late '70s Colleen and I both moved to Southern California. She was heading west to be with a new man she'd met on a cruise, I was trying to put my marriage to Will behind me. Then, after a few years, Colleen returned home to Bethlehem—again for a man—while I stayed in California. We both went to graduate school and tried a variety of careers before ending up in some form of education. We both found love again and lost it more than once. Through visits, phone calls, letters, and eventually email, Colleen and I saw each other through life's ups and downs. These included marriage and divorce for both of us, an

abusive relationship with a broken nose for her, a cheating relationship with broken trust for me, exhausting back-breaking
single parenthood for her, and crushing, heart-breaking infertil-
ity for me. I spent three weeks in Pennsylvania so I could be
there to coach her through the birth of her second child. She was
indispensable to me when I returned there to face the deaths of
my parents.

Every friend old and new who heard the story of me, JT, and
Colleen wondered how I could remain close to her. It was hard
to explain, and sometimes I even wondered myself. Was I too
forgiving? Or like Colleen used to say, too "placid"? I'd tried to
understand how her fiancé Kenneth breaking up with her must
have devastated her self-esteem. She had meant so much to me
for so long that one mistake—however huge, and granted, it was
huge—wasn't enough to give up on her. Over several decades,
we'd seen each other through so much.

And every five years, we went to the reunion together.
Sometimes I had a date, sometimes she did. Either way, I stayed
at her house and looked forward to our late-night talks. She'd
light a candle on the kitchen table and I'd pour juice glasses of
vodka on ice. We'd lean forward on our elbows, legs crossed or
wrapped around the spindly chair legs, just like high school girls.

We'd go over all the latest about our men (or lack thereof),
her kids and their dads, our parents when they were still alive,
my little sis who had grown up and followed her big sis to LA
(and had not become a racist during her year in Texas).

"Show me your dress," I'd say, and we'd hop up and head into
her bedroom.

Or "Let's look at the yearbook," she'd suggest, and we'd pore
over the funny hairstyles and nerdy glasses from our high school
days.

She knew she could call me anytime late at night to cry over a breakup or unload about the constant fatigue of parenting. I knew that the copious letters, and later emails, that I wrote would be replied to, with no detail of my life too small to comment on. Maybe I didn't entirely forgive Colleen, but I clung to the fact that she'd saved me in high school and, with that one exception of JT, had been there for me more than anyone else had.

We remained best friends.

♡

Now in 2014, with a trip to Pennsylvania coming up, I had two tasks. The first was to find out if JT would agree to meet me. Following my move to California I had written to him, and from then on we'd stayed in touch. Sometimes a few years went by in between, but we always had an address, a phone number, and eventually an email to contact. Our conversations tended toward the superficial, mostly information about work or sharing music, with occasional reminiscing.

I checked our email history. Our last exchange had been in 2012, two years prior. JT didn't always reach out first, but that time he had, and I'd gotten teary when I saw the subject: "Hello Like Before." He'd included a link to a YouTube video of that song, and I guessed this now took the place of JT's formerly copious lyrics. The poignant words and Bill Withers's melancholy voice, reminiscing about a lost young love, were perfect for our situation.

Now I emailed JT. I told him about my plan to visit the East Coast, and how I hoped he would understand my desire to lay eyes on him. Distance and age meant that maybe it would be for the last time.

To my surprise, because he didn't always answer right away either, he emailed me right back:

Subject: *You Don't Know Me*

My heart sank a little. What did he mean by that? I knew it was a song title, but I didn't know the lyrics. I thought maybe he meant that, with so many years under the bridge, there might not be very much that we shared anymore. Inside was another You-Tube link. I clicked on it and heard Ray Charles's soulful voice telling me he couldn't speak because his heart was beating so.

His wasn't the only heart beating faster. Because his words told me he was a friend who had loved me secretly all these years.

Wow. I'd feared that he might not want to meet, and now he'd come out with this. Was it true? I didn't know. But I did know that he also said yes. Yes let's meet, yes keep me posted about your plans:

I would be thrilled to see your beautiful face one more time.

Just like that, it was going to happen. I was going to see JT! And I wasn't exaggerating when I said that it might be our last. Four decades of living had gone by. A couple of my friends had already died. Nothing was promised.

... thrilled ... your beautiful face ...

With that, I booked my flight in and out of DC and a hotel room for the first and last nights. In between I would drive to Pennsylvania and stay three days, which would include the re-union activities. I pictured JT and me only meeting for dinner but didn't want our visit to be rushed. My fantasy was that he would agree to dinner both of the days I'd be there. And he said yes.

I didn't tell Colleen about the plan to see Jon. For once I wanted something that was only mine.

My next task, though, was to decide whether to stay with her during the course of the reunion. I always had. We'd weathered JT and decades of friendship, and for most of our relationship I'd been able to count on her for support and encouragement.

But about ten years before our 45th reunion, I'd started to notice some negativity creeping in.

It was subtle at first, little digs about this or that. How I drank too much, even though she'd been a daily pot smoker for many years. How my men were "too feminine," even though most of them were athletic. Diet was her favorite obsession, so she thought I should sacrifice to stay slim the way she did, but I knew she also had the metabolism of a hummingbird. Criticism and its companion advice had come to seem like a way for her to feel superior. When I called her on it, she would only admit that, yes, she could be too critical.

"Too critical"? For most of our lives, people had said that Colleen was "crazy." Usually they were referring to the way she couldn't sit still, pushed herself into the center of attention, and said provocative things to get laughs or get laid: "That Colleen is crazy!" But there had been a few more serious incidents over the years when I had worried about her. Once when she was unhappily married and attempted to reconcile with her old Baltimore flame, Rich, the attorney, he actually called me to say that he was concerned about her, too.

But now, as I considered whether to book a hotel or stay at her house, her bouts of "crazy" faded into the background. She was responsible about work, paid her bills, and had raised happy, accomplished kids. She was pretty normal most of the time, I decided.

I remembered the morning coffees, evening nightcaps, and

many stories we had shared over her cozy kitchen table. I decided to stay with Colleen.

Chapter 32

AFTER JT SAID YES TO MEETING AND TOLD ME—BY WAY of Ray Charles—that he was the one who dreamt of me at night, I emailed back (at night):

I'm speechless.

Really? I'm surprised you're not more sure of yourself with me.

I'm so glad you're going to indulge my wish for two days. It's not required; I'm not an extortionist. ☺

I am so happy to give you what you want. But could you be an exhibitionist? ☺

What fun to wake up to his latest in our playful, sexy banter. But he had promised me something:

Hey, where's that picture from the awards dinner that you said you'd send?

I changed my mind. Me and a bunch of other old dinosaurs? You might be attracted.

To what? Other old dinosaurs? Believe me, you would always rise to the top like cream.

Good response. But I still might be just a wee bit possessive of you.

That's kind of charming.

Charming, maybe; silly, absolutely.

I enjoyed his obvious attraction to me. But it did weigh on my mind a bit that I was no longer the fit young girl he'd once known:

As far as meeting, I should warn you, I'm not exactly the slim sylph I used to be.

You obviously don't remember how absolutely lovely that clever, sexy, creative little mind of yours is.

Whoa!

Yeah, and I have to admit I'm only about two thirds as manly as I was way back when.

How did you calculate that two thirds?

Combination of fantasy and nightmare.

I drank it up like fresh spring water. But I didn't want to overdo things:

I hope I'm not writing too much, I don't want to be in trouble before I even see you.

Suavecito, don't you know that I could never punish you, ever, for anything?

Suavecito—of course I loved that. And his generosity of spirit toward me. Well, except for that time when I had another man, and I didn't end things with that other man, and JT had finally had enough and fucked my best friend. Retaliation, even he had said so. I hadn't been able to *suave* that one away. But that was the past and this was the present and I was on my way to see JT one more time.

♡

In DC, I drove my rental car to the hotel. The first thing I did after checking in was to turn the A/C to high. Whew, how did people on the East Coast ever have good hair days? I freshened up and started to think about what to wear.

With that one sentence about how "absolutely lovely that clever, sexy, creative little mind" of mine was, JT had allayed the nervousness I felt about showing up in my sixty-two-year-old skin. Yet I still wanted to remind him of the girl I'd been. I picked out a pair of skinny jeans; a "retro" top, diaphanous with a lacy camisole visible underneath, and sandals. I still colored my hair brown and wore it long. Although I had some good jewelry, my favorite was a silver peace sign dangling from a colored ribbon, plus hoop earrings. And now I wore glasses.

We'd agreed to meet in the cocktail lounge downstairs. I got there a little early and sat at the bar. Was I nervous? Yes. But I didn't expect much—a nice dinner, maybe some wine, whatever reminiscences came up.

JT was a few minutes late. And then I caught the eyes of a tall man looking at me from the wall of mirror along the bar. He was standing behind me, in shadow. He looked different, but I knew it was him. How long had he been there?

The years had not been totally kind to JT's looks, either. His beautiful 'fro was gone. What little hair he had left he wore in a short gray fringe. And he was missing the beard and moustache I'd always loved. He'd already told me he didn't play basketball anymore, and I could see that his muscle tone wasn't what it once was. But he was tall and lean, dressed in a nice short-sleeved shirt over slacks and sandals. He wore glasses, too.

I turned my barstool around and gave JT the big genuine smile of my heart that he deserved.

"Have you been waiting long?" he asked.

"No. Have you been watching long?" I countered. He grinned, stepped in to give me a hug, and didn't let go.

His hard chest. His scent. His hands on me.

"Should we move to a table?" he suggested. We walked to a corner booth near the back. It was a quarter-moon booth, and without hesitation, we both slid in close to the middle. A waiter brought menus.

"Hmmm, would you like some wine?" JT asked. Yes, I certainly would.

"I don't drink much," he added. "Is there anything you'd recommend?"

We conferred over the selections and ordered two different reds to compare. We did the same with dinner, a pasta and a salad to share. I knew I didn't want to be overstuffed . . . just in case . . . and I wondered if he had the same thought.

"So, our first black president," I said. "Did you ever think we'd see it? Are you thrilled?"

"Yes," he smiled. "But no, too," his smile faded. "I think there's so much more he could be doing for black folks."

"I know what you mean," I said. "Maybe he's just trying to keep from being murdered." That had been my fear upon Obama's election—that he would be assassinated. Knowing about JT's work for racial justice, I figured he was thinking of all the other black men and women who had been murdered.

"Here's to surviving," he said and we clinked glasses. We knew bits and pieces of each other's history and we recapped some things.

"Remember I bounced around after college," JT said, "trying to figure out what I wanted to do." I remembered. Something similar had happened to me. But the bulk of his work had been his own business as a researcher for non-profit justice organizations.

"I've been lucky," he mused. "I've been to almost every state."

I wondered how many times he had come to Los Angeles and not called me. But then, I hadn't called him when I was on the East Coast, either. Our calls were sporadic and always from a safe 3000-mile distance. Things had changed for him, though, since the recession. There was little money for either non-profits or justice, and his business folded. For the few available jobs, most employers were not interested in hiring a sixty-two-year-old black man. He was deeply depressed about all of this, even though none of it was his fault.

"But let's talk about you," JT said. It was obvious he wanted to change the subject. I told him that I taught health and human sexuality in a college biology department and was only a year or two away from retiring.

He frowned when I told him that I'd started the book. "I really value my privacy," he said. But he didn't ask me not to write it.

He did stop me when I started to say something about Colleen. "I don't want to talk about her," JT said. "I can't even stand to hear both your names in the same sentence." Now *that* was something I wanted to ask more about. But he made clear that it was off limits.

We were eating from the same plates and sipping from the same glasses as easily as if we'd done it all our lives. It felt so intimate, the way JT's arm brushed mine, the feel of his thigh against my thigh. Our lips were inches apart as we savored the flavors and conversation.

When our meal was done, we digested in a comfortable silence. But my mind wondered, now what? Is he just going to say goodnight and go?

"Did you bring your computer?" JT asked. Sure.

"Why don't we go listen to some music then?"

JT, so smooth, so easy, still my *suavecito*, too. That sounded so good to me.

♡

At the desk in my room, JT brought up YouTube on my laptop. "Remember this?" he asked and clicked on a song. He leaned back in the chair, man-style, hands laced behind his head, legs spread. I sat on the edge of the bed and tried not to stare at every inch of him.

JT: Al Green, "Look what you done for me . . ." Oh, did I remember.

We took turns, just like the first night I'd gone to his room.

Me: Malo, "I never met a girl like you . . ."

"Yeah," he said, "I'd have to say '*Suavecito*' was 'our song.'"

I knew he'd never married, but I didn't know why. "Did you know I had a ten-year relationship?" he asked. I shook my head no. "Yeah, five good years and five bad ones."

I wanted to ask more. What made the five good? What made the other five bad? He said "had," so that implied it was over, but was it? How long ago? And why hadn't he married her? Given his privacy issues, I didn't want to spook him more than I already had.

After a while he said, "Let's lie down," and we stretched out in the middle of the king bed. He pulled me close to him, looked into my eyes, and kissed me.

"Was I a good kisser, back in the day?" JT asked, a little shyly, when the kiss ended.

"Oh, yeah." We kept kissing, and pretty soon our clothes were coming off. My mind flowed back and forth between those long-ago nights in his bed and this night in this bed—so different, yet somehow so much the same.

After making love—and yes, I could call it that, he was JT, my first love, not some hookup—we ended up with me cocooned in his arms, until, like the older people we'd become, we gravitated to our own sides. He slept quietly. From time to time I felt his hand reach for me as if to make certain I was still there. Or I rolled over and softly laid my cheek against his back.

I barely slept. The room was hot, and I was thirsty and keyed up—heart awash with emotions, body lethargic from the long, tiring day. I wanted to drink water and turn up the A/C again, but I was afraid that if I stirred too much, he might get up and leave me. I wasn't ready to have him get up and leave me.

In the morning we ordered room service. As normal as it was, staying in a hotel and ordering room service was something JT and I had never had the chance to do. Many of the hotel staff were black, and an African-American man brought our food. I wondered what he thought of us, a black man in his boxers and a white woman in her nightgown, or whether he thought anything at all. He probably saw all manner of guests, but it seemed to me that mixed race couples were still not all that commonplace.

We nibbled, while JT sat at the desk and I reclined on the bed.

"There have been a few songs through the years that made me think of you," he said. He searched for one on YouTube.

The song started off, lazy and soulful, with a deep voice speaking to background music. It was a poem to his lady, telling her how she, barefoot in a sundress, was all that he would need.

As the song wound on, full of sensuality and metaphor, JT got out of his chair and ambled over to my side of the bed. He murmured along with the words that he obviously knew well, asking nature to send a breeze to lift that dress so gently away from my thighs.

JT slipped two long fingers under the lace edge of my chemise. He pushed the fabric higher to expose more and more of my legs. His eyes never left my eyes. And I was mesmerized.

Oh, my fucking god. Older, balding, and bespectacled, this man was still so sweetly, powerfully attractive to me. So, "Sundress," this spoken word piece by Coco Brown and the Phat Cat Players, recorded in 2000, had reminded him of me? Had he been in or out of his ten-year relationship at the time? And where was I in 2000? Married (again), soon to be divorced (again), and buying the house in the foothills where the threat of fire had finally sent me in search of JT's letters. Fire igniting fire.

He went back to the desk. "Here's another one," he said, and clicked. It was Arthur Prysock, "This Is My Beloved," another spoken word piece I had never heard before. Yet it was from 1968. Why didn't we know it back in the day? JT sat on the edge of the bed and watched me listen from the first solemn note, about hate that is legislated and time that is slipping away, and what is left to us besides love?

The violins settled over us like grace. I felt like I'd just heard the truest call to arms my rebel heart had ever known. I needed love more than a drink. I needed his love. And my eyes, like no other eyes, worshipped him. JT.

"You know what?" he said after the last note sounded, his voice wistful, his finger still trailing lightly on my skin. "I don't think I've ever loved anyone as much as I loved you."

☮

Chapter 33

"IT'S TIME TO GET YOU ON THE ROAD," JT SAID. "AND FOR me to get back to my job search."

If it were up to me, I might never have left. But that was not the deal we'd made. And someone else was expecting me: Colleen.

As I drove, I couldn't help but reflect on the past.

Throughout the years I had questioned a lot of it. Like what had sent me into the arms of not one, but two, black men all those years ago when most of my friends didn't go there. My mom knew about only one of them, Will, and she had seemed to think my lack of a true father was "to blame." That she perceived my loving a black man as a bad thing made no sense to me then and made no sense to me now.

Various friends through the years had asked whether I might have been rebelling. It was true that I hadn't wanted to be trapped in the same narrow world view as my parents. Was I trying to hurt them? I didn't believe that I'd wanted to hurt them any more than when I'd used drugs or been cavalier about school. I wanted to be self-determining, to write my own story in a time when that wasn't a common script for a woman. It was all about me trying to find my way, an explorer without a map.

What bothered me about the question of rebellion, though, was that it too implied there was something wrong with dating outside my ethnic group. As if Will and JT were not people but just an experiment. I knew better. I had true feelings for both of them. Yeah, maybe I hadn't really been in love with Will, but I'd thought I was. If my family's strong reaction hadn't pushed me even further under his wing, maybe we would have just run our course and broken up early like so many young couples do, leaving me free for JT. My parents' hate drove me to feel I had to say, "I love Will." Otherwise, it would just seem like gratuitous sex with a black man, and I knew it wasn't that. I admired Will's intelligence, work ethic, and integrity, and I thought that was enough. It wasn't, and what was missing was what I found in JT. The timing sucked, and I didn't have the tools to handle it.

If there was anything shallow about my interest in JT, it could have been his good looks and notoriety. But from the first night I'd also gotten to know his heart, and deeply. I could feel that his connected with mine in a mysterious way. That's what had really made me fall in love and still love him forty years later. So why, why, why had I/he/we fucked it all up?

I genuinely hadn't wanted to hurt Will. I'd seen where he'd come from, up close. He deserved only good things, and I'd intended to create that life with him. After my near miss with Curtis and his gangbang, Will's protectiveness had felt good to me.

And in spite of my strong attraction to JT, I'd been uneasy about his reluctance to say "I love you," his periodic urge to just cut and run. As time went on, I found out that my fork in the road was one faced by many women and even other species, whether to choose the more exciting mate who is statistically more likely to leave me or the solid, steady man who doesn't make my heart race.

A cowardly part of me had been frightened of ending up alone. But why? JT's admission now, that I was the woman he'd loved, was mirrored in all those torn up, taped up letters. Yet as an insecure young woman, I'd paid more attention to his reticence than to his declarations. If I'd had more confidence, in myself and my ability to keep the interest of a man like JT, maybe that reluctance on his part wouldn't have loomed so large. And who could blame him for sometimes holding back, considering that I had another man?

As much as I had wanted to blame JT and Colleen for their part in hurting me, it was a sobering thought to realize that the root cause was mine—my inability to break up with Will.

As I matured, I spent time in counseling to examine my early history with men—a deserting father, a disinterested stepfather, and the grandfather who'd loved me but had turned his back on me. I'd finally come to realize that I had serious abandonment issues, issues that had allowed me to languish in limbo while Colleen moved in.

Sometimes, in moments of despair, I'd even wondered miserably if both men would have been better off had they never met me. Maybe Will would have gone to England and stayed on in London with Brenda, as she'd wanted. Maybe JT would have married his ten-year-relationship, in year five before it turned bad. Was she black or white, and did it matter? Would a black woman have handled my situation differently—maybe never gone behind Will's back in the first place or more readily left him for Jonathan instead of letting things drag on? Probably some women—black or white, wiser than I—would have made such choices. But in those early talks with my black girlfriend Linda, I saw that she was just as confused about her life as I was about mine.

Science teaches now that there's no such thing as race, that we're all just part of the species Homo sapiens. I saw that race as we knew it then played only a small part in the early triangle that had so impacted my life, and it was almost totally in the form of outside pressures. I hadn't been with Will and JT because they were black, and I hadn't left them because they were black; I had loved them for the men they were.

JT's and mine was a true love story, and what ended it was what ends love for many young people: confusion, fear, hurt feelings, infidelity, and foolish pride. I thought, if only there had been a parents' guidebook for teaching kids how to deal with those things. If there was, it must have been published too late for me.

♡

As I drove to Pennsylvania, and away from JT, I started getting texts from him that made me wonder if it really was too late:

> Where are you? I feel like I need to watch over you when you're in my town.

> Don't worry, I am safely on my way.

> Wow, that was such a nice evening.
> I felt like I just couldn't stop talking.
> But I've been waiting so long.

> And I'm still coming back for one more! 😊

It was all I could do not to turn the car around. A bit later, my phone dinged again:

> I was so excited about coming that I forgot to pack my blood pressure medication. That's not good!

> Oh no. So is your BP OK?

Fine for now. Maybe that new wine
and fitness program we tried out. 😜

And a bit later, another ding:

I haven't heard back about that
job interview.

Did you know that being out of work lowers a
man's testosterone level, but having sex raises
it and makes him more successful at work?

That's perfect! I think my star is rising!

Yes, I bet you'll have a job in a minute.

And finally, JT's last message of the day:

What in hell brought you back to me?

Dealing with my abandonment issues.

Hold up, I thought it was your reunion.

Secondary, I'm sure.

You are so adorable.

Oh my god. He thought I was so adorable. The only woman
he ever loved. I didn't turn the car around, but I sure found it
hard to stop smiling.

♡

Colleen wouldn't be home from work until around nine that
night, so I was in no rush to get to her house. I stopped for a late

lunch and found a liquor store to buy a hostess offering for her. Then I looked forward to some quiet time in her house. I needed to center my thoughts and feelings about JT before she came flying in like a human tornado.

The liquor I'd picked was a slightly pricey potato vodka called Boyd & Blair, made in Pennsylvania. In the cupboard where she usually kept her vodka was a half-empty bottle of Stoli. Good, I'd drink that and the gift bottle would be all hers. Then I saw an empty bottle of Boyd & Blair in her trash. I poured a little Stoli and sat down to wait for her.

The door flew open. "Oh my god, girl, you made it!" Colleen flung down her purse and keys and swooped me up in a quick hug. "How was your flight?" She knew I didn't like to fly. She just didn't know that I'd actually flown the day before.

"Good. I just chilled out with my Kindle." Which had been true—the day before. I felt no guilt about keeping the real story to myself.

I got out the bottle of vodka I'd bought.

"Boyd & Blair?" Colleen gave me a quizzical look. "That's my favorite brand. How did you know?"

"It was just chance. And then when I saw an empty in your trash, I didn't know if it was because you liked it or hated it and threw it out."

"I love it," she said. "How strange that you picked this. But thanks." She opened the bottle. "Want to try it?"

She poured a little for me and more for her. We clinked glasses: "Here's to a great reunion!"

"Yum, that is good," I said, "but you drink it. I'll have the Stoli."

We started catching up on news and then going over details of the reunion. There were always two parties—an informal gathering at a bar on Friday and a fancier dinner with dancing at a hotel on Saturday.

In the midst of our girl talk, Colleen gave me a sly, sideways glance. "Soooo. Are you gonna wear that dress that I've seen six times on Facebook?"

Wow. There it was, that thing that had been happening more and more in recent years. The sly tone, the sidelong look, the words that sounded like a dig. Was it competitiveness or what? Should I call her on it? I didn't want to start our visit on a confrontational note, and really, how important was a dress?

"Maybe I will," I said. "Wanna see?" When I showed her the dress I was planning to wear, she said, "No, I've never seen that one before." Was it my imagination or did she sound disappointed?

Still, I didn't like the feeling of being so scrutinized. I didn't like the way she watched my alcohol intake like a probation officer, either. I decided to drink lightly at her house.

It didn't stop there. The next morning over coffee Colleen said, "Soooo . . ." *Uh oh.*

"How much do you weigh these days? I bet I could guess your weight within three pounds." There was that same sly tone and appraising sideways look.

"Why would you want to do that?" I asked.

"Ohhhh . . ." she trailed off. I knew her vagueness meant she either didn't want to answer or was trying to figure out how to spin it. "I'm just curious about people's weights. I'm always guessing what people weigh." She chuckled. "I tell everyone I should have a job guessing weights in the circus."

In over forty years of friendship, I'd never heard her guess anyone's weight or say that she belonged in a circus.

"I'm really not interested in talking about my weight,

Colleen." I made a mental note to eat and drink more like I did at home rather than how I indulged when I was on vacation, because I just didn't want to hear any more shit. So much for being on holiday. And now she was off work until I left. I was beginning to wish I'd booked a hotel for my whole stay instead of just the one night of the reunion.

After our coffee, she was headed to the farmers' market. "You don't have to go," she said. She knew I wanted to take a walk before the day got too hot. "But what should I get? I don't have salad, do you want some?" Sure. I offered to contribute, but she refused.

I put on my sneakers and started out around the neighborhood. Good old hometown. Her place was more rural than where we'd lived as teenagers, and I admired the lush foliage that helped compensate for all the rain and humidity. But I lived in California because I preferred to skip the rain and humidity. I came to a little stone bridge across a stream, sat down on the edge, and dangled my feet. The air felt a bit cooler there, and the trickling water sounded like nature's bells. A man on a tractor mower rode around on the property. He smiled and waved. I waved back.

I took out my phone and checked messages. There was one from JT:

> It's probably a good idea if I don't text or email much. I want you to enjoy your reunion and your friends.

> No, please! Things here are not so good. Hearing from you is a bright spot in my day. And shouldn't I be in charge of what's in my best interest?

> Touché. OK, I'm on the case. Consider this
> the first of an at least daily barrage.
>
>> Barrage away! 😊

Oh, thank god. And a bit later, another:

> Ready for the countdown? 4, 3 . . .
>
>> You're so good at math Dr. Thomas. But I
>> thought you studied psychology.
>
> I did. I just want to impress you with my
> myriad skills.
>
>> I'm always impressed by you.
>
> Honest? I wonder how my life might have
> gone if I'd realized.

How could he not have realized? Probably because I'd done nothing instead of choosing him. Yes, JT, just imagine how your life would have turned out. Because I was wondering the same thing about mine.

♡

When Colleen got back, she started preparing lunch—homemade pea soup, one of my favorites. She refused any help. "Tell me about your walk," she said.

"There isn't much to tell. It's so pretty and green, but I'm not used to the humidity anymore. I sat on this little bridge over a stream."

"Well, I hope you realize you were trespassing. That's private property." To me it was dubious whether the bridge, which was part of the road, was "private property." Maybe, maybe not; I wasn't a surveyor. But I didn't feel like arguing the point. "The owner saw me," I said. "He waved, so I'm sure it was OK."

The soup was delicious. She had two bowls. I had one bowl and a side salad. She wouldn't let me help clean up, either.

That afternoon we rested and then got ready for the informal get-together at the bar. We went separately.

"I won't drink as much as you, and I'll probably go home early," Colleen said. She was right on there. I might curtail my celebrating at her house, but I saw no reason to do it elsewhere.

I knew Sharon would come, and I was really looking forward to seeing her. Sharon who had first started partying outside Philly with me, who had intercepted JT's summer letters, and who had surprised him with my "I love you" at the department store opening all those years ago. She and I had lost touch for some years and later reconnected. Her first marriage hadn't lasted, but she'd married again, moved to Lancaster in the Pennsylvania Dutch area, and she and her husband had visited me in California a couple times. I planned to spend one night at her place before going back to JT.

Sharon and I sat in the bar having our first drink as Colleen flitted around like she always did.

"So how are things at Colleen's?" Sharon asked. She knew about the difficulties we'd had in recent years. I told her about the snide dress comment and the weight conversation.

"I should have gotten a hotel room or stayed with you," I concluded regretfully.

"You're always welcome," Sharon said with a big smile, and we clinked glasses. I felt sad that I'd spent so much time with Colleen over the years and so little with Sharon. It had been easier to stay in Bethlehem when my parents were still alive. But it was also my mindset that Colleen was my "best friend." Now I felt that designation was about to change; it seemed that it already had.

Sharon caught me up on her life. I told her about my night with JT, quietly in between pit stops from Colleen.

Colleen rushed up and pretended to swoon. "I heard Dell is gonna come tomorrow! Oh, I've always had it bad for that guy."

And a bit later: "Did you gals look at the photo table? There's a good one of me when I was in the school play."

Then Colleen would dash off while Sharon and I continued. "So, what do you think is gonna happen with JT?" Sharon asked.

"I don't know," I said. "But no matter what, I'm just grateful that I got the answer to my biggest question all these years, how he really felt about me." I shared his mind-blowing comment about my being the only woman he had ever loved. "And I still get to see him one more time," I grinned. She raised her glass again.

The next morning, I woke to a text from JT:

> BP is up. I may need to hear more of
> our music, plus that wine and fitness program.

> Is it at least within a normal range?

> That's funny! Like it's ever going to be
> normal with you around.

And a little bit later:

> Like I said, what brought you to me?

> The universe called me, just like
> that first time.

> Damn, apparently the universe is more
> in tune with me than I ever realized. ❤

It was reunion day. Soon I got a text from my old high school friend Jim. "Looks like I can meet you for a drink in the hotel bar at 6," it said. Even though I stayed with Colleen, on the night of the reunion I usually slept at the hotel. I'd go there in the afternoon to get ready, giving Colleen and me a break from each other, which I needed more than ever this year.

Jim and I had gotten to be friends as high school seniors. We were both up for the Poetry Award that I'd been happy to win, but I'd always thought that he was the more deserving poet. He had given up his counterculture lifestyle to raise kids but was wicked smart and still a liberal thinker. We'd stayed in touch over the years.

Without meaning any disrespect to his wife, I liked it when he came to the reunions alone. He'd sit with me, we'd dance, and sometimes we'd grab a private drink before the event. This year his wife had opted to stay home.

But first I still had to lunch with Colleen. While she cooked, I wrote in my journal at the kitchen table. I felt like discouraging conversation with her. Besides, she wouldn't let me do anything but fix my salad. She made rice and black beans.

"I like to keep busy," she said. "Just talk to me." She seemed to believe that her constant motion was a discipline she practiced to keep her weight in check, but I knew it wasn't a choice; she just couldn't sit still.

"Okayyyy . . ." I said. "What do you want to talk about?" In years past our conversations had flowed. Now I felt guarded.

"Well, having you here has made me think about Jon Thomas."

Whoa! What the fuck? For a minute I wondered, did she see my phone? Read my journal? But I knew that whatever her faults, she wasn't a snoop.

"Did I ever tell you about the last time I saw him?" she asked.

I knew she and JT had met up about five years before. Because of his scoring records, JT's college had invited him to an awards banquet at which they'd "retired his jersey." It meant that his basketball shirt would be displayed and the number wouldn't be used again. Colleen had sent me an article about him that appeared in the paper afterward and said they'd had lunch or a drink or something.

In the newspaper picture, his hair was thinning, but he still sported a graying goatee and the most gorgeous smile I'd ever seen. The article called him "a 6'9" player in a 6'2" body" and raved about his basketball skills and stats. As usual, he gave credit to the whole team.

Now it didn't surprise me if my presence had brought him back into Colleen's mind. Unlike me, she wasn't one to spend time analyzing the past. Aside from that visit when he'd come to collect his award, I doubted if Colleen had thought much about Jon Thomas since 1975. "On to the next one!" was usually her motto.

"Yeah, you told me," was all I said. I really didn't want to encourage her.

"I'll tell you what, though," she continued. She buzzed around the stove, stirring beans, checking rice. "He sure did look goony. Goony, goony, goony." She shook her head, as if trying to shake the image away.

"What do you mean?" I didn't want to hear her talk about him, but now I had to ask.

"Oh, his face was just so goony. He's not handsome anymore." Yes, we'd all changed, including her. But the picture in the article she'd sent had still looked good. I thought about telling her how handsome his face had been lying next to mine on a pillow two nights before.

"And you know how he is, the way he talks in circles, always so ambivalent about things. That boy needs some serious help." I thought about revealing the words he'd said in our hotel room: "I've never loved anyone the way I loved you." Nope, no ambivalence there.

"His hands, though?" Colleen added, getting down plates, pouring iced tea. "Those are the one thing that haven't changed. He still has the most beautiful hands." I closed my eyes and silently agreed. I could describe the way those hands had looked searching the keyboard for our songs, how they had felt playing over my body.

But all I said back to her was, "Hmmmm."

Thank goodness I had my journal to scribble in, and soon I would escape to the hotel.

After I'd checked in, bathed, and dressed, Jim texted that he was in the bar. We ordered cocktails and chatted about the directions our lives had taken since we'd last met.

In the dining room, we sat together at a table that included Sharon and her husband, Gerry, and Colleen and one of her girlfriends. The cocktails flowed, the traditional chicken dinner was served, neckties and conversation loosened up, and the disc jockey played oldies as requested. Fewer people every year hit the dance floor as weight gain, joint problems, and a longing to be home in bed increased in our once agile, Motown-obsessed crowd. But some of us were still happy to shake our booties in tribute to our teen years until we closed the place down. Colleen didn't last that long. I told her I'd see her at her house later the next day. I was glad for my hotel bed.

I wasn't going straight back to Colleen's the next morning. On the night of the fire, when I'd found JT's letters, I'd also found some from Charlie, a guy I'd become friends with in college who was now a high school principal in Philly. I'd contacted him on LinkedIn, and he'd said he wanted to meet. He was willing to drive to a restaurant just outside Bethlehem while I was visiting. I brought his letters and a few other mementos, thinking it would be fun to share them with his wife, but Charlie said she hadn't wanted to come.

"You told her, right?" I asked. I wouldn't be comfortable if he had concealed our visit.

"Yeah, and I asked her again this morning, but she just said 'No, you go on, have fun.'"

We caught up, and I showed him the things I'd brought. Soon Charlie said he had to get back. I approved because it meant that he had his priorities straight when he told me that this was his "last" marriage.

I drove to Colleen's. She was already preparing dinner, a "Lynda's favorite," her homemade mac and cheese. I had her recipe, but it always tasted better when she made it. While she boiled noodles and grated cheese, we rehashed the reunion, and then I described my visit with Charlie.

"Soooo," she said with that conspiratorial tone, those eyes cutting off to the side. *Oh boy, what now?*

"Have you had your fill of married men yet?"

What the fucking hell?

I knew that my liberal values weren't for everyone. But they had never included dating, fucking, or even flirting with a man who was committed elsewhere.

"What does *that* mean?"

"Well, you just spent time with two men, and both of them are married. I was wondering if you had enough."

"Enough of what, exactly? I had two short get-togethers to catch up with old friendships that predated their marriages. And as far as I know, their wives knew about it. Why are you trying to make something more out of it?"

"Ohhhh . . ." she said with that predictable vague tone. I waited for her spin, but I guess she couldn't think of one. God, she made someone want—no, need!—a drink. How many hours were left in this motherfucking long-ass day anyway?

She put the casserole in the oven and set the timer. "I'm tired," she said. "I think I need a nap."

That sounded good to me. Then dinner and only one more morning before Colleen would go back to work, and I would leave for Sharon's.

Instead of napping, I read my Kindle and then checked messages.

Countdown 3, 2 . . .

And then 1, 0! Wheee!

Wheee!

♡

The next morning, I was quiet while Colleen and I had our coffee. She was up and down as usual, fixing her supper to take to work later. But quiet was not something that sat well with her.

"Let's have a 'best of your life' quiz," she suggested. "Like, who was the best kisser of your life?"

Oh, Jesus. Did I have to play this? I knew it would involve

talking about JT again. But now I was curious about what she'd say.

"I don't think I can name just one," I said. "I've had 'best' kissers at different times of my life. Like JT was the first." Then I named two others.

"Mine was Rico," she sighed with a dreamy faraway look. Rico was a married Latino doctor who she had hoped would leave his wife and kids for her. From the first, I had doubted that his Catholic values would allow him to leave his family. And they hadn't.

"OK, what about best fuck?" she went on. "Who was the best fuck of your life?"

"Hmmm. Well, JT and I had passion, but we were also young and inexperienced." Then I named the man after JT who had encouraged me to talk and explore, and my most recent serious love who relit my flame when I thought menopause had put it out.

"Mine was Wes the Mess," she said. He was a married cop who, once again, she'd hoped would leave his wife and marry her. She was a basket case when he left his wife and married someone else. Jesus! I hadn't approved of those married men then, and I approved even less now. Especially since she had just accused me of doing it.

"All right, last one," she said. "Who was the love of your life? Mine was Mickey," she sighed. "He was good in bed, he was smart, and he was creative. He had everything." I had thought that he was funny looking, but at least he was single. She had pushed him to let her and her preteen son move in. Just when she was ready to sell her home, he got the balls to say no.

I named the same three men I already had and didn't elaborate. I was tired of her game. It made me sad and angry that she hadn't listed JT in any of her categories. At one time, he had seemed "best of" to be worth wreaking havoc in our lives. Now he didn't even warrant a mention.

I got up to go pack and answer a text tapped out by goony JT's still-beautiful fingers.

♡

Later, after I'd returned home to LA, I would email Colleen. I'd thank her for the things I'd enjoyed and repeat her comments that had hurt or made me uncomfortable, asking only, why?

She would say that I drank too much at her house. (I did sometimes drink more than I should, but with her watching me like a parole officer, I never had more than two at her place.)

She would say that of the meals she prepared, I ate twice as much as she. (I ate half as much, plus a small salad—but why did it matter?)

She would say that I had trespassed on her neighbor's property. (It took me a while to even remember the bridge and the owner's friendly wave.)

She would say that I passive-aggressively brought her a bottle of vodka when I knew that she didn't drink anymore. (I didn't know that. And so why did she rave about it, drink it, and have an empty in the trash?)

When I asked her to explain, she said, "Let's just move on through like we have in the past." But I didn't want to ignore our problems this time, with her twisting truth to fit her versions of reality. I knew that this friendship—which had rescued me in high school, destroyed me in college, and slowly helped me to heal over many years, only to begin to eat away at me again— finally had to end.

Others would tell me it was forty years overdue.

☮

Chapter 34

GOD, IT FELT GOOD TO GET TO SHARON'S. LIKE I COULD DRAW a full, free breath for the first time since I'd arrived in Pennsylvania. She showed me to my room while I filled her in on my final hours with Colleen.

When Gerry got home from his work as a contractor, we took a walk around their considerable historic property in Pennsylvania Dutch farm county. We sampled bottles from an impressive wine cellar while Gerry grilled steaks and Sharon steamed veggies from their garden. I felt relaxed to be away from Colleen's eagle eyes and judgments.

Before going to sleep, Sharon sat on my bed. We were both tipsy. We shared a few giggles over our adventures of long ago. "I love you," she said with a warm hug. Had Colleen ever told me she loved me? Her own brother had told her she chewed men up and spit them out, and I was aware of a number of girlfriends she had traded out, too. I knew she loved her children, but who else did she ever really love?

The next morning, I hung out with Sharon and then got ready to leave. I'd arranged an early check-in at the hotel.

"OK, girl," I said, "I'm gonna get going. Tell Gerry good-bye and thanks again for me."

"I'm glad you've still got one more adventure to look forward to," Sharon said with a hug. "Make sure you tell me all about it." Oh, I would.

I got back on the road.

While driving, I turned an idea over in my mind. Was there

any chance that JT and I could pick up where we had left off? Was it crazy to wonder if we could find in older age what we had lost in our youth? There were a lot of barriers—home, family, work, history, geography. He'd made a couple comments about not feeling very connected to his city or to his family.

"They act like somehow what's happened with my job situation is my fault, but it isn't." I believed him; it was a global economic crisis, and in that environment, jobs for justice fell by the wayside. Yet, did that mean he'd be willing to leave? It seemed unfair to ask if I weren't equally willing to move to DC. I hated gray skies, rain, and humidity, and I loved LA. But what else did I love? Did I really still love JT?

He'd also startled me with an unexpected question. "Are you happy?"

That was a hard one. There was so much good in my life, and yet. "I would say I'm content," I answered. "But not happy. And you?"

He shook his head sadly. "No. Maybe content if I find work. But not happy."

Was he wondering whether we could be happy together?

Even if he were willing to try, what would it be like? Did I want him to know the woman I really was now? Or remain infatuated with the young woman I'd been? Was the man I saw—the man I'd had only glimpses of over the years—the man he truly was?

Or was I really getting ahead of myself?

I called a therapist friend of mine in LA and asked, "Do you think I should bring this up with him?"

Her answer was on point: "How far did it get you when you didn't tell him how you felt?" *Touché.*

As I flashed between past and present, thoughts of my parents came to my mind. They were both dead now. What would it be like if they were alive and I were with JT? They'd eventually reached grudging acceptance of Will, but then Will and I didn't last. I suspected now that they'd have accepted JT more readily. Will was darker-skinned, JT was lighter; Will was articulate, JT was eloquent.

Mom would've liked JT because he was handsome and charming. And she had mellowed over the years. When she died, one of the black women from her church lamented Mom's loss. "Your mother was just a dear soul," she said.

It saddened me now that my dad had never gotten a chance to know JT. God, how they would've loved talking basketball. They had such a common history: both stars at the same small college, in the local newspapers all the time, and tall but not quite tall enough for the big time.

Maybe JT would've been able to explain to Dad why Lew Alcindor became Kareem Abdul Jabbar.

Maybe Dad would've bet that the Lakers would never win an NBA championship with Shaq at the helm. (He would've lost.)

Maybe JT would've agreed with Dad that basketball players should not lift weights but instead remain light and fast.

Maybe they both would've enjoyed seeing Magic still smiling.

In Dad's later years, long after I'd moved to California, long after my mom was gone, he told me that he wished he'd been a better husband and father. Right before he died, he said that if he lived, he would probably vote for Barack Obama. I thought, *You've come a long way, Dad.*

♡

With an early check-in at my DC hotel, I was able to relax and take my time getting ready. Then JT texted me from the bar.

We sat at the same table.

"That might have been the best pasta I've ever had," he said.

"The salad and wine were good, too," I agreed. We ordered exactly the same meal as on our previous night.

"Is that weird?" he asked.

"No, I seem to have a tendency to go back to something I liked before," I said. JT raised his eyebrows and pointed to himself and we both laughed.

"Look, I've got something to show you," he said when our wine arrived. He got out his phone. "This is a picture of my basketball jersey that they retired."

I'd only seen him wear it once, in that game I saw the night he stood me up at Hannah's and we broke up. The tank top draped across his muscled shoulders as he dribbled down the court. The snug gym shorts that showed off his tight thighs as he danced up for the jump shots. (Whose idea had it been to change basketball uniforms to baggy board-style shorts? Bad decision.)

"They gave it to you?" I asked. He nodded. "Where is it?"

"On the wall in my office at home," he said. "It's really the only thing I have from those days."

He asked about the reunion, but I knew he didn't want to hear about Colleen. Maybe he should know the kinds of things she had said about him, but that just seemed unkind.

We didn't dawdle over dinner this time, now that it was understood we would retire to "our" room.

We played music. Bobby Womack. Stevie and Syreeta. Santana. "Ordinary Joe" by Terry Callier, a tribute to blues singer

Joe Williams but also to the "ordinary" black man struggling with self-esteem. I'd included it in a mixtape I'd made for JT a couple of decades before. "I think you get exposed to better music in LA than I do," he'd said. I enjoyed turning him onto songs the way he had done for me in college.

Now I introduced JT to Mayer Hawthorne, "The Walk," about a girl with luxurious hair, long legs, and cocoa butter skin.

"Someone once told me that's my type," JT said.

I pointed down at my summer tan. "Oh, am I too dark, then?" I teased.

JT smiled and showed me what he thought of my cocoa butter.

By the time we finished loving, we could hear a rainstorm outside. He got up and looked out the one large window.

"It's really raging out there," he said. I could hear the thunder crack and see the lightning from the bed.

"Remember the terrible storm that last night at Harvey House?" I asked. He nodded. "I thought we might die there," I said. Then I added softly, "A part of me wanted to."

"There's a song like that," JT said. "5th Dimension. 'Requiem: 820 Latham,' I think."

"What does that mean?"

He shrugged. "An address, I guess. Let's see if we can listen to it."

Of course, he found it on YouTube, and time seemed to stop. The song said almost exactly what I felt and what I'd just said. Our hot young blood, so tempered by age now. Would I have to wait ten million years before he took me up that mountain again? And why had I not just died there?

"Jonathan." He looked at me from the desk. I patted the other side of the bed.

"I have something to say and I think I should say it now before I lose my nerve."

JT slipped into bed. We lay on our sides, with our faces nearly touching on the pillow.

"Why do you think we lost each other, way back then?" I asked.

His eyes never left mine.

"Youthful folly. Poor communication." He paused. "And a bit of malfeasance on the part of Colleen."

Wait. Had he actually said that? "Malfeasance on the part of Colleen"? I felt my eyes prick with tears of relief: he knew and understood the whole story, that I had loved him, that I hadn't planned to choose Will over him, that I'd been foolish and had waited too long because I didn't know what the hell to do. In his brief answer I heard it all, that he'd been hurt, so he hurt me back. That in spite of all our words, we hadn't told each other everything we felt. And that Colleen had manipulated us.

"Maybe it's not too late to recover from those things," I said. We lay very still. I wondered if he could feel the pounding of my heart across the bed. "We're sixty-two years old, Jon. You're going to be sixty-three in just a few days; you're *really* old," I teased, and he smiled. "But it's not easy getting old. It's lonely. And even more important, at least to me, is the sense that I lost something valuable that I haven't been able to get back. Yes, I've lived. And I've even loved again. But you were the first, and in some ways, I feel I've never gotten over you." The tears were still threatening; I felt my throat constrict. "What if we decided to just go for it?" I finished.

JT's long fingers reached out and smoothed hair from my face. His eyes were deep damp pools.

"Funny you should say that. Did you see what shirt I had

on?" I had noticed that he was dressed more casually this time. He got up and held up his T-shirt.

"It's my Vegas shirt," he said, pointing to the design. "My gambling shirt. Remember that song by Kenny Rogers, 'The Gambler'?"

"Yeah, sure." I started singing, "You gotta know when to hold 'em."

He continued, "Know when to fold 'em."

I smiled. "Know when to walk away."

We finished together, "Know when to run!"

"So, what are you saying, Jonathan?" I thought about how charming I found this conversation—and how much Colleen would hate it. "Just spit it out already," she'd say.

"I'm saying maybe it's not so bad to take a chance."

I beckoned him back to the bed and he laid the T-shirt down. He climbed under the covers and resumed our face-to-face position.

"So, you're not running," I said.

"Do I look like I'm running?" His free hand played with my free hand.

"And you're not walking away," I said.

"Not yet." He smiled.

"And you haven't folded?"

"Right now I'm holding. That's all I can tell you, Lynda. I'm holding." And then JT pulled me in and held me close until we fell asleep.

♡

The next morning, I woke him to the sound of Aretha singing from my laptop. I danced around the bed, swaying my hips.

JT propped himself up on pillows, arms behind his head, and leaned back into his crossed hands. I saw how hairy he was, by today's standards, and wondered, *was he this hairy back then?* But of course, it was the times of "Hair." Hair was normal; we barely even noticed.

JT was grinning. I smiled and winked and sang and danced some more. Aretha and I told of how much I'd be missing him until he came back to me.

Have I ever felt as free as I did at that moment? It didn't matter that I was sixty-two or that I had a belly. It didn't matter that my lipstick had been kissed off or that I had mascara under my eyes. I was with JT, and I was the only woman he had ever really loved.

We decided that instead of room service, we'd go someplace and grab lunch and talk about next steps. I started packing my stuff and took a quick look at my itinerary.

"Holy shit!" I exclaimed. "My plane leaves earlier than I thought. I don't have time for lunch. I've gotta get to the airport."

I felt cheated. My careless lack of attention was going to make our last moments together rushed.

"That's OK," JT said. "Finish packing, and then we'll go down and print your boarding pass." I liked his calm demeanor and the protective way he took charge.

"Wow," he said when we got to my rental car. "Look at this hot rod." I had gotten a black Challenger.

"Yeah, I just figure that if I have to drive, it might as well be fun."

"Did you know I got a car senior year?" he asked. Yes, Colleen had told me, in one of the letters from her that I couldn't bring myself to answer back then. I'd tried not to think about them driving around in it, free in a way that he and I had never been.

"Yeah, and you wrecked it almost immediately, right?" I'd been relieved that JT hadn't been hurt in that accident.

"Yup." He shook his head. "Talk about youthful folly."

The seconds were ticking by. Neither of us wanted to go, but we had to.

We faced each other. "Do you know how to Skype?" JT asked.

"I never have. But I can learn."

"OK," he said. "We'll learn to Skype together." He put his arms around me and drew me close.

I tilted my head back and tried to memorize him. "How do you feel about PDA?" I asked.

"PDA? What's that?"

"Public Display of Affection," I said.

"I hate it," JT said, as his lips slowly came down to meet mine. It was a kiss as long and deep as the years we'd missed out on, and as sweet as the promise of what we might still be able to recapture.

☮

Epilogue

I LOVE A HAPPY ENDING, DON'T YOU? AND I SO WANTED a happy ending to this story. As I stood with JT in that parking lot, I felt almost young again, like so many possibilities could still open up. But in a relationship marked by many twists and turns, this time was no different.

JT and I did Skype as soon as I returned home and throughout that summer. I remember the quiet excitement I felt on the days we'd agreed to talk. How I'd get ready almost as if I were going on a date. I decided the best location was the bar in my family room. Behind me would be the karaoke system and conga drums my friends and I liked to play with. And beyond that was the view of the pool, sparkling in the moonlight. Yes, I loved my home in the California foothills. I barely let myself fantasize that if JT and I somehow made it, he might come there. In DC he had agreed to a visit.

I'd fix my hair and wear a little makeup. Put on my hippie-inspired jewelry and pick out a pretty top. I'd have a martini and a glass of water ready. And then suddenly there was JT on my computer. Skype didn't offer the best visual. He looked kind of distorted, and I wondered if that was how he saw me, too. But he was still my JT. And there on the wall behind him was his basketball jersey that Moravian College had "retired" from use, that he said was the only thing he had from those days.

We shared music old and new, of course. We also flirted.

JT said, "I'm finding it hard to get motivated these days."

"Remember what we learned about testosterone increasing motivation?"

"Yeah, but how can I raise my testosterone with you 3,000 miles away?"

I lowered my computer screen to reveal my black lace bra. JT laughed so hard he almost tipped his office chair over. But he sure liked that bra.

Serious subjects came up as well. JT had still not been able to find employment, and already the assets he had spent a lifetime working so hard for were in danger of disappearing. At his age, that didn't bode well for the future.

To my mind, if we pooled resources, the financial picture would be comfortable. He had a house that was paid for and he could soon begin collecting Social Security. I had a house that wasn't paid for, but I could soon retire and begin collecting a pension. Many couples had less. But work had been his life, and I suspected that it was too strange for him to contemplate simply relaxing into retirement, especially given that he wasn't choosing it. I feared that he would never feel we were both contributing equally.

We also talked some about work, mine in public health and his on behalf of quality of life for minorities. He had dedicated his life to consulting with government and justice organizations. I was no doubt more naïve than he, hoping that the slow trudge of civil rights had at least made some things better. We had a black president, something I didn't think I'd see in my lifetime.

But suddenly that summer of 2014, while JT and I Skyped, Ferguson, Missouri, exploded. An unarmed young black man was killed by police and people took to the streets in protest. Then came counter-protests, rioting and looting, and terrifying YouTube images of a burning city.

I felt like we'd just been thrown back into the '60s—and not the good parts of the '60s:

"What's going on, Jonathan? (Pause) Oh hey, that's Marvin. Remember?" "What's Going On" was the Marvin Gaye song that many would say was the anthem of our youth.

"(Big sigh) Sure do. And it still fits today, unfortunately. Nothing new that police have been beating up on black folks since forever. But sometimes there's a perfect storm and people just can't stand it anymore."

And people didn't just stand for it. Black Lives Matter was born, a huge grassroots movement like some of the better parts of the '60s. But still the cycle of murder-protest-violence continued. And JT couldn't help but wonder if all his work on behalf of his community had just wound back to the same shitty place.

I'm not sure what happened with JT and me or why. All I know for sure is that he was feeling down. But when my sixty-third birthday was coming up, he specifically said he wanted to Skype that day.

"And what if I want to Skype with you before that?" he teased.

"All you have to do is call," I responded happily.

My birthday came. I'd already celebrated with my sister and friends, and now I was looking forward to seeing the guy I loved, even if visually distorted on Skype. I got myself and my little spot at the bar ready for his call.

A call that never came.

Of course, I called him. Several times. And got no answer. I was reminded of a night in 1972 when I had waited for his call.

1972 and the night I sat at Hannah's after watching JT play basketball for the first time. Wearing the scratchy alpaca skirt that he would need to help me take off. Working on his school paper that my old friend and new nemesis Colleen had told him she would write and then asked me to write for her. (I always wondered if she confessed to him that I wrote it, or kept quiet and took the credit.) Waiting for his call, until Hannah came back from a party and told me she saw him there. The night that I ended things with JT by putting a FUCK YOU note on his dorm room door.

In 2014, the morning after my birthday, JT emailed me first thing:

> *I am so sorry for messing up your birthday. I hope you were*
> *still able to enjoy your day. Please know that it had*
> *nothing to do with you or us. I don't know how I can make*
> *it up to you. But I will try.*

Sadly, he never did make it up to me. No make-up Skype, and soon after came an email in which he said that he needed to concentrate on his job search and had no energy left to pursue a relationship. He was no longer "holding"; instead, he had folded his cards and walked away.

Now, once again, I had to walk past loving him. Past the tears that still threatened every time one of our songs came on.

At least I was stronger this time. I had lived through so much. And I realized that my reconciliation fantasies had been premature, although he had certainly fed them. Maybe JT still loved me, but even if he did, he couldn't act on that love.

♡

Friends tell me I hang onto people I've loved, and it's true. JT and I still stayed in touch. I was working on my book, and when

I took a memoir workshop at a conference, I was shocked to learn that I couldn't use his letters without his permission: "You own the physical letters, but he owns the words, like a copyright," the lawyer/presenter said. I wrote JT and asked him for permission; while he responded to the email, he didn't answer the question. I tried asking him if he would consider collaborating with me; again, he didn't respond to my request. I accepted that. I would have to paraphrase his beautiful words from all those years ago. I doubted whether I could do them justice.

Eventually he found work, but he didn't invite me to be closer than occasional emails. Imagine my surprise then in 2019, when I asked him if he wanted to meet up again when I came east for my 50th reunion, and he not only said yes but that he would like more time than last time. He invited me to come to DC for five days, and he would pay for my hotel:

Unless you are just playing with me, that's what I'd like.
Crazy huh? Probably the most time we ever spent together.

Huh! Thus, five years after our 2014 visit, I was once again on my way to see Jonathan Thomas. This time I didn't read too much into it or have high expectations. As I told him when he asked what I did hope for:

"To see your face, hear your voice, share some music, a little word play, maybe some footsie under the table."

Before my trip arrived, though, I realized I had one more wish. I had completed a draft of my book, and JT was the first person I wanted to read it. I was so proud of it! Maybe it was foolish, but I thought that if he saw the sweetness of our story, he'd realize why I needed to write it. I took his copy to our first dinner and told him that I hoped he would read it. He accepted the manuscript graciously and said that he'd read it after I left.

At dinner that night we both shared something incredible that we had done with our phones. He'd made his screen image a photo of me from back in the day, wearing the blue hot pants that I'd worn to my first party in Philly. I had changed my ring tone to our favorite music line ever: "*Suavecito, mi linda. Suavecito!*" Every time he made a call, he saw my long legs in those hot pants. And every time my phone rang, I heard Our Song. It touched my heart that, without conferring, we'd both set up our phones to remind us of those days.

That might have been the high point of our visit. We spent time together, mostly dinners and sleepovers, and it was pleasant enough but lacked the intensity of our previous encounter. The past came up many times, and eventually he told me that he was tired of talking about years gone by.

It got worse. After I got home, he emailed that he would not read my book, that he wondered if my whole trip had been orchestrated to get his permission to use his letters. It didn't make sense to me because I'd stopped asking about that for some time, and he was the one who'd requested the extra days together. It finally became clear that, for whatever reason, he didn't want the book to exist at all.

JT's final words:

I don't want to hear from you ever again.

Whaaat? No! I couldn't believe it. I felt like I had been punched in the stomach. And losing the enduring friendship added a fresh cut next to the scars of our failed romance. Hadn't he said, "*Suavecito*, don't you know that I could never punish you, ever, for anything?"

But this time he folded his cards and ran. I could hardly stand knowing that we would never again share music or memories or flirtatious wordplay. The worst punishment of all.

I'd really hoped that JT and I could write a new chapter and a new ending together. Instead, I spent years working on understanding the story we'd had, one I couldn't give up on until I learned what it had to teach me. I've forgiven myself (mostly) for the mistakes I made, for being young and scared and not holding on to the great love I was given. And I've forgiven JT (mostly) for making the missteps he did and for being so private that he felt he finally had to close the door between us.

I know that I'm richer for having loved him. That I still cherish the answers to my long-ago questions. And if JT ever changes his mind, reads the book, misses the friendship we shared until we didn't, he knows how to find me.

Afterword

The name used in my book to identify Jonathan Thomas, as well his various nicknames (Jon, Johnny and JT), are fictional. Other identifying details have also been fictionalized.

As the reader now knows, the real person who inspired my account of the individual called JT objected to direct quotations from his various writings over the years. For that reason, his letters, emails, text messages, and journal entries have been summarized or very loosely paraphrased. No direct quotations are used.

The names used for the following characters, and some of their identifying details, are also fictionalized: Will, Colleen, Hannah, Roy Green, Ditto, Tucker (and the nickname Tuck), Curtis, Tim, Cathy, Pam, Jamie, Linda, Ricardo, Rich, Dell, Rico, Wes, Mickey, Buddy and Davy, Mr. Reynolds (and the nickname Rah Rah).

In the writing of this book, most of my research involved letters, notes, and emails, with occasional forays into old sports pages and internet searches. Three online searches about songs turned up some very interesting information that I'd like to share.

The first song I wanted to know more about was, of course, "*Suavecito*" by Malo. To my surprise, there were several online articles about either the song or the band or both. Ian S. Port wrote in the alternative newspaper *SF Weekly* that the song was a love poem written to his crush by singer and timbales player Richard Bean. The girl broke his heart but brought about the song that reached No. 18 on the Billboard singles chart and gave Malo national recognition. (I wonder if she knows!) Unfortunately, the song was a one-hit wonder. But Port writes that to some, it was so much more:

"For Americans of Mexican descent, however, 'Suavecito' is iconic, a core piece of a shared culture. Released at a time when Chicanos were struggling for basic rights and recognition in the US, 'Suavecito' is a symbol of unity still widely played and enjoyed today. (It) has even been dubbed the Chicano national anthem."

I can certainly believe that, for it has long been my personal anthem. Not just because it was JT's and my song, or even because it has my name in it. The crossover mix of Latin and rock and soul music is just beautiful, and so emblematic of what was going on in society and in music at the time.

Read the whole article at:

https://www.sfweekly.com/music/smooth-pride-the-legacy-of-malos-suavecito/

Another song I wanted to see if I could find out more about was "Requiem: 820 Latham" by the 5th Dimension. I found an article in the music essay publication *Pop Matters* by author Christian John Wikane. The focus of the article, an interview with group founders Marilyn McCoo and Billy Davis, Jr., is on songwriter Jimmy Webb. McCoo and Davis were in complete awe of his lyrics:

"Davis: Jimmy is probably one of the best songwriters I ever worked with. It was just amazing to talk to a young guy with that much depth.

McCoo: I always ask people if they are familiar with "Requiem: 820 Latham". Most of the time they aren't. When you start reciting those lyrics . . .

Davis: ... they bring tears to your eyes."

McCoo quotes one of her favorites. My favorites are paraphrased in the book. But there are so many good ones that it was hard to choose. My ultimate tribute: I wish I'd written them.

Here's the whole interview:

https://www.popmatters.com/the-magic-garden-revisited-marilyn-mccoo-billy-davis-jr-on-jimmy-webb-2496174334.html

Finally, I looked into the song by Bobby Taylor and the Vancouvers, "Does Your Mama Know About Me." I'd considered it as a possible title for my book, partly because it's a beautiful song, and partly because JT had written the lyrics to me. I was in for a surprise! It was written by Tommy Chong of comedy duo Cheech and Chong, when he was a musician prior to getting into comedy. In fact, he plays guitar on the song. And the group is one of few interracial groups recorded by Motown.

According to the online music website *Songfacts*, "This song is about the worries of a young black man dating a white girl." But reader comments state that Chong, half Chinese, wrote it when he was nervous about meeting the parents of an African-American woman he was courting, Maxine Sneed, ultimately Maxine Chong and the mother of their daughter, actor Rae Dawn Chong. And some readers even think that it could describe a same-sex relationship.

Whatever the reason behind the song, the fact that so many readers can relate on so many levels—well, here's to all the star-crossed lovers who love the song as I do.

Here's one link:

https://www.songfacts.com/facts/bobby-taylor-the-vancou-vers/does-your-mama-know-about-me

It's really amazing what can turn up when you start research-ing the background of a song. I've included the list of wonderful songs featured in this book. Happy listening!

Song Playlist

40,000 Headmen – Blood, Sweat & Tears

Ike's Rap III/Your Love Is So Doggone Good – Isaac Hayes

So Far Away – Carole King

Smiling Faces – The Undisputed Truth

The Ghetto – Donny Hathaway

Ungena Za Ulimwengu (Unite the World) – The Temptations

The Harder I Try (The Bluer I Get) – The Free Movement

Love the One You're With – Stephen Stills

Does Your Mama Know About Me – Bobby Taylor & the
Vancouvers

Here I Go Again – Smokey Robinson & the Miracles

Too Late to Turn Back Now – Cornelius Brothers & Sister Rose

Taboo – Santana

Everything's Coming Our Way – Santana

Sunlight – Jesse Colin Young

Suavecito – Malo

Pretty as You Feel – Jefferson Airplane

Mommy, What's a Funkadelic? – Funkadelic

Don't Cry My Lady Love – Quicksilver Messenger Service

Jackson-Kent Blues – Steve Miller Band

Black Thighs – The Last Poets

Sugar Man – Rodriguez

Inner City Blues – Rodriguez

Ain't No Mountain High Enough – Marvin Gaye and Tammi
Terrell

Day Dreaming – Aretha Franklin

Where Is the Love – Donny Hathaway and Robert Flack

Look What You Done for Me – Al Green

Goodnight My Love (Pleasant Dreams) – The Fleetwoods
Under the Boardwalk – The Drifters
The First Time Ever I Saw Your Face – Roberta Flack
Do What You Gotta Do – Roberta Flack
I'll Be Around – The Spinners
I Can Understand It – Bobby Womack
Woman's Gotta Have It – Bobby Womack
Did You Hear What They Said? – Gil Scott-Heron
The King Alfred Plan – Gil Scott-Heron
Ohio – Crosby, Stills, Nash & Young
To Know You Is to Love You – Syreeta featuring Stevie Wonder
That's the Way I Feel About 'Cha – Bobby Womack
Traffic – The Low Spark of High Heeled Boys
(If You Don't Want My Love) Give It Back – Bobby Womack
Lady Day and John Coltrane – Gil Scott-Heron
Long Train Runnin' – The Doobie Brothers
Oh! No Not My Baby – Rod Stewart
Ain't No Woman (Like the One I've Got) – Four Tops
Hello Stranger – Barbara Lewis
Hello Like Before – Bill Withers
You Don't Know Me – Ray Charles
Sundress – Phat Cat Players featuring Coco Brown
This Is My Beloved – Arthur Prysock
Ordinary Joe – Terry Callier
The Walk – Mayer Hawthorne
Requiem: 820 Latham – The 5th Dimension
The Gambler – Kenny Rogers
Until You Come Back to Me – Aretha Franklin
What's Going On – Marvin Gaye

Acknowledgments

So many people contribute to the birth of a book, and like a new parent I am afraid I will forget that night nurse or maintenance person who also deserves the box of chocolates. My apologies if that happens.

I have to start with my writing mentor, award-winning author (of thirteen books), botanist, and teacher Susan J. Tweit. I met her by chance in a nature writing workshop in 2003, at which point my own writing had been floundering for decades. Everything I have done since, including my website, publications, and more, has been thanks to her guidance. She is the one who recommended She Writes Press to me. I am so deeply grateful for all of it.

And of course, many bows to my progressive indie publisher, Brooke Warner, and her talented She Writes Press team. I am thrilled to have made their cut and for all the learning experiences regarding an industry I knew nothing about that have followed.

For the five years plus that it took me to write this book, I was fortunate to have my writing group Tres Libras, with sister memoirists Frances Borella and Juanita Mantz. Our meetings always included wine, dinner, and one of earth's most precious resources, women's talk. They generously critiqued every chapter, often more than once, and my writing has grown from their input.

Speaking of generous, who is more generous than a beta reader, who has much to give and little to gain from reading our manuscripts? My loving thanks to Abi Fuesler, Riah Fuesler, Jennifer Hoggan, Jim Schaffer (high school poet competitor),

Jenna Carpenter, Ena Ellis, Diana Mamot, and sister Barbara Smith (li'l sis Barbie). Special mention goes to Fran Kissel-Powell (college roomie Frannie) and Jack Miller, as they actually did a complete reading twice!

As I started to get back into creative writing after a long hiatus, the name John Brantingham kept coming up as someone I should know. I found out that he is a (THE?) big writing honcho at Mt. San Antonio College, where I teach as well. He would blush at that characterization, but never has there been a more generous mentor, not only to his students but to anyone who comes his way with writing and publishing questions.

And through John I met authors Bonnie Hearn Hill (the first to read a chapter of this book and write "Yes!" in encouragement), Jo Scott-Coe, and many more who inspired me to tell my stories.

This may sound like an odd acknowledgment, but to me, it's an important one. I was pitching my first book idea to agent Angela Rinaldi when she asked, "Is this the book of your heart?" My answer was no, and I immediately flashed on the story of JT and me. "Then write that one," she said. So I did.

I have to thank the late novelist Carolyn See for some of the best writing advice I've gotten. On a weekend getaway with a family member, I learned, to my disappointment, that she hadn't read a story I'd recently published. How serendipitous that I had brought with me a copy of Carolyn's wonderful book *Making a Literary Life*. In the first chapter she tells us, "Don't expect your friends and family to love your work. Instead, find a writing community that does." So I did. (My family member subsequently did read my story, though.)

Besides my beta readers, my support team included close friends Bruce Jacobs, Callie Hurd, and Naluce Santana—thank you for listening to my thoughts about the book for years. Special recognition to wise friend and therapist Dr. Vena Blanchard, who at times seemed to understand my book even better than I did. More than once I'm sure my writing "borrowed" some of her words.

And what writer is not indebted to those queens and kings of book and research, our librarians?

Lastly, I have to gratefully acknowledge some very deep and meaningful influences on my book and my life:

People of my generation who explored without a map, gave the finger to the rules, and really tried to influence our country to live up to its ideals. We didn't fully succeed, but our movement continues. I loved growing my values along with you and am grateful for the person you helped me to become. Peace, and keep the faith!

Writers of the literature that taught me about words, about worlds near and far, and about the potential that is in all of us. Different ways to think, different ways to live and love. I can't get enough of you, and I have yet to meet the movie that is better than the book.

Makers of the music whose pioneering lyrics and rhythms fueled our young lives and loves in the '60s and '70s. I hope the young'uns who followed appreciate you. And I hope I did justice to your words and meanings. I still listen to you every day.

About the Author

Photo credit: Julie Hood Portraits

LYNDA SMITH HOGGAN is Professor Emeritus of Health and Human Sexuality at Mt. San Antonio College in Southern California. She has also been a professional gift shop duster, bra strap counter, playground instructor, army base secretary, garment district house model, barmaid, go-go dancer, high school teacher, technical writer, sex educator, and amateur martini taster. Her writing has appeared in *Westwind: UCLA Journal of the Arts*, the *Los Angeles Times*, *Cultural Weekly*, and more. She blogs at www.lyndasmithhoggan.com.

SELECTED TITLES FROM SHE WRITES PRESS

She Writes Press is an independent publishing company
founded to serve women writers everywhere.
Visit us at www.shewritespress.com.

Postcards from the Sky: Adventures of an Aviatrix by Erin Seidemann.
$16.95, 978-1-63152-826-2. Erin Seidemann's tales of her struggles, adventures, and relationships as a woman making her way in a world very much
dominated by men: aviation.

Queerspawn in Love by Kellen Kaiser. $16.95, 978-1-63152-020-4. When
the daughter of a quartet of lesbians falls in love with a man serving in the
Israeli Defense Forces, she is forced to examine her own values and beliefs.

Peanut Butter and Naan: Stories of an American Mother in The Far East by
Jennifer Magnuson. $16.95, 978-1-63152-911-5. The hilarious tale of what
happened when Jennifer Magnuson moved her family of seven from Nashville to India in an effort to shake things up—and got more than she bargained for.

Blue Apple Switchback: A Memoir by Carrie Highley. $16.95,
978-1-63152-037-2. At age forty, Carrie Highley finally decided to take on
the biggest switchback of her life: upon her bicycle, and with the help of
her mentor's wisdom, she shed everything she was taught to believe as a
young lady growing up in the South—and made a choice to be true to herself and everyone else around her.

Times They Were A-Changing: Women Remember the '60s & '70s edited by
Kate Farrell, Amber Lea Starfire, and Linda Joy Myers. $16.95,
978-1-938314-04-9. Forty-eight powerful stories and poems detailing the
breakthrough moments experienced by women during the '60s and '70s.

Fire Season: A Memoir by Hollye Dexter. $16.95, 978-1-63152-974-0. After
she loses everything in a fire, Hollye Dexter's life spirals downward and she
begins to unravel—but when she finds herself at the brink of losing her
husband, she is forced to dig within herself for the strength to keep her
family together.